AMERI
MEDIC
ASSOCIATION

FUNDAMENTALS OF CODING, PAYMENT, AND DOCUMENTATION

Understanding their role and impact in health care

Susan E. Garrison

American Medical Association

Executive Vice President, Chief Executive Officer: James L. Madara, MD

Chief Operating Officer: Bernard L. Hengesbaugh

Senior Vice President, Publishing and Business Services: Robert A. Musacchio, PhD

Vice President, Business Operations: Vanessa Hayden

Vice President, AMA Publications and Clinical Solutions: Mary Lou White

Senior Acquisition Editor: Elise Schumacher

Manager, Book and Product Development and Production: Nancy Baker

Senior Developmental Editor: Lisa Chin-Johnson

Production Specialist: Meghan Anderson

Director, Sales Marketing & Strategic Relationships: Joann Skiba

Director, Sales and Business Products: Mark Daniels

Manager, Marketing and Strategic Planning: Erin Kalitowski

Marketing Manager: Lori Hollacher

Reviewers: Karen O'Hara, Grace Kotowicz, Danielle Pavloski, Nancy Spector

Order Information

To order additional copies of *Fundamentals of Coding, Payment, and Documentation*,
call the American Medical Association toll free at (800) 621-8335
or access the secure AMA Web site at *www.amabookstore.com*.
Mention product number OP077010.
ISBN: 978-1-60359-337-3

Library of Congress Cataloging-in-Publication Data

Garrison, Susan E.
Fundamentals of coding, payment, and documentation : understanding their role and impact in health care / Susan E. Garrison.
p. ; cm.
Includes bibliographical references and index.
ISBN 978-1-60359-337-3
1. Nosology--Code numbers. 2. Clinical medicine--Code numbers. 3. Health insurance claims--United States. I. American Medical Association. II. Title.
[DNLM: 1. Clinical Coding--United States. 2. Insurance Claim Reporting--United States. W 80]
RB115.G373 2012
616.001'2--dc23

2011014408

BP54: 11-P-094:09/11

About the Author

In her role as Executive Vice President for Med Law Advisors, Inc, Susan Garrison, CHCA, CHCAS, CHC, PCS, FCS, CCS-P, CPC, CPC-H, CPAR, has attracted clients including solo practicing physicians, large teaching facilities, freestanding ambulatory surgery centers, hospitals, national associations, publishers, and over 100 other leading facilities and affiliated organizations. Garrison serves on the board of directors of the Association of Health Care Auditors and Educators. She is also past president of the American Academy of Professional Coders National Advisory Board and past chair of the American College of Medical Coding Specialists.

With over 25 years of experience, Garrison has expertise in documentation, coding, billing, litigation support, expert witness services, revenue enhancement, revenue cycle operations, and professional communications. Her prolific publishing career includes hundreds of articles and several books.

Garrison is a nationally acclaimed and highly sought speaker, having presented to small and large groups at hundreds of educational sessions for professional organizations (Association of Health Care Auditors and Educators [AHCAE]; American College of Medical Coding Specialists [ACMCS]; American Academy of Professional Coders [AAPC]; Healthcare Financial Management Association [HFMA]; American Health Information Management Association [AHIMA]; Medical Group Management Association [MGMA]), teaching university health systems, health care providers of all sizes, and payers. Garrison's audiences include physicians, nonphysician providers, residents, chief executive officers (CEOs), chief financial officer (CFOs), coding professionals, and attorneys.

Contents

Preface

If you glance around, it is easy to see the chaos of health care payment. Providers struggle with submitting claims correctly and payers struggle with paying appropriate levels of payment. Rejected claims, denials, appeals, patient copayments, varying payment systems—the process can be quite confusing and unpredictable, perhaps even slightly intimidating and depressing. *Fundamentals of Coding, Payment, and Documentation* is devoted to providing a simple overview of the key coding issues facing health care providers and how documentation and payment are intertwined with coding.

This book is about understanding the basics of medical coding, payment, and documentation. It does not teach how to code. Instead, it provides a foundation for understanding the various elements and the impact of coding, and the importance of coding in health care. In short, this book will stimulate and rouse further interest.

Although medical coding is not rocket science, the intricacies and importance of medical coding should not be undervalued. Mastering medical coding may seem like an overwhelming prospect. But to understand the fundamentals of coding and its impact on a health care provider or payer is an achievable feat, one that can be accomplished by studying the overview and the core fundamentals of each payment model and coding system.

Within this book, there are specific examples of coding, payment, and documentation issues, but the book will primarily focus on a high-level view of medical coding and how it affects payment and documentation. The book presents generalities for overall understanding and provides specific examples for real-life application. We hope that this format will help readers improve the accuracy and completeness of the documentation, coding, billing, and payment for each medical encounter.

Although *Fundamentals of Coding, Payment, and Documentation* can be used by those who are learning how to code, it is intended for individuals such as the practice administrator, clinician, business office manager, or CFO who need to understand the basic concepts and constructs of coding without having to actually code. For these individuals, building an understanding of the structure of coding and how coding is related to payment through documentation is more important than learning to code from the ground up.

The book's content is arranged according to three different aspects of coding and payment. The first group of chapters provides an overview of medical insurance elements (claim forms, payment systems), while the second group covers the different coding systems (Current Procedural Terminology [CPT®] codes, International Classification of Diseases, Ninth Revision, Clinical Modification [ICD-9-CM] codes). The final group of chapters provides additional information on fraud and abuse issues and pulls all the information together into a final, big-picture review.

Like moles in the arcade game *Whac-A-Mole*, health care issues jump out when you least expect them to, and we hope that this book will serve as a guide to hitting the mole cleanly and quickly on the head.

Good luck and happy reading and understanding!

Susan Garrison, CHCA, CHCAS, CHC, PCS, FCS, CCS-P, CPC, CPC-H, CPAR
Executive Vice President
Med Law Advisors, Inc.
susan@medlawadvisors.com

Chapter 1

Fundamentals of Medical Coding, Payment, and Documentation

This chapter introduces the fundamentals of coding, payment, and documentation. Coding is incredibly complex, and therefore, this book does not teach how to code. It will introduce the different available coding systems, some general guidelines and rules around using each system, and how the system is used in health care. Throughout the book, common examples will be incorporated to demonstrate the true scenarios in health care coding, payment, and documentation.

What Is Medical Coding?

Medical coding is the conversion of information (clinical documentation) that describes medical services, supplies, and diagnoses into numeric or alphanumeric codes. This conversion helps provide adequate information to explain the services and medical condition of the patient, but in a condensed format. Having a method of converting what can be a voluminous amount of data from the medical record's documentation into a concise 3-9 digit code(s) enables an efficient, yet accurate view of the health care episode.

For example, the diagnosis code for mitral and aortic valve insufficiency is concisely reflected by using ICD-9-CM code 396.3. By using a code, space is saved and the medical record does not have to be submitted as the code is a sufficient indicator of the medical story. Another example would be for an operation in which the documentation is lengthy (see excerpted texts below), but the surgeries performed can be condensed into a couple of 5-digit procedural codes and a couple of diagnosis codes. More information about medical coding is provided later in this chapter.

Preoperative Diagnosis: Infected left tibia fracture, status post open reduction and internal fixation.

Postoperative Diagnosis: Infected left tibia fracture, status post open reduction and internal fixation.

Procedures:
1. Excision of osteomyelitis, left tibia.
2. Removal of hardware, left tibia.
3. Application of hybrid external fixator, left tibia.

Anesthesia: General endotracheal.

Estimated Blood Loss: Minimal.

Drains: One Hemovac.

Complications: None.

Description of Procedure: The patient was brought to the operating room and after the successful induction of general anesthesia, a tourniquet was applied to the left upper thigh. The left leg was prepped and draped to a sterile field.

The left leg was elevated, exsanguinated with an Esmarch bandage, and the tourniquet was inflated to 300 mmHg. The patient had an open wound with purulent exudate from the proximal anterolateral tibia and the distal intermedial tibia. The patient's previous surgical incision on the anterolateral leg was utilized and extended distally the full length of the previously applied plate. Soft tissues were elevated. The plate was identified and removed without difficulty. There was a large amount of purulent material and granulation tissue that was debrided. Fibrous tissue, granulation tissue, and infection from between one of the major fracture lines were also debrided. The wound was thoroughly irrigated with saline using Simpulse irrigation. The Hemovac drain was then placed and brought out through a separate stab wound. The fascia was closed with 0 Vicryl, subcutaneous layer with 2-0 Vicryl, and skin with 3-0 nylon and a 3-0 Monocryl. Next, through stab wounds two 4-mm titanium self-drilling Shanz pins were placed into the tibial shaft. A hybrid external fixator was applied to these 2 pins with a three-quarter ring at the top. A single wire was placed from lateral to medial and then two 4-mm Shanz pins were placed into the proximal tibia under image-intensifier control. Sterile dressings were applied. The tourniquet was released. AP and lateral plain X-rays were obtained. The patient was then awakened from anesthesia and transported to the recovery room in stable condition.

Revenue Cycle of Health Care

The revenue cycle encompasses the entire process from the point of initial patient contact for care through the collection of payment for that care. See Figure 1-1 for a

FIGURE 1-1 *Normal Revenue Cycle for a Health Care Provider*

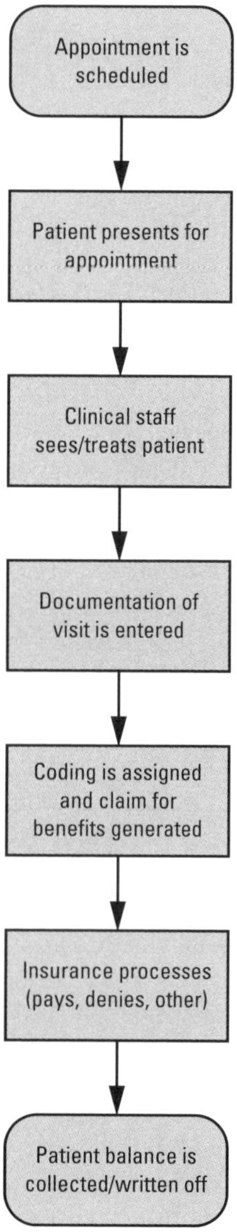

quick review of the revenue cycle. Note that coding is an essential part of the revenue cycle, and it usually drives the level of payment received.

Revenue cycles can vary from provider to provider. For example, the patient's portion of the visit might be, at least in part, collected prior to services being rendered; while at other practices, the patient's portion will be collected at the end of the encounter or perhaps after insurance has been collected.

Each step of the revenue cycle is critical to and for an accurate payment of the health care encounter. Figures 1-2A–1-2E delineate and outline some of the key pieces from each

FIGURE 1-2A *Important Steps in Revenue Cycle*

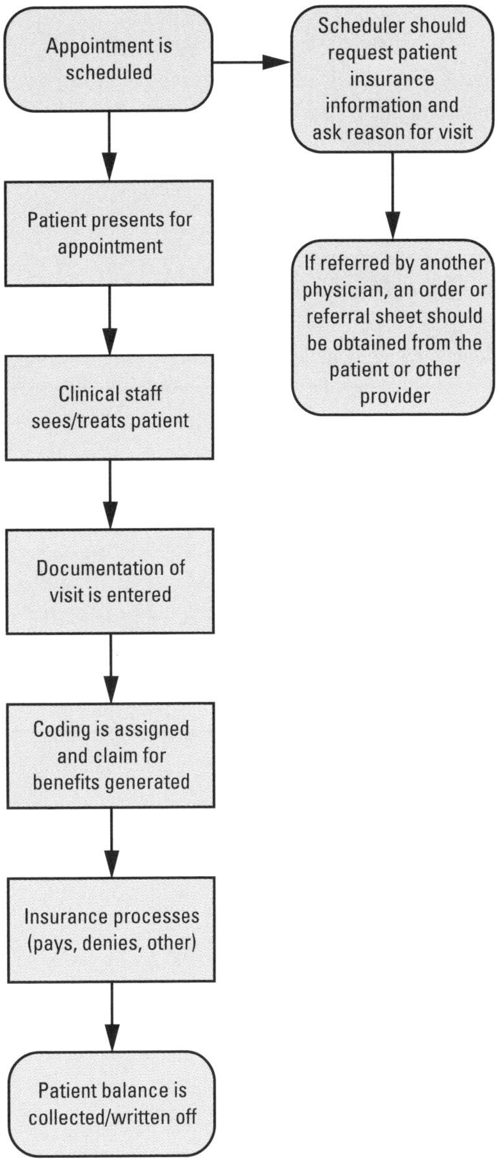

FIGURE 1-2B *Important Steps in Revenue Cycle*

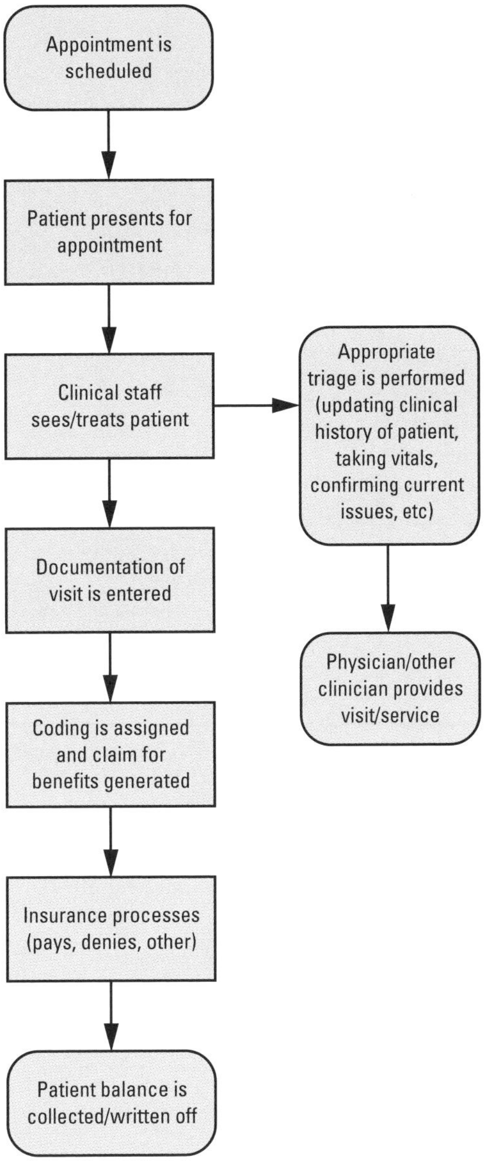

FIGURE 1-2C *Important Steps in Revenue Cycle*

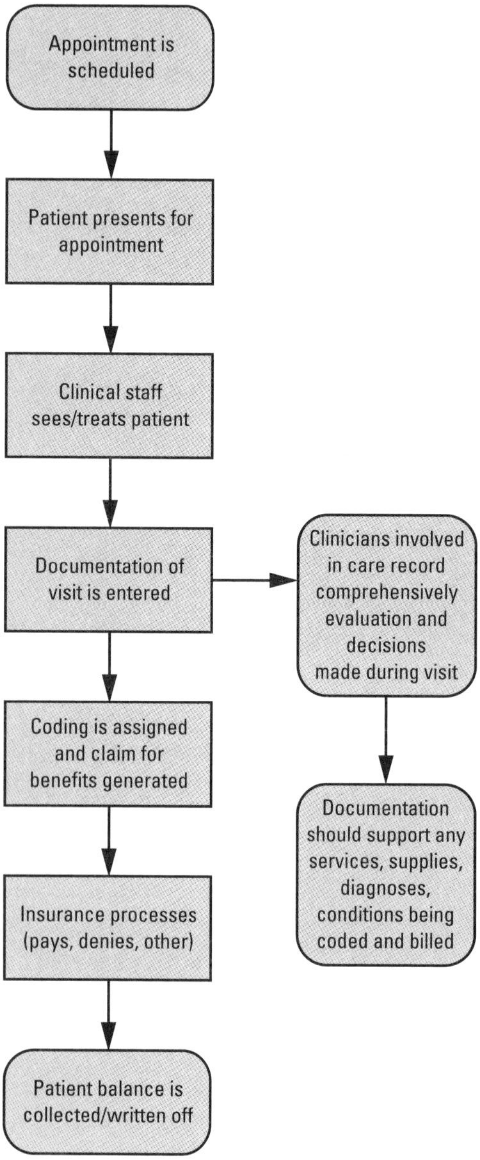

step of the revenue cycle to highlight important processes that should be followed.

Obviously, all necessary steps are not included here, but this should provide a general overview of some of the main processes in order to receive payment appropriately. Notice the insurance verification, documentation of services, and coding are all essential to appropriate payment. Documentation of the encounter determines the coding for the encounter and the coding of the encounter drives the level of payment as illustrated in Figure 1-3.

If a patient is scheduled or registered appropriately, that impacts the payment. If proper verification is not made at the point of scheduling and registration, an incorrect coinsurance/copayment might be charged (or not charged), the wrong insurance company could be billed, or the benefits of the patient's policy could be misunderstood—all of which costs the provider time and money to resolve later. If the clinical care is not well documented, it will affect payment and might put the patient care in dispute. If the documentation is not coded correctly, that impacts payment. Every element can put a provider's reputation, financial sustainability, and legal compliance at risk.

Payment for Health Care Providers

The largest portion of a health care provider's income—hospital, physician, or others—is derived from third-party payment. The mechanics of this payment are determined by individual payer contracts and policies, and medical coding. Different payers have various methods of determining the level of payment to be made on any single claim.

Medicare payment, for example, is established by the type of provider (hospitals are paid differently than physicians, and skilled nursing facilities are paid differently than either hospitals or physicians), coding (ICD-9-CM drives the inpatient facility payment for Medicare, but the Healthcare Common Procedure Coding System [HCPCS] decides the outpatient facility payment), and coverage criteria (Medicare's overarching criteria for payment is determined by ensuring that the level of care matches the patient's need and is neither under- nor overprovided). Private payers, however, may have different payment policies from Medicare, and a few may even pay based on the charged amounts rather than codes.

FIGURE 1-2D *Important Steps in Revenue Cycle*

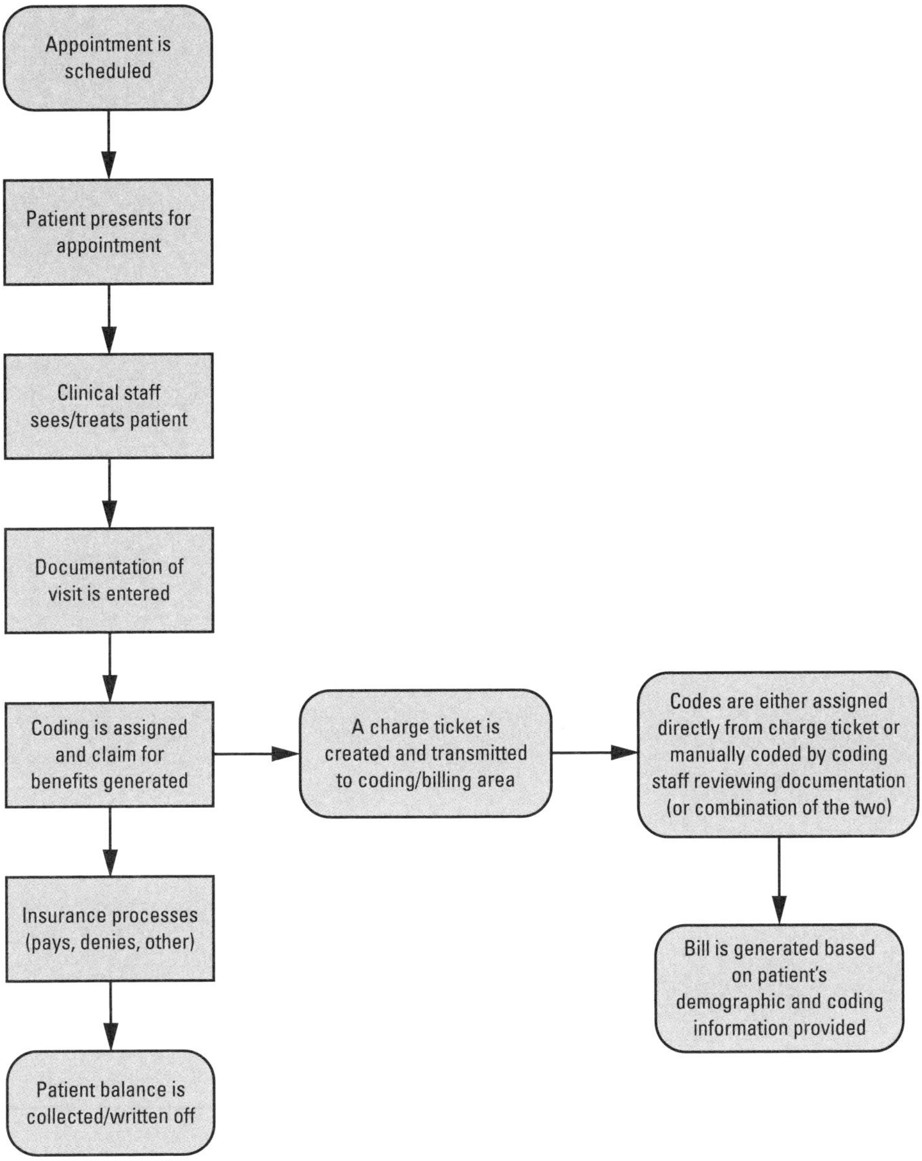

Learning Break

Keep a list of the payers with whom the facility provider has the most patients. Include the Web site for the payer, any relevant billing, coding, and payment guidelines related to that payer, and a copy of the contract (or at least how to access the contract). This way there should be few cases where much research has to be completed on a claim-by-claim basis.

HIPAA Coding Classifications

The Health Insurance Portability and Accountability Act of 1996 (HIPAA) established standards for the classification systems that providers, payers, and other covered entities must use. These classification standards include specific code systems to identify and

FIGURE 1-2E *Important Steps in Revenue Cycle*

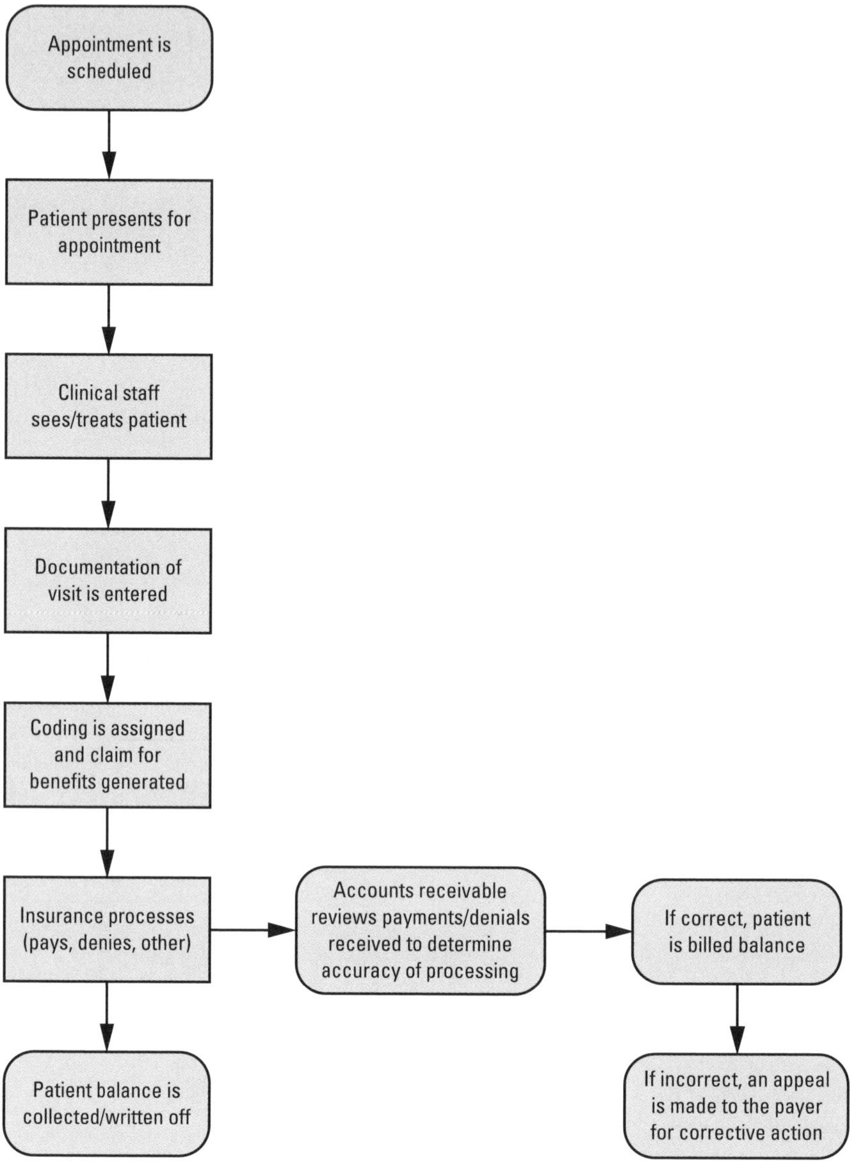

diagnose medical services and procedures for claim submissions as well as electronic transactions.

The following are the code sets that must be used based on HIPAA:

- Current Procedural Terminology (CPT), 4th Edition: Level I HCPCS primarily including codes for physician services and performance measurements. CPT is "a numeric coding system maintained by the American Medical Association (AMA). The CPT is a uniform coding system consisting of descriptive terms and identifying codes that are used primarily to identify medical services and procedures furnished by physicians and other health care professionals. These health care professionals use the CPT

FIGURE 1-3 *From Documentation to Payment*

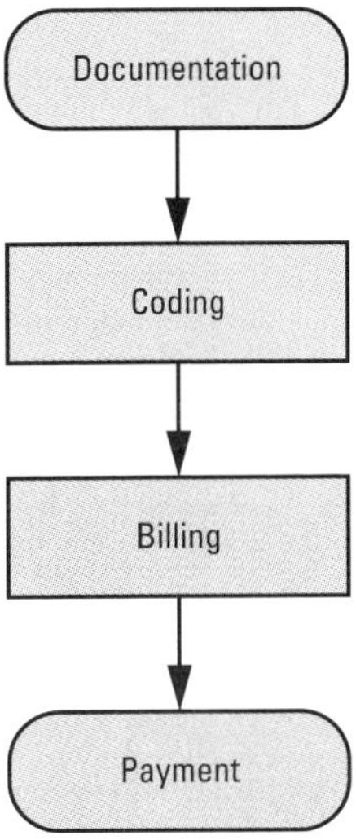

to identify services and procedures for which they bill public or private health insurance programs. Decisions regarding the addition, deletion, or revision of CPT codes are made by the AMA. The CPT codes are republished and updated annually by the AMA."[1]

- Healthcare Common Procedure Coding System (HCPCS): The HCPCS is divided into two principal subsystems, referred to as level I and level II of the HCPCS, and the Centers for Medicare and Medicaid Services (CMS) maintains this code set including CPT level I and level II HCPCS codes. Level I of the HCPCS comprises CPT codes, and it does not include codes needed to separately report medical items or services that are regularly billed by suppliers other than physicians. "Level II of the HCPCS is a standardized coding system that is used primarily to identify products, supplies, and services not included in the CPT codes, such as ambulance services and durable medical equipment, prosthetics, orthotics, and supplies (DMEPOS) when used outside a physician's office. Because Medicare and other insurers cover a variety of services, supplies, and equipment that are not identified by CPT codes, the level II HCPCS codes were established for submitting claims for these items. The development and use of level II of the HCPCS began in the 1980's. Level II codes are also referred to as alpha-numeric codes because they consist of a single alphabetical letter followed by 4 numeric digits, while CPT codes are identified using 5 numeric digits."[1]
- International Classification of Diseases, Ninth Revision, Clinical Modification (ICD-9-CM): Maintained by the National Center for Health Statistics, Volumes 1 and 2 represent diagnosis codes. Maintained by CMS, Volume 3 represents procedure codes used by hospitals for inpatient procedure reporting.

The two primary medical coding systems, CPT/HCPCS and ICD-9-CM, will be discussed more completely in later chapters, but Figure 1-4 provides a snapshot of how the most common health care providers (physicians, hospitals, ambulatory surgery centers) code and are paid under CMS regulations. There are many types of provider (skilled nursing facilities, ambulance providers, dentists, home health care agencies, etc) and many types of payers (other than Medicare and Medicaid), all of which may vary the method of coding and payment. Regardless of payer and system, CPT/HCPCS and ICD-9-CM are the principal coding systems used.

Importance of Coding

Medical coding is used for many reasons, including:

- to submit claims to insurance companies for payment
- to enter data into a repository for research use
- to store the data within a facility for analysis of patient care, financials, etc

Without medical coding, an entire medical record would need to be provided or accessed to communicate and understand the information in sufficient detail. This is impractical.

FIGURE 1-4 *Current Coding Systems Used in the United States*

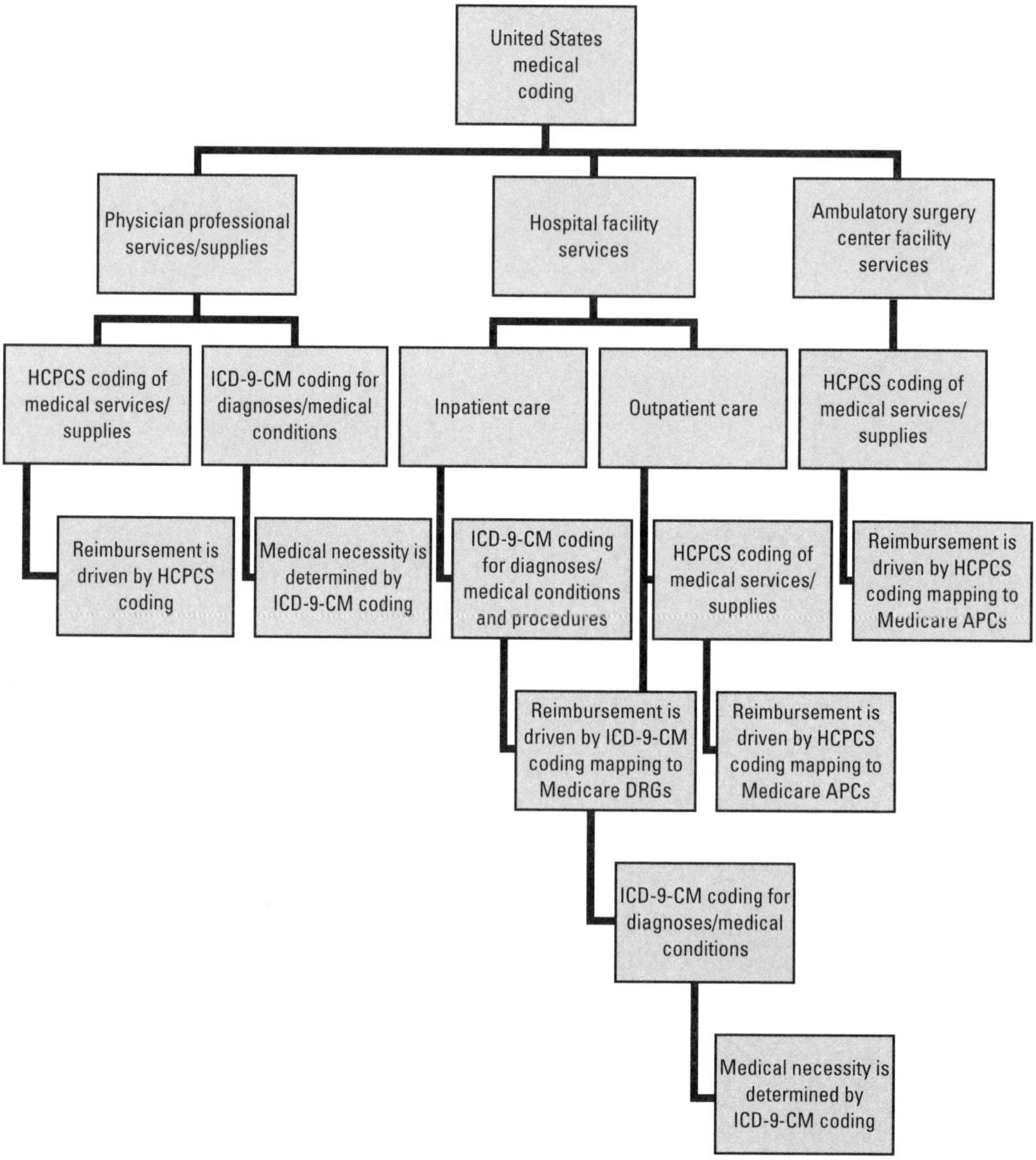

Learning Break

It's important to note that ICD-9-CM will be replaced by ICD-10-CM and ICD-10 Procedure Coding System (ICD-10-PCS) in 2013. Providers and payers are currently using ICD-9-CM in the United States, so overall, this will be a major change in medical coding. This book contains a chapter devoted to ICD-10-CM and ICD-10-PCS, and it is important to begin learning this system and adapting documentation to make the transition as seamless as possible.

Medical coding embodies every aspect of a patient's health history; therefore, accuracy is critically important. If incorrectly coded, a patient's diagnoses and procedures can be misstated, which could affect the patient's future insurability or quality of health care. Additionally, accurate coding is necessary to help ensure that the facility's payment is appropriate and that no compliance risks exist.

In the coding piece of the revenue cycle, clinical documentation (whether hardcopy or electronic) is analyzed by an individual and converted into CPT/HCPCS or ICD-9-CM codes (using a manual or a software program) and then entered into a database.

Accurate medical coding is one of the biggest challenges providers (and payers) face today.

Medical coding is challenging for many reasons:

- Codes are updated at least annually (with some changing more often), which requires coding personnel to stay current. This can be time consuming and costly.
- Some facilities use coding software (encoders, scrubbers, etc) that may provide erroneous information, may be used incorrectly, or may not be updated appropriately. This could lead to errors in coding.
- Coding is complex and requires ongoing education, good documentation, and experience.
- Coding includes all spectrums of health care from a simple incision and drainage of an abscess to complicated pediatric cardiovascular surgeries. A clinical understanding of what is being coded is important.
- If documentation is incomplete or unclear, it could potentially negatively impact the coding accuracy.
- The individual coding an encounter is often not the clinician providing the care. Coders must rely on the documentation in the medical record, a charge ticket, a superbill, or other billing document in which the clinician indicates the essentials of the medical encounter. A superbill (charge ticket or encounter form) is a form used by health care providers to quickly indicate what was involved in the patient's encounter for billing purposes. In addition to demographic information (patient's name, medical record number, date of service), the form includes the diagnoses being addressed during the encounter, the services and/or supplies provided, and charges for the encounter. This form rarely includes detailed information regarding the encounter. Therefore, the individual billing for the encounter is not truly coding but rather entering data into the billing information. See Figure 1-5 for a generic example of a superbill, which is usually provider-specific (eg, an obstetrics-gynecology practice's superbill would be substantially different from an orthopedist's superbill). Also, a hospital's billing would be done electronically by the specific department that performs the services (eg, laboratory, emergency department, cardiology); therefore, the charge ticket for the laboratory department would differ from that of the emergency department.

Coding Resources

It is helpful to have access to as many coding resources as possible. Because this book's purpose is not to teach how to code, the resources listed in this book should be considered integral to effectively understanding coding and payment. The experienced coder will understand the value and necessity of good, current resources. It is unwise to code using outdated manuals, and it is important to remember that the codes change on at least an annual basis. In addition to suggested resources, checklists (see boxed-texts on page 11 and 12) are provided to help a facility ensure that its resources are current and optimized. Coding resources can range from printed resources to software and online resources.

Software

Coding software can help supplement manual review and translation. As electronic

FIGURE 1-5 *Sample Physician Superbill*[2]

[Company Name] YOUR LOGO HERE

Outpatient Encounter Form

Patient Information		Payment Method		Visit Information	
Patient ID number		**Primary**		Visit date	
Patient name		Primary ID number		Visit number	
Address		Primary group number		Rendering physician	
City/State		**Secondary**		Referring physician	
Social Security number		Secondary ID number		Reason for visit	
Phone number		Secondary group no.			
Date of birth		Cash/credit card			
Age		Other billing			

E/M Modifiers	Procedure Modifiers	Other Modifiers
24 — Unrelated E/M service during postop.	22 — Unusual, excessive procedure	
25 — Significant, separately identifiable E/M	50 — Bilateral procedure	
57 — Decision for surgery	51 — Multiple surgical procedures in same day	
	52 — Reduced/incomplete procedure	
	55 — Postop. management only	
	59 — Distinct multiple procedures	

CATEGORY	CODE	MOD	FEE	CATEGORY	CODE	MOD	FEE
Office Visit — New Patient				**Wound Care**			
Minimal office visit	99201			Debride partial thick burn	11040		
20 minutes	99202			Debride full thickness burn	11041		
30 minutes	99203			Debride wound, not a burn	11000		
45 minutes	99204			Unna boot application	29580		
60 minutes	99205			Unna boot removal	29700		
Other				Other			
Office Visit — Established				**Supplies**			
Minimal office visit	99211			Ace bandage, 2"	A6448		
10 minutes	99212			Ace bandage, 3"-4"	A6449		
15 minutes	99213			Ace bandage, 6"	A6450		
25 minutes	99214			Cast, fiberglass	A4590		
40 minutes	99215			Coban wrap	A6454		
Other				Foley catheter	A4338		
General Procedures				Immobilizer	L3670		
Anascopy	46600			Kerlix roll	A6220		
Audiometry	92551			Oxygen mask/cannula	A4620		
Breast aspiration	19000			Sleeve, elbow	E0191		
Cerumen removal	69210			Sling	A4565		
Circumcision	54150			Splint, ready-made	A4570		
DDST	96110			Splint, wrist	S8451		
Flex sigmoidoscopy	45330			Sterile packing	A6407		
Flex sig. w/ biopsy	45331			Surgical tray	A4550		
Foreign body removal—foot	28190			Other			
Nail removal	11730			**OB Care**			
Nail removal/phenol	11750			Routine OB care	59400		
Trigger point injection	20552			OB call	59422		
Tympanometry	92567			Ante partum 4–6 visits	59425		
Visual acuity	99173			Ante partum 7 or more visits	59426		
Other				Other			

Vitals:
B/P ______
Pulse ______
Temp. ______
Height ______
Weight ______

Other Visit Information:
Lab Work to Order: ______
Referral to: ______
Provider Signature: ______
Next Appointment: ______

Fees:
Total Charges: $______
Copay Received: $______
Other Payment: $______
Total Due: $______

Company Name, Street Address, City, State, ZIP Code, phone number health records (EHRs) flourish, many providers employ software to assist in coding. There are different types of software to assist in coding:

- Encoding products. Encoders help assign the correct code by using a series of questions and answers to help drill down to the correct code. Often, hospitals will use encoders in their health information management department to determine the correct diagnosis or surgery coding.
- Computer-assisted coding (CAC). There are computer software applications that offer suggestions for medical codes based on the medical record documentation. There are several advantages to CAC such as increased productivity and consistency, but it can be expensive and might not be as accurate as manual coding. During the implementation of CAC, a provider should assign the computer-assisted coding only after an experienced individual has reviewed and validated the codes.
- Claims scrubbing software. Software that can review claims for potential problems at the point of billing has become increasingly popular in the last decade. This software essentially runs the bill through Medicare edits to see if bundling issues might exist, if the demographic information appears accurate, or if there are incongruous codes (CPT and ICD). In short, the scrubber helps ensure the claim will be processed correctly without having a rejected claim from the payer. Examples of claims scrubbers are the McKesson Health Solutions *ClaimCheck* software and the National Correct Coding Initiative (NCCI) edits.
- Electronic coding manuals. Electronic coding manuals take all the hardcopy resources (eg, *CPT Assistant*, CPT codebook, ICD-9-CM manual, HCPCS) and put them in electronic form so individual users can access them more easily from different locations. The AMA offers the CodeManager[3] software as an electronic coding reference resource.

Quick questions to check on your coding software:

1. What software does your facility use?
2. What is the purpose of the software (coding, encoding, replacing manuals)?
3. Is the contract current?
4. Does the contract include updates?
5. How often are updates provided?
6. Do those responsible for coding, billing, and accounts receivable understand how to use the software effectively?

Print Resources

Several vendors sell printed resources (ie, books and manuals) for coding. When a practice uses a print resource, it must ensure that staff uses the correct set of data for the date of service in question. It is best to check with vendors to learn how updates are dispersed. The manuals that a facility must have for coding are:

- Current CPT codebook*: This resource will have all the current year's CPT codes except for semi-annually updated Category III codes, which can be obtained through the AMA's Web site (see next section).
- Current HCPCS Level II manual*: This resource will have all the current year's HCPCS Level II codes except for payer-specific updates, which should be obtained through individual payer Web sites (see next section).
- Current ICD-9-CM manual (Volumes 1 and 2 for nonhospital coding; Volumes 1, 2, and 3 for inpatient hospital coding)*: This resource will have all the current year's ICD-9-CM codes.

---

* Past issues of codebook and manuals may be needed if you either review, audit, or appeal older service dates. Therefore, it is a good practice to save any older manuals for later access, and it is also important to keep track of your print resources.

- Past issues of *CPT Assistant*[4]: This resource will include all *CPT Assistant* articles since 1990. It is also helpful to search for reporting instructions that have been updated due to subsequent code revisions/additions/deletions in the CPT code set.
- Current CPT *Insiders View*[5]: This resource will explain the annual changes in CPT codes. The code change details, rationale, and clinical examples are included.

Questions to ask include:

1. Does your facility have all appropriate coding manuals necessary (see above list)?
2. If not, what is missing?
3. How are updates obtained?
4. Are these resources current?

Online Resources

There are hundreds if not thousands of Web sites devoted to coding, payment, and documentation. Listed below are Web sites that are recognized for their authority in coding guidelines and regulations.

AMA Web Site

AMA, the official administrator of CPT coding, has a great deal of information related to coding on its Web site, which can be accessed at www.ama-assn.org/ama/pub/physician-resources/solutions-managing-your-practice/coding-billing-insurance/cpt/about-cpt.shtml. If seeking further confirmation/clarification of CPT code set errata published during a given CPT cycle, visit www.ama-assn.org/ama/pub/physician-resources/solutions-managing-your-practice/coding-billing-insurance/cpt/about-cpt/errata.shtml.

CMS Web Site

CMS, the major payer for physicians and health care professionals, has a wealth of information on its Web site, which can be accessed at www.cms.hhs.gov. In addition to accessing the national CMS Web site, be sure to visit the Web sites of all the individual payers who you bill.

CDC Web Site

The National Center for Health Statistics (NCHS) is a part of the Centers for Disease Control and Prevention (CDC); therefore, ICD-9-CM related information is found at the CDC Web site. The guidelines on the CDC Web site are important to coding and are available at www.cdc.gov/nchs/icd/icd9cm_addenda_guidelines.htm.[6]

Questions that will help to keep track of the Web sites include:

1. Which Web sites do you (or your staff) access? Keep a list.
2. Have you bookmarked these on your computer?
3. How often do you check for updates?
4. Do you look closely to determine any pertinent changes?
5. Are any of these resources duplicative? If so, make sure the most up-to-date is the one accessed.

Definitions and Acronyms

American Medical Association (AMA). This is an association whose mission is to promote the art and science of medicine and the betterment of public health.

Centers for Medicare and Medicaid Services (CMS). This is a branch of the Department of Health and Human Services (HHS) responsible for overseeing the Medicare and Medicaid federal health care programs.

Healthcare Common Procedure Coding System (HCPCS). This is a coding system that includes medical procedures, pharmaceuticals, supplies, ambulance services, and CMS-established temporary codes. HCPCS includes CPT codes maintained by the AMA and non-CPT codes maintained by CMS.

International Classification of Diseases (ICD).[7] This is the classification (ie, coding) system maintained by the World Health Organization. ICD is used for international comparability of mortality statistics. Medical conditions are translated into codes through use of the classification structure and the selection and modification rules contained in the ICD.

International Classification of Diseases, Ninth Revision, Clinical Modification (ICD-9-CM). This is used in the United States and is based on the World Health Organization's International Classification of Diseases, Ninth Revision (ICD-9). It is the official system of assigning codes to diagnoses and procedures associated with hospital utilization in the United States. *Note that ICD-9-CM is used for both inpatient and outpatient diagnoses, but it is only used for inpatient prescriptions.*

International Classification of Diseases, Tenth Revision, Clinical Modification (ICD-10-CM). This is the replacement for ICD-9-CM, Volumes 1 and 2, scheduled for implementation on October 1, 2013.

International Classification of Diseases, Tenth Revision, Procedure Coding System (ICD-10-PCS). This is the replacement for ICD-9-CM, Volume 3, scheduled for implementation on October 1, 2013.

Medicare Severity Diagnosis Related Groups (MS-DRGs). This is the CMS payment system for inpatient hospital care.

REFERENCES

1. Centers for Disease Control & Prevention. HCPCS—General Information. Overview. Available at: www.cms.gov/medhcpcsgeninfo/. Accessed April 5, 2011.
2. Microsoft Templates. Outpatient Encounter Form. Available at: http://office.microsoft.com/en-us/templates/outpatient-encounter-form-TC001204517.aspx?AxInstalled=1&c=0. Accessed January 5, 2011.
3. American Medical Association. *CodeManager* [software]. Available at: www.codemanager.com. Accessed January 15, 2011.
4. American Medical Association. *CPT Assistant 1990-2009*. Chicago, IL: American Medical Association; 2010.
5. American Medical Association. *CPT Changes: An Insider's View*. Chicago, IL: American Medical Association; 2010.
6. Centers for Disease Control & Prevention. ICD-9-CM Guidelines. Available at: www.cdc.gov/nchs/data/icd9/icdguide10.pdf. Accessed January 3, 2011.
7. Centers for Disease Control & Prevention. International Classification of Diseases, Ninth Revision. Available at: www.cdc.gov/nchs/icd/icd9.htm. Accessed January 3, 2011.

Chapter 2

Insurance Payment Overview

Health Insurance Overview

Providers (physicians, hospitals, etc) submit health insurance claims to insurance companies to receive payment for the services they provide to patients. Patients are billed directly if they have no insurance. Coverage for services and the amounts paid by the insurance company (insurer) depend on the patient's health insurance policy.

There are thousands of options for individuals and employers when choosing health insurance, and with those options come thousands of guidelines surrounding claim payment. The health care provider is subject to following those guidelines and must have a level of understanding of how to properly bill.

Most of the different policy types are summarized in Table 2-1.

The health insurance policy is an agreement (contract) between the insured and the insurer. The agreement outlines what health care services and supplies the insurer will pay for in exchange for a payment of a premium. Usually the policy includes a listing of services and supplies that will be covered, as well as those that are not covered or are conditionally covered. If health care is provided that is not covered by the policy, the insured are typically responsible for paying for the service themselves. The insurance company is only responsible for paying benefits that are covered under the policy.

With so many options, insurance billing is quite complex, and providers should understand the type of insurance a patient has and the billing guidelines for that policy. If providers are unfamiliar with the specifics of a patient's insurance, they should investigate the particulars before services are rendered. It is best to determine insurance coverage as early as possible within a medical encounter, or ideally, when the patient schedules the appointment. A lack of this information prior to rendering care can mean lost payment for the provider. Also, because the patient is often responsible for any noncovered services or at least a copayment or deductible, it is important to know what patients should be paying and encourage them to render payment at the time of service rather than billing them later.

Tip: *It is helpful to keep a chart of benefits by payer type as a quick reference when filing a claim or collecting a copayment. That information should stay in each patient's file, and a grid of the most common payers/policies should be maintained and stored electronically so staff can quickly check whether a copayment is to be collected, if benefits are limited in some way, or if a referral is needed prior to coverage.*

TABLE 2-1 *Types of Insurance Policies*

Government Health Insurance	
Health Plan	**Brief Description**
Medicare	Federal program to provide coverage for elderly and disabled persons.
CHAMPVA	Civilian Health and Medical Program of the Department of Veterans Affairs provides benefits to veterans (and dependents of veterans) who are completely and permanently disabled from a service-related condition or died as a result of a service-related condition, or died on duty with fewer than 30 days of active service.
Medicaid	Federal- and state-sponsored program providing health care coverage for low-income populations.
TRICARE	Military health care coverage for active duty and retired members of the military.
FEHBP	Federal Employee Health Benefits Program is a voluntary program covering federal employees, retirees, and their dependents.
IHS	Indian Health Service provides federal health care for American Indians and Alaska natives.

Managed Care Health Insurance	
Health Plan	**Brief Description**
Managed Care General	Health care is reimbursed through capitation, which occurs when pre-established fees are agreed upon. The fees can be per member per month or otherwise. By participating in the plan, the physician agrees to accept the pre-established payment to provide care for the patient.
HMO	Health maintenance organizations provide comprehensive health care to enrolled members. The patients go to the HMO providers, so HMOs eliminate some patient selection by narrowing the choice of providers to those who are participating or employed by the HMO.
PPO	Preferred (or participating) provider organizations are networks of health care providers who join together and contract with insurance companies and provide health care at predetermined discounted fees. Patients have more flexibility in selecting physicians within a PPO than an HMO.
EPO	Exclusive provider organizations are similar to PPOs; however, the insured must use the providers within the EPO to have benefits covered. There are usually fewer providers within an EPO to make it enticing to the providers, thus the "exclusiveness" of the plan.
POS	Point-of-service plans offer more flexibility than an HMO in that the provider can make referrals for the patient to see out-of-network physicians. If out-of-network physicians are seen, the costs (copayment, deductible, etc) are increased.

(continued)

TABLE 2-1 *(continued)*

Other Health Insurance Options	
Health Plan	**Brief Description**
Employer Self-Insured	Through a third-party administrator (TPA) an employer assumes the responsibility for paying for the employees' health care rather than buying a policy from an insurance company.
Workers' Compensation	This is a state-mandated insurance that reimburses health care and lost wages if an employee suffers a work-related injury or condition.
CDHP	Consumer-driven health plans encourage the insured to take more responsibility for their health care and the costs. Insureds may use Health Savings Accounts (HSAs) or Health Reimbursement Arrangements (HRAs) to pay for smaller or routine services combined with a high-deductible policy (with lower premiums) to help protect against catastrophic medical expenses.

How the Revenue Cycle is Key to Accurate Claims Submission

As outlined in Chapter 1, each step of the revenue cycle is important in receiving appropriate payment for services provided. The practice has a lot of control over the revenue cycle, and to help guarantee successful collection of payment from insurers and the patients, a few easy steps can be implemented.

Scheduling and Registration

When scheduling a visit make sure you have this information:

- Correct spelling of patient's name
- Current address and phone number
- Social Security Number
- Date of birth
- Employer's name, address, and phone number (if applicable)
- Guarantor's information (name, address, number, employer, etc)—this is the person responsible for paying the charges
- Spouse or significant other's information
- Referring provider's name and address, if applicable
- Emergency contact information
- Health insurance information
  - Name and phone number of insurance company
  - Policy number
  - Policy holder's name
  - Group number

In addition, send patients any appropriate paperwork (registration form, history or patient intake forms, etc) or direct them to a Web site where they can download the appropriate documents for completion prior to their arrival for care.

Confirm with the patient's insurance company what benefits are available and any copayment or deductible due. A preauthorization may be needed for services rendered, which means the service must be approved in advance for it to be covered.

When registering a patient presenting for services, the key is to verify the information collected during scheduling. Request the insurance card and copy it (front and back) to file in the patient's financial record. Collect the copayment from the patient, if known. See Figure 2-1 for an example of a registration form.

Clinical Care for the Patient

When the clinician is treating the patient, it is imperative that the encounter be well documented within the record (ie, so that it will support payment for the services)

FIGURE 2-1 *Sample Patient Registration Form*[1]

[Name of Practice]

REGISTRATION FORM

(Please Print)

Today's Date:			PCP:		
PATIENT INFORMATION					
Patient's last name: First: Middle:	☐ Mr. ☐ Mrs.	☐ Miss ☐ Ms.	Marital status: Single☐ Mar ☐ Div☐ Sep☐ Wid ☐		
Is this your legal name? ☐ Yes ☐ No	If not, what is your legal name?	(Former name):	Birth date:	Age:	Sex: ☐ M ☐ F
Street address:	Social Security no.:	Home phone no.: ( )			
P.O. box:	City:	State:	ZIP Code:		
Occupation:	Employer:	Employer phone no.: ( )			
Chose clinic because/referred to clinic by (Please check one box):	☐ Dr.	☐ Insurance plan	☐ Hospital		
☐ Family	☐ Friend	☐ Close to home/work	☐ Yellow Pages	☐ Other	
Other family members seen here:					

INSURANCE INFORMATION						
(Please give your insurance card to the receptionist)						
Person responsible for bill:	Birth date:	Address (If different):	Home phone no.: ( )			
Is this person a patient here? ☐ Yes ☐ No						
Occupation:	Employer:	Employer address:	Employer phone no.: ( )			
Is this patient covered by insurance? ☐ Yes ☐ No						
Please indicate primary insurance	☐ [Insurance]	☐ [Insurance]	☐ [Insurance]	☐ [Insurance]	☐ [Insurance]	
☐ [Insurance]	☐ [Insurance]	☐ [Insurance]	☐ Welfare *(Please provide coupon)*	☐ Other		
Subscriber's name:	Subscriber's S.S. no.:	Birth date:	Group no.:	Policy no.:	Co-payment: $	
Patient's relationship to subscriber:	☐ Self	☐ Spouse	☐ Child	☐ Other		
Name of secondary insurance (If applicable):	Subscriber's name:	Group no.:	Policy no.:			
Patient's relationship to subscriber:	☐ Self	☐ Spouse	☐ Child	☐ Other		

IN CASE OF EMERGENCY			
Name of local friend or relative (not living at same address):	Relationship to patient:	Home phone no.: ( )	Work phone no.: ( )

The above information is true to the best of my knowledge. I authorize my insurance benefits be paid directly to the physician. I understand that I am financially responsible for any balance. I also authorize [Name of Practice] or insurance company to release any information required to process my claims.

_______________________________ _______________

Patient/Guardian signature *Date*

and appropriate charges be selected. See Chapter 8 on documentation.

Billing the Encounter

Upon conclusion of care, the services and/or supplies and diagnoses will be coded and billed to the insurance company. The billing may be sent through a clearinghouse that validates the claims data and electronically transmits the claim.

Health Insurance Claim Forms

In order to receive payment, providers will submit a health insurance claim (form CMS-1500 or UB-04) to the insurance company. The CMS-1500 form is illustrated in Figure 2-2 and the UB-04 form in Figure 2-3.

The CMS-1500 form is used to submit claims for professional services by physicians and other clinicians (eg, nurse practitioners) and for Medicare and freestanding surgery centers (for non-Medicare payers, most surgery centers submit the UB-04). The UB-04 is used to submit facility (eg, hospital) services. Both of these forms will be reviewed in detail in Chapter 3.

Claims are usually submitted by electronic data interchange (EDI) using specialized software.

Time Limitations for Filing a Claim

Payers generally have filing deadlines for claims. Because payments, coverage benefits, etc, change over time, it is important to submit the claim as soon as possible. The longer the delay in submitting claims, the greater the chance of a problem occurring in processing the benefits. For Medicare, claims must be filed within 12 months from the date of service for fee-for-service claims. When a provider fails to file a timely claim, a patient may not be charged for the services except for deductibles and/or coinsurance amounts that would have been appropriate if Medicare payment had been made. Also, the provider may **not** appeal a rejection based on timely filing errors.

Insurance Processing of Claims and Accounts Receivable

Accounts Receivable Management

When the claim is processed by the insurance company, the accounts receivable staff will validate that the payment is appropriate and post or appeal the payment.

It is hoped that everything goes smoothly and the claims are processed correctly and promptly; however, on occasion there likely will be a claim that is denied or underpaid. This can cause problems for the provider because the work and costs of providing the care have been expended but not paid for adequately.

There are many reasons for claims to be rejected by a payer. Some of the common reasons for denied, rejected, or underpaid claims are:

- The plan might not cover the procedure, drug, or supply.
- The insurance company believes the service is not medically necessary.
- The service, drug, or supply is considered experimental.
- There was no preauthorization for the service.
- The claim contains errors (missing information, wrong insured).
- The claim was not filed within time limits specified by the policy.
- The insurer processes the claim erroneously.
- Services were unbundled (submitting multiple services when one comprehensive service is correct).
- Patient's coverage is cancelled prior to service date.
- Payer believes they are not the primary insurer for the services.
- There are incongruencies between the insured's benefits and the billed claim.

FIGURE 2-2 *CMS-1500 Health Insurance Claim Form*

1500

HEALTH INSURANCE CLAIM FORM

APPROVED BY NATIONAL UNIFORM CLAIM COMMITTEE 08/05

PICA | PICA

CARRIER

1. MEDICARE (Medicare #) MEDICAID (Medicaid #) TRICARE CHAMPUS (Sponsor's SSN) CHAMPVA (Member ID#) GROUP HEALTH PLAN (SSN or ID) FECA BLK LUNG (SSN) OTHER (ID)

1a. INSURED'S I.D. NUMBER (For Program in Item 1)

2. PATIENT'S NAME (Last Name, First Name, Middle Initial)

3. PATIENT'S BIRTH DATE MM DD YY SEX M F

4. INSURED'S NAME (Last Name, First Name, Middle Initial)

5. PATIENT'S ADDRESS (No., Street)

6. PATIENT RELATIONSHIP TO INSURED Self Spouse Child Other

7. INSURED'S ADDRESS (No., Street)

CITY STATE

8. PATIENT STATUS Single Married Other

CITY STATE

ZIP CODE TELEPHONE (Include Area Code) ( )

Employed Full-Time Student Part-Time Student

ZIP CODE TELEPHONE (Include Area Code) ( )

9. OTHER INSURED'S NAME (Last Name, First Name, Middle Initial)

10. IS PATIENT'S CONDITION RELATED TO:

11. INSURED'S POLICY GROUP OR FECA NUMBER

a. OTHER INSURED'S POLICY OR GROUP NUMBER

a. EMPLOYMENT? (Current or Previous) YES NO

a. INSURED'S DATE OF BIRTH MM DD YY SEX M F

b. OTHER INSURED'S DATE OF BIRTH MM DD YY SEX M F

b. AUTO ACCIDENT? YES NO PLACE (State)

b. EMPLOYER'S NAME OR SCHOOL NAME

c. EMPLOYER'S NAME OR SCHOOL NAME

c. OTHER ACCIDENT? YES NO

c. INSURANCE PLAN NAME OR PROGRAM NAME

d. INSURANCE PLAN NAME OR PROGRAM NAME

10d. RESERVED FOR LOCAL USE

d. IS THERE ANOTHER HEALTH BENEFIT PLAN? YES NO *If yes*, return to and complete item 9 a-d.

READ BACK OF FORM BEFORE COMPLETING & SIGNING THIS FORM.

12. PATIENT'S OR AUTHORIZED PERSON'S SIGNATURE I authorize the release of any medical or other information necessary to process this claim. I also request payment of government benefits either to myself or to the party who accepts assignment below.

SIGNED ________ DATE ________

13. INSURED'S OR AUTHORIZED PERSON'S SIGNATURE I authorize payment of medical benefits to the undersigned physician or supplier for services described below.

SIGNED ________

PATIENT AND INSURED INFORMATION

14. DATE OF CURRENT: MM DD YY ILLNESS (First symptom) OR INJURY (Accident) OR PREGNANCY(LMP)

15. IF PATIENT HAS HAD SAME OR SIMILAR ILLNESS. GIVE FIRST DATE MM DD YY

16. DATES PATIENT UNABLE TO WORK IN CURRENT OCCUPATION MM DD YY FROM TO MM DD YY

17. NAME OF REFERRING PROVIDER OR OTHER SOURCE

17a. 17b. NPI

18. HOSPITALIZATION DATES RELATED TO CURRENT SERVICES MM DD YY FROM TO MM DD YY

19. RESERVED FOR LOCAL USE

20. OUTSIDE LAB? YES NO $ CHARGES

21. DIAGNOSIS OR NATURE OF ILLNESS OR INJURY (Relate Items 1, 2, 3 or 4 to Item 24E by Line)

1. ___ . ___ 3. ___ . ___

2. ___ . ___ 4. ___ . ___

22. MEDICAID RESUBMISSION CODE ORIGINAL REF. NO.

23. PRIOR AUTHORIZATION NUMBER

24. A. DATE(S) OF SERVICE From MM DD YY To MM DD YY	B. PLACE OF SERVICE	C. EMG	D. PROCEDURES, SERVICES, OR SUPPLIES (Explain Unusual Circumstances) CPT/HCPCS MODIFIER	E. DIAGNOSIS POINTER	F. $ CHARGES	G. DAYS OR UNITS	H. EPSDT Family Plan	I. ID. QUAL.	J. RENDERING PROVIDER ID. #
1								NPI	
2								NPI	
3								NPI	
4								NPI	
5								NPI	
6								NPI	

25. FEDERAL TAX I.D. NUMBER SSN EIN

26. PATIENT'S ACCOUNT NO.

27. ACCEPT ASSIGNMENT? (For govt. claims, see back) YES NO

28. TOTAL CHARGE $

29. AMOUNT PAID $

30. BALANCE DUE $

31. SIGNATURE OF PHYSICIAN OR SUPPLIER INCLUDING DEGREES OR CREDENTIALS (I certify that the statements on the reverse apply to this bill and are made a part thereof.)

SIGNED DATE

32. SERVICE FACILITY LOCATION INFORMATION

a. NPI b.

33. BILLING PROVIDER INFO & PH # ( )

a. NPI b.

PHYSICIAN OR SUPPLIER INFORMATION

NUCC Instruction Manual available at: www.nucc.org

APPROVED OMB-0938-0999 FORM CMS-1500 (08-05)

Source: www.cms.gov.

FIGURE 2-3 *UB-04 Health Insurance Claim Form*

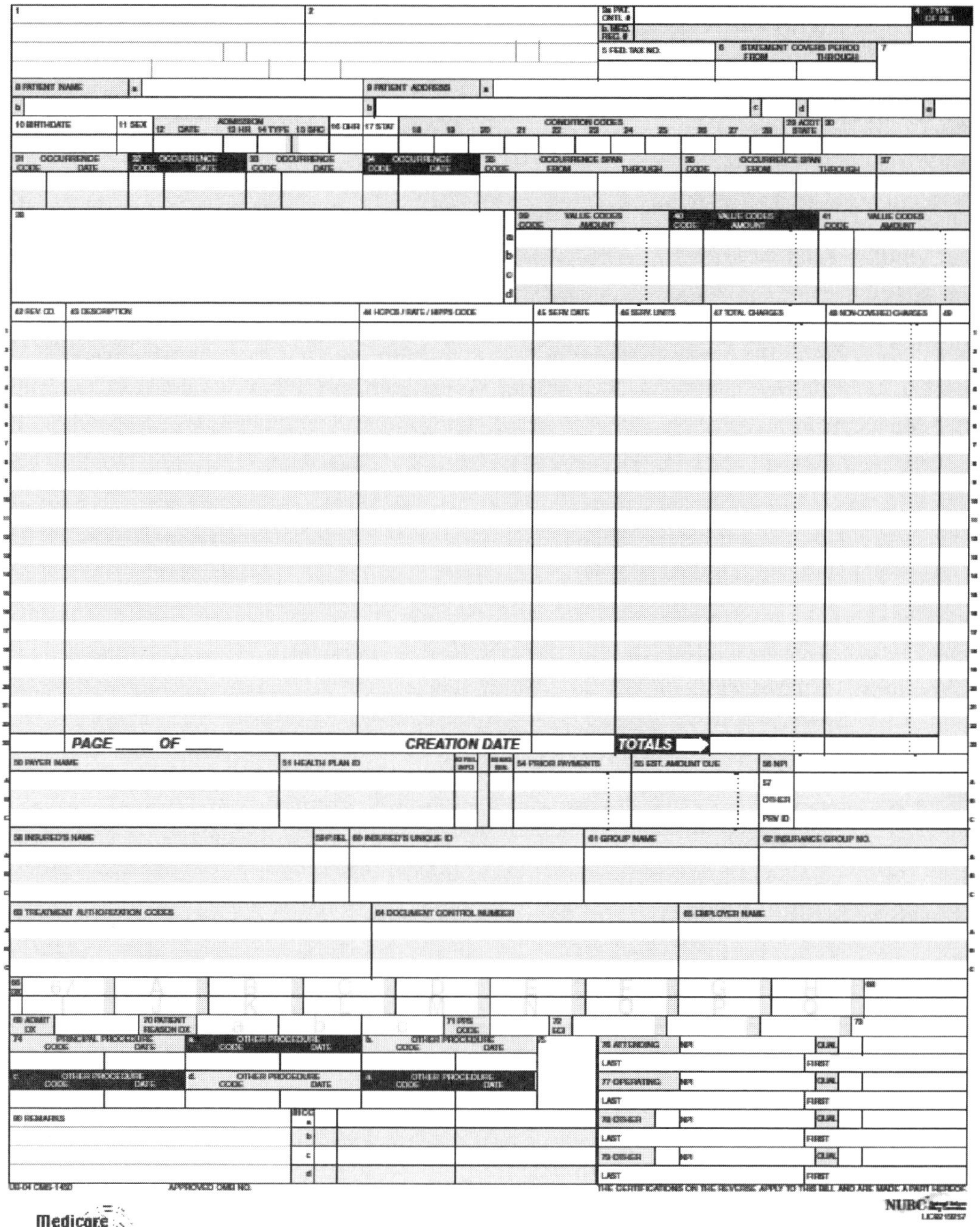
1
2
3a PAT. CNTL #
b. MED. REC. #
4 TYPE OF BILL
5 FED. TAX NO.
6 STATEMENT COVERS PERIOD FROM THROUGH
7
8 PATIENT NAME a
b
9 PATIENT ADDRESS a
b c d e
10 BIRTHDATE
11 SEX
ADMISSION 12 DATE 13 HR 14 TYPE 15 SRC
16 DHR
17 STAT
CONDITION CODES 18 19 20 21 22 23 24 25 26 27 28
29 ACDT STATE
30
31 OCCURRENCE CODE DATE
32 OCCURRENCE CODE DATE
33 OCCURRENCE CODE DATE
34 OCCURRENCE CODE DATE
35 OCCURRENCE SPAN CODE FROM THROUGH
36 OCCURRENCE SPAN CODE FROM THROUGH
37
38
39 VALUE CODES CODE AMOUNT
40 VALUE CODES CODE AMOUNT
41 VALUE CODES CODE AMOUNT
a b c d
42 REV. CD.
43 DESCRIPTION
44 HCPCS / RATE / HIPPS CODE
45 SERV. DATE
46 SERV. UNITS
47 TOTAL CHARGES
48 NON-COVERED CHARGES
49
PAGE ____ OF ____
CREATION DATE
TOTALS
50 PAYER NAME
51 HEALTH PLAN ID
52 REL. INFO
53 ASG. BEN.
54 PRIOR PAYMENTS
55 EST. AMOUNT DUE
56 NPI
57 OTHER PRV ID
A B C
58 INSURED'S NAME
59 P. REL
60 INSURED'S UNIQUE ID
61 GROUP NAME
62 INSURANCE GROUP NO.
63 TREATMENT AUTHORIZATION CODES
64 DOCUMENT CONTROL NUMBER
65 EMPLOYER NAME
66 DX
67 A B C D E F G H
I J K L M N O P Q
68
69 ADMIT DX
70 PATIENT REASON DX a b c
71 PPS CODE
72 ECI
73
74 PRINCIPAL PROCEDURE CODE DATE
a. OTHER PROCEDURE CODE DATE
b. OTHER PROCEDURE CODE DATE
75
76 ATTENDING NPI QUAL
LAST FIRST
c. OTHER PROCEDURE CODE DATE
d. OTHER PROCEDURE CODE DATE
e. OTHER PROCEDURE CODE DATE
77 OPERATING NPI QUAL
LAST FIRST
80 REMARKS
81CC a b c d
78 OTHER NPI QUAL
LAST FIRST
79 OTHER NPI QUAL
LAST FIRST
UB-04 CMS-1450
APPROVED OMB NO.
THE CERTIFICATIONS ON THE REVERSE APPLY TO THIS BILL AND ARE MADE A PART HEREOF.
NUBC

Medicare Learning Network

Source: www.cms.gov.

In addition, when a claim is denied, rejected, or underpaid incorrectly, there are remedies the practice can pursue. However, before challenging the way a claim was processed, the provider should track and validate how claims should have been adjudicated versus how they were adjudicated. Sometimes when reviewing how a claim was processed, providers can feel like they are putting together a jigsaw puzzle, but there are no corner pieces and the puzzle is all white. Most payers are open to inquiries from a provider for clarification of benefits paid, rejections, or denials; however, there are usually processes to follow to expedite the handling of such queries. The accounts receivable staff is obligated to verify that claims are processed correctly. Be certain the appropriate personnel are taking the time to review payments for accuracy prior to posting them. If payments are received as expected, they can be posted and any secondary insurance filed or the patient billed for any applicable coinsurance. However, if there is an error with the payment, the provider should call the insurance company to discuss the problem, and this might quickly resolve the issue. If a phone call doesn't work, then a formal review can be requested; there are additional levels of appeal to pursue as well.

Levels of Appeal Claims

Figure 2-4 highlights the levels of appeal for Medicare claims. Non-Medicare can be appealed as well but might have different processes.

There are five levels of appeal for Medicare claims processing, as shown in Figure 2-4. Level 1 is Redetermination. This is where the Medicare Administrative Contractors (MAC) personnel (different from those who made the initial determination) review the claim. The individual appealing has 120 days from the date of the initial claim determination, and there is no minimal dollar threshold to be met. The CMS-20027[3] form can be used to make the request, but the form is not mandatory as long as the necessary information (beneficiary name and policy number, specifics on service for which the request is made, name and signature along with supporting documentation) is provided in writing.

Level 2 is Reconsideration by a Qualified Independent Contractor (QIC). If the requester is dissatisfied with the results of the redetermination, a reconsideration request may be made. A QIC will conduct the reconsideration. This ensures an independent review. There is no minimal dollar threshold for reconsideration, and the written request must be submitted within 180 days of the redetermination decision. The redetermination decision will be sent on a Medicare Redetermination Notice (MRN) and will provide instructions on requesting reconsideration. The CMS-20033[4] form is mailed with the MRN and can be used to make the request, but the form is not mandatory as long as the necessary information (beneficiary name and policy number, specifics on service for which the request is made, name and signature along with supporting documentation, name of contractor that made the redetermination decision) is provided in writing.

Level 3 is Hearing by an Administrative Law Judge (ALJ). Within 60 days of the reconsideration decision, an appeal may be made for an ALJ review as long as at least $130 is in dispute. The reconsideration letter will provide details as to how to request this level of appeal. The CMS-20034[5] form may be used.

Level 4 is Review by a Medicare Appeals Council. If the requester is still dissatisfied after the ALJ's decision, a request for review by a Medicare Appeals Council may be made. This request must be made within 60 days of the ALJ's decision. The ALJ's decision will provide details as to how the Appeals Council review can be solicited.

Level 5 is Judicial Review in US District Court. If the amount in controversy is at least $1,260, a request for Judicial Review may be submitted. This request must be filed within 60 days of the Appeals Council's decision. The Appeals Council's decision will provide details as to how the Judicial Review can be requested.

FIGURE 2-4 *Medicare Appeals Process*[2]

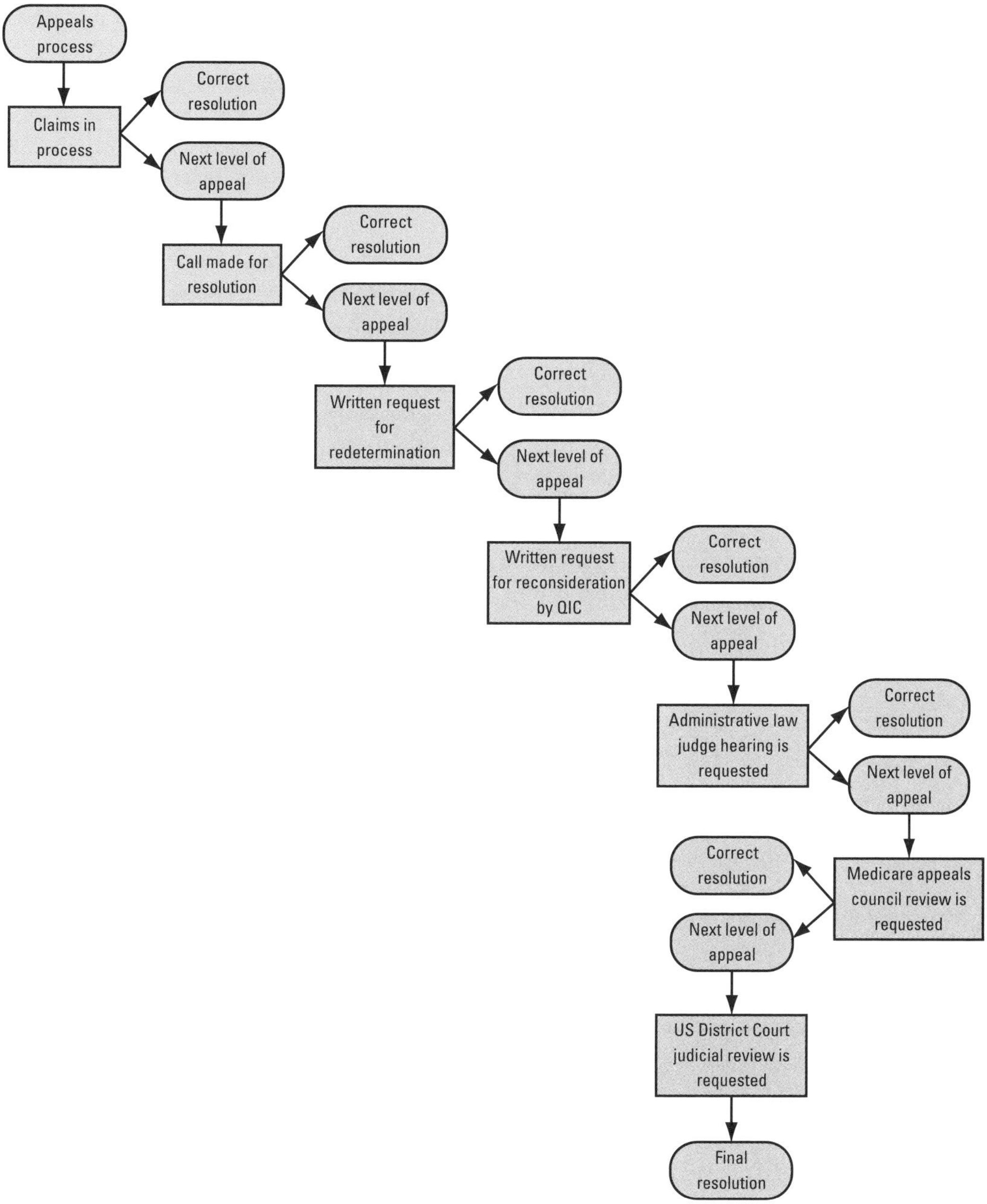

Correct payment should not require any effort beyond submitting a claim and posting payment, but practically speaking, providers pursue at least the lower levels of appeal (phone call, redetermination) fairly commonly.

Definitions and Acronyms

advance beneficiary notice (ABN). A written notice to patients explaining they will have responsibility for paying claims should they be denied by Medicare. Patient should be presented with information prior to services being rendered and acknowledge acceptance by signing.

assignment. Indicates that a health care provider agrees to the allowed amount of the insurance company and will bill the patient only for copayments, deductibles, coinsurance, or noncovered services.

coinsurance. A percentage of the covered allowed amount for health care that the insured is responsible for paying.

copayment. Fixed amount the insured pays at the time of medical service.

deductible. Fixed amount that the insured must pay before the insurance company pays any benefits.

fee for service (FFS). Provider is paid a set amount for each covered service provided.

fee schedule. List of maximum fees by procedure that is usually used in a fee-for-service payment arrangement.

health maintenance organization (HMO). A form of health insurance providing coverage on a group basis. A group of doctors and other medical professionals offer care through the HMO for a flat monthly rate with no deductibles.

Medicaid. Provides health insurance coverage for low-income individuals through a combined state and federal program.

Medicare. Provides health insurance coverage for seniors and disabled individuals funded at the federal level.

Medicare Administrative Contractors (MACs). Insurance companies responsible for processing Medicare claims replacing fiscal intermediaries and carriers.

Medicare Secondary Payer (MSP). When Medicare is not responsible for paying as primary (or first).

Medigap. Supplemental insurance to Medicare coverage.

participating provider. A physician who chooses to enter into a contract for a specific health insurance program.

preferred provider organization (PPO). A health care organization composed of physicians, hospitals, or other providers that provides health care services at a reduced fee.

third-party payer. The party who is responsible for processing and paying for health care claims but is not involved in the health care relationship.

REFERENCES

1. Microsoft Generic Patient Registration Form. Available at: http://office.microsoft.com/en-us/templates/CT010143320.aspx?tl=2#ai:TC001036511. Accessed January 5, 2011.
2. Centers for Medicare and Medicaid Services. Medicare Appeals Process information. Available at: www.cms.gov/MLNProducts/downloads/MedicareAppealsprocess.pdf. Accessed January 4, 2011.
3. Centers for Medicare and Medicaid Services. Medicare Appeals Process Redetermination request form CMS-20027. Available at: www.cms.hhs.gov/CMSForms/CMSForms/list.asp#TopOfPage. Accessed January 4, 2011.
4. Centers for Medicare and Medicaid Services. Medicare Appeals Process Reconsideration request form CMS-20033. Available at: www.cms.gov/cmsforms/downloads/cms20033.pdf. Accessed January 5, 2011.
5. Centers for Medicare and Medicaid Services. Medicare Appeals Process Reconsideration request form CMS-20034. Available at: www.cms.gov/cmsforms/downloads/cms20034ab.pdf. Accessed January 5, 2011.

Chapter 3

Insurance Billing Claim Forms

Claim Forms Overview

As mentioned in the last chapter, to receive payment for services delivered, health care providers must submit health insurance claims to insurance companies. These claims should explain the services, supplies, and pharmaceuticals provided to the patient during a medical encounter. *For the purposes of this book,* medical encounter *will be used to describe anything from a visit to a physician's office for routine care to a multiday stay at a hospital.* The claims essentially serve as requests for payment for care provided.

Exception to Claim Forms

An exception to using claim forms (eg, CMS 1500, UB-04) would be when a patient does not have health insurance and is billed directly by the provider as a "self-pay." In this case, providers would normally bill the patient using a different form, perhaps a superbill or detailed bill.

Precision in completing claims is critical to prompt and accurate payment. If claims have missing or invalid information, they likely will be returned as unprocessable, which will delay payment and create more work for the billing provider, as well as the payer.

There are dozens of reasons why a claim may be returned, and some of the common reasons may include:

- No valid health insurance claim (HIC) number was provided.
- The patient's name does not match the HIC number given.
- Dates of service are missing or invalid.
- The claim is not appropriately authorized by signature.
- ICD-9-CM or HCPCS coding is obsolete or invalid.

***Tip:** Many payers will notify providers of the commonly seen reasons for claim denials or returns. Every provider should sign up to receive information from payers. These notices, usually sent via e-mail, often have changes in benefits, coverage, payment, claims processing, coding, and so forth. Figure 3-1 illustrates a generic electronic notification from a payer.*

There are two methods of submitting claims: electronic data interchange (EDI) and hardcopy claim submissions. EDI is simply the claim form translated into electronic data and electronically transmitted to the payer or clearinghouse, whereas hardcopy submission requires mailing or faxing the data to the payer. This chapter will review both of these in detail. In order to best understand EDI billing, it is helpful if the hardcopy claims are discussed first. A hardcopy claim form is used only when the provider is not required to submit electronically. Payers do not supply claim forms, so providers must purchase the forms from vendors.

FIGURE 3-1 *Example of an Electronic Notification From Payer*

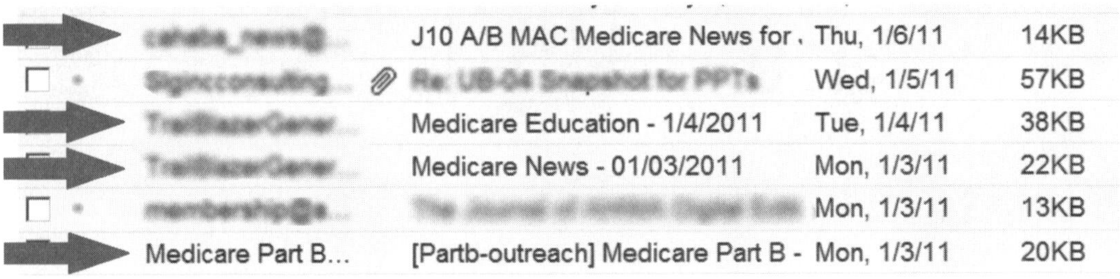

CMS 1500 Claim Form

The CMS-1500 form is the standard claim form used by physicians and suppliers to file insurance claims. For Medicare, ambulatory surgery centers (ASCs) also use the CMS-1500 form. However, for most other payers, ASCs usually use the UB-04 form. The National Uniform Claim Committee (NUCC) is responsible for maintaining the CMS-1500 form, which can be downloaded from CMS (see Figure 2-2). Note that photocopies may not be used to submit claims. Always use original forms.

CMS provides detailed instructions on completing the claim form,[1] but this chapter will review only the highlights of the claim form. Most payers follow the same instructions as CMS, thus these will hold true across the patient population.

Tips for Completing the CMS 1500 Form

Make sure the information is:

- Legible
- In black ink
- In Pica or Arial 10-, 11-, or 12-point font
- In CAPITAL letters

The information should not include:

- Broken characters
- Script, italics, or stylized font
- Red ink
- Dot matrix printing
- Corrections made with liquid correction fluid
- More than six service lines per claim (use a new form for additional services)
- Narrative descriptions of procedures, modifiers, or diagnosis (codes are sufficient)
- Handwriting (except signatures)

The claim form must be:

- An original CMS 1500 form printed in red (photocopies are not acceptable)
- Size should be 8½" × 11"

Patient Demographic and Insurance Information

Patient demographic and insurance information is reported in item numbers 1 through 13.

Item 1 (see Figure 3-2) is the selection of insurance being billed (Medicare, Medicaid, TRICARE). Remember, this form is used by most payers, so "Other" might indicate BlueCross BlueShield, Aetna, or another insurer.

Item 1a is where the patient's insurance policy number is entered. For Medicare, this would be the HIC number. This should be exactly as shown on the patient's insurance card.

FIGURE 3-2 *CMS 1500 Header Information*

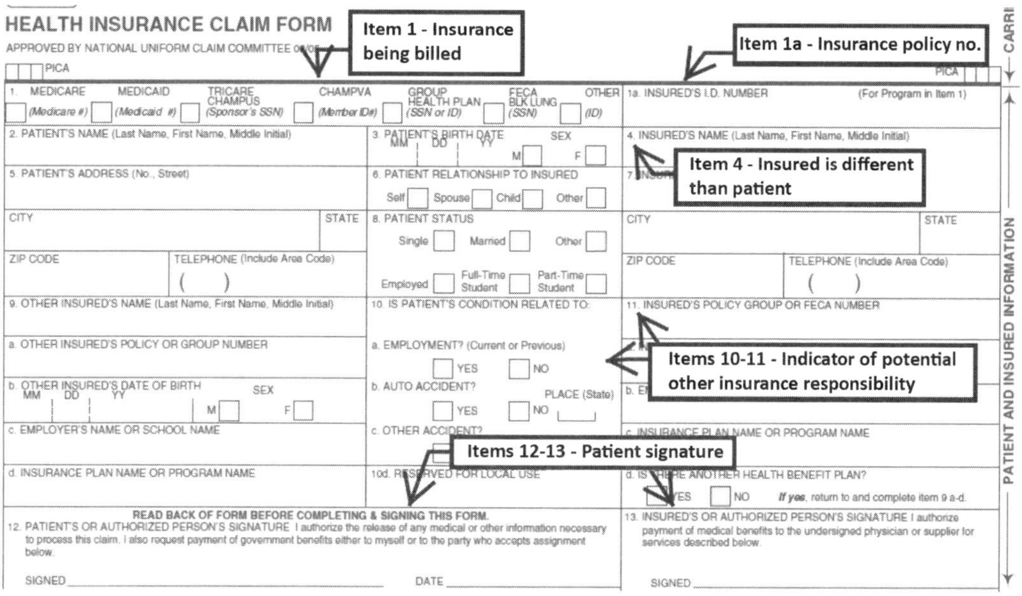
HEALTH INSURANCE CLAIM FORM
APPROVED BY NATIONAL UNIFORM CLAIM COMMITTEE 08/05
PICA PICA
1. MEDICARE (Medicare #) MEDICAID (Medicaid #) TRICARE CHAMPUS (Sponsor's SSN) CHAMPVA (Member ID#) GROUP HEALTH PLAN (SSN or ID) FECA BLK LUNG (SSN) OTHER (ID)
1a. INSURED'S I.D. NUMBER (For Program in Item 1)
2. PATIENT'S NAME (Last Name, First Name, Middle Initial)
3. PATIENT'S BIRTH DATE MM DD YY SEX M F
4. INSURED'S NAME (Last Name, First Name, Middle Initial)
5. PATIENT'S ADDRESS (No., Street)
6. PATIENT RELATIONSHIP TO INSURED Self Spouse Child Other
7. INSURED'S ADDRESS
CITY STATE
8. PATIENT STATUS Single Married Other
CITY STATE
ZIP CODE TELEPHONE (Include Area Code) ( )
Employed Full-Time Student Part-Time Student
ZIP CODE TELEPHONE (Include Area Code) ( )
9. OTHER INSURED'S NAME (Last Name, First Name, Middle Initial)
10. IS PATIENT'S CONDITION RELATED TO:
11. INSURED'S POLICY GROUP OR FECA NUMBER
a. OTHER INSURED'S POLICY OR GROUP NUMBER
a. EMPLOYMENT? (Current or Previous) YES NO
b. OTHER INSURED'S DATE OF BIRTH MM DD YY SEX M F
b. AUTO ACCIDENT? PLACE (State) YES NO
c. EMPLOYER'S NAME OR SCHOOL NAME
c. OTHER ACCIDENT?
c. INSURANCE PLAN NAME OR PROGRAM NAME
d. INSURANCE PLAN NAME OR PROGRAM NAME
10d. RESERVED FOR LOCAL USE
d. IS THERE ANOTHER HEALTH BENEFIT PLAN? YES NO *If yes*, return to and complete item 9 a-d.
READ BACK OF FORM BEFORE COMPLETING & SIGNING THIS FORM.
12. PATIENT'S OR AUTHORIZED PERSON'S SIGNATURE I authorize the release of any medical or other information necessary to process this claim. I also request payment of government benefits either to myself or to the party who accepts assignment below.
SIGNED DATE
13. INSURED'S OR AUTHORIZED PERSON'S SIGNATURE I authorize payment of medical benefits to the undersigned physician or supplier for services described below.
SIGNED

Tip: *Remember to copy the patient's card to have the insurance number for later reference when billing.*

Item 4 will be completed if the insured is someone other than the patient, for example, patients who are covered through their spouse, parent, or other. If the patient is the insured, leave this item blank. For Medicare claims, if Medicare is the primary payer, leave this blank as well, but if Medicare is the secondary payer to another insurer, complete this item. When item 4 is completed, item 6 (patient's relationship to insured) should also be completed.

Item 10 on the form is to be completed for each claim submitted to indicate whether employment, an automobile accident, or another accident caused the patient's condition. This can be an indicator of another insurance being liable for the costs of care. If any answer in item 10 is "Yes," item 11 should be completed with the other policy information. If all the answers in item 10 are "No," item 11 should still be completed by writing the word "NONE" in the space.

The patient (or the authorized representative) must sign the claim, unless the provider has a signature on file indicating the patient has agreed for the provider to file for claim payment and to release any necessary information to the insurance company to obtain payment. In that case, entering "Signature on File" is sufficient in these sections. Most providers will have signatures on file and will not have patients sign individual claim forms.

Patient Diagnosis/ Condition Information

Items 14 through 20 furnish information on the current illness and referring physician information.

Item 17 (see Figure 3-3) is where the name of the referring or ordering physician or health care professional should be given, if the service or item was ordered or referred by a physician or health care professional. When a claim involves multiple referring and/or ordering physicians, a separate CMS 1500 should be used for each ordering/ referring physician. Item 17a is left blank for now, but item 17b is a mandatory field for

FIGURE 3-3 *CMS 1500 Item 17*

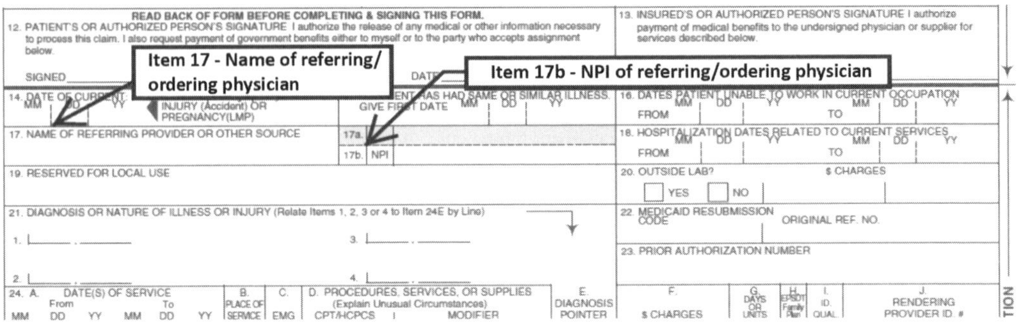

completion. For item 17b, the national provider identification (NPI) of the referring and/or ordering physician listed in item 17 should be entered.

National Provider Identifier

A national provider identifier (NPI) is an identification number assigned to health care providers by the Centers for Medicare and Medicaid Services (CMS). It is a unique 10-digit number used by HIPAA-covered health care providers.[2] The NPI number system was established by Congress in the Health Insurance Portability and Accountability Act (HIPAA) in 1996, and CMS began issuing NPI numbers in 2006. As a result of HIPAA Administrative Simplification provisions, the National Provider Identification (NPI) is a mandatory requirement for claims submission. The NPI number officially replaced the UPIN (unique provider identification number), which was used in the past. Covered health care providers and all health plans and health care clearinghouses must use the NPIs in the administrative and financial transactions adopted under HIPAA. A national registry for the NPI number, which can be accessed online and was made available on September 4, 2007, can be utilized to find the NPI of another provider, if necessary.

Medical Encounter Diagnoses and/or Services

Items 21 through 24 are very specific to the medical encounter being billed.

Item 21 is used to enter the ICD-9-CM codes for the patient's diagnosis and/or condition. On the CMS 1500 form, there is space for up to four diagnoses. The diagnoses should be listed in priority order (list the most important or primary to the encounter first, followed by the secondary, and so forth). Figure 3-4 illustrates a blank item 21.

Figure 3-5 is an example of a completed item 21. ICD-9-CM code 401.9 is the code for hypertension. Placing it in the first position tells the payer that hypertension was the primary reason for the visit. ICD-9-CM code 250.00 indicates diabetes, and V15.82 indicates the patient has a history of tobacco abuse. If a payer requested the medical record, these diagnoses should all be indicated within the documentation for this date of service, and it should show that the patient was evaluated, treated, or otherwise impacted by the care. Detailed information on ICD-9-CM codes will be provided in Chapter 10.

For items 24A-J, the services provided are detailed here. There are a total of six lines for services to be billed. See Figure 3-6 for this section. If it is necessary to submit more than six services, a second CMS-1500 form may be attached.

The six service lines in item 24 are divided horizontally with the upper half

FIGURE 3-4 *CMS 1500 Item 21: ICD-9-CM Codes*

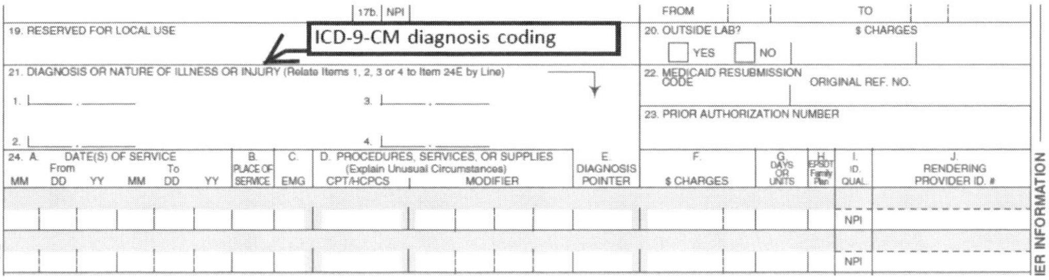

FIGURE 3-5 *CMS 1500 Item 21: ICD-9-CM Codes Example*

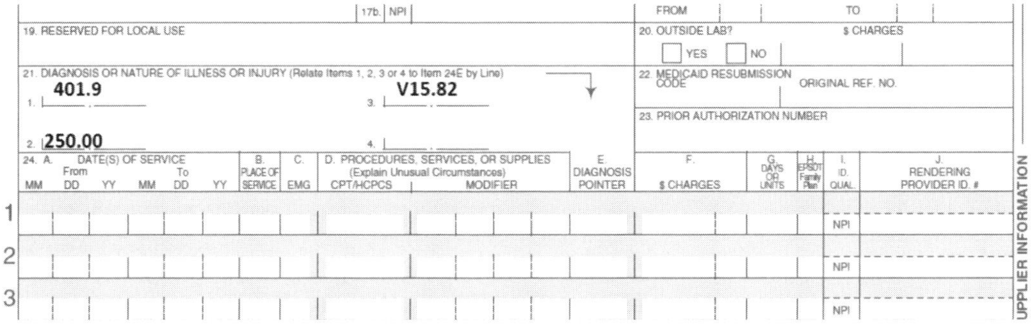

FIGURE 3-6 *CMS 1500 Items 24A-J*

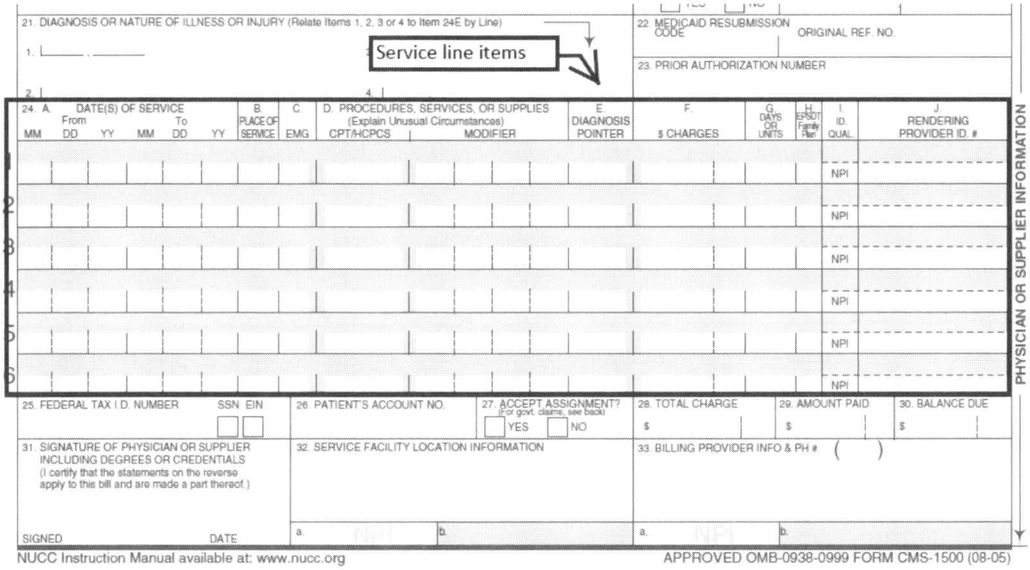

shaded. The shaded areas in items 24A-J allow for reporting supplemental information, such as the national drug code or a description of an unspecified procedure code.

Item 24A is for the date of service, and if identical services spanning multiple dates are being billed together, different "from" and "to" dates may be entered. When that is the case, item 24G should have the appropriate number entered to represent the total number of services.

Item 24B is to indicate the place where services were provided. See Table 3-1 for a list of place of service codes and their descriptions.

TABLE 3-1 *Place of Service Codes and Descriptions*

Code(s)	Place of Service	Place of Service Description
01	Pharmacy	A facility or location where drugs and other medically related items and services are sold, dispensed, or otherwise provided directly to patients.
02	Unassigned	N/A
03	School	A facility whose primary purpose is education.
04	Homeless Shelter	A facility or location whose primary purpose is to provide temporary housing to homeless individuals (eg, emergency shelters, individual or family shelters).
05	Indian Health Service Freestanding Facility	A facility or location, owned and operated by the Indian Health Service, which provides diagnostic, therapeutic (surgical and nonsurgical), and rehabilitation services to American Indians and Alaska Natives who do not require hospitalization.
06	Indian Health Service Provider-based Facility	A facility or location, owned and operated by the Indian Health Service, which provides diagnostic, therapeutic (surgical and nonsurgical), and rehabilitation services rendered by, or under the supervision of, physicians to American Indians and Alaska Natives admitted as inpatients or outpatients.
07	Tribal 638 Freestanding Facility	A facility or location owned and operated by a federally recognized American Indian or Alaska Native tribe or tribal organization under a 638 agreement, which provides diagnostic, therapeutic (surgical and nonsurgical), and rehabilitation services to tribal members who do not require hospitalization.
08	Tribal 638 Provider-based Facility	A facility or location owned and operated by a federally recognized American Indian or Alaska Native tribe or tribal organization under a 638 agreement, which provides diagnostic, therapeutic (surgical and nonsurgical), and rehabilitation services to tribal members admitted as inpatients or outpatients.
09-10	Prison/Correctional Facility	A prison, jail, reformatory, work farm, detention center, or any other similar facility maintained by either federal, state, or local authorities for the purpose of confinement or rehabilitation of adult or juvenile criminal offenders.
11	Office	Location, other than a hospital, skilled nursing facility (SNF), military treatment facility, community health center, state or local public health clinic, or intermediate care facility (ICF), where the health professional routinely provides health examinations, diagnosis, and treatment of illness or injury on an ambulatory basis.
12	Home	Location, other than a hospital or other facility, where the patient receives care in a private residence.

(continued)

TABLE 3-1 *(continued)*

Code(s)	Place of Service	Place of Service Description
13	Assisted Living Facility	Congregate residential facility with self-contained living units providing assessment of each resident's needs and on-site support 24 hours a day, 7 days a week, with the capacity to deliver or arrange for services including some health care and other services. (effective 10/1/03)
14	Group Home	A residence, with shared living areas, where clients receive supervision and other services such as social and/or behavioral services, custodial service, and minimal services (eg, medication administration).
15	Mobile Unit	A facility/unit that moves from place to place equipped to provide preventive, screening, diagnostic, and/or treatment services.
16	Temporary Lodging	A short-term accommodation such as a hotel, campground, hostel, cruise ship, or resort where the patient receives care, and which is not identified by any other POS code. (effective 4/1/08)
17-19	Unassigned	N/A
20	Urgent Care Facility	Location, distinct from a hospital emergency room, an office, or a clinic, whose purpose is to diagnose and treat illness or injury for unscheduled, ambulatory patients seeking immediate medical attention.
21	Inpatient Hospital	A facility, other than psychiatric, which primarily provides diagnostic, therapeutic (both surgical and nonsurgical), and rehabilitation services by, or under, the supervision of physicians to patients admitted for a variety of medical conditions.
22	Outpatient Hospital	A portion of a hospital that provides diagnostic, therapeutic (both surgical and nonsurgical), and rehabilitation services to sick or injured persons who do not require hospitalization or institutionalization.
23	Emergency Room—Hospital	A portion of a hospital where emergency diagnosis and treatment of illness or injury is provided.
24	Ambulatory Surgical Center	A freestanding facility, other than a physician's office, where surgical and diagnostic services are provided on an ambulatory basis.
25	Birthing Center	A facility, other than a hospital's maternity facilities or a physician's office, that provides a setting for labor, delivery, and immediate postpartum care as well as immediate care of newborn infants.
26	Military Treatment Facility	A medical facility operated by one or more of the Uniformed Services. Military Treatment Facility (MTF) also refers to certain former U.S. Public Health Service (USPHS) facilities now designated as Uniformed Service Treatment Facilities (USTF).
27-30	Unassigned	N/A
31	Skilled Nursing Facility	A facility that primarily provides inpatient skilled nursing care and related services to patients who require medical, nursing, or rehabilitative services but does not provide the level of care or treatment available in a hospital.

(continued)

TABLE 3-1 *(continued)*

Code(s)	Place of Service	Place of Service Description
32	Nursing Facility	A facility that primarily provides residents skilled nursing care and related services for the rehabilitation of injured, disabled, or sick persons, or, on a regular basis, health-related care services above the level of custodial care to other than mentally retarded individuals.
33	Custodial Care Facility	A facility that provides room, board and other personal assistance services, generally on a long-term basis, and that does not include a medical component.
34	Hospice	A facility, other than a patient's home, in which palliative and supportive care for terminally ill patients and their families are provided.
35-40	Unassigned	N/A
41	Ambulance—Land	A land vehicle specifically designed, equipped, and staffed for lifesaving and transporting the sick or injured.
42	Ambulance—Air or Water	An air or water vehicle specifically designed, equipped, and staffed for lifesaving and transporting the sick or injured.
43-48	Unassigned	N/A
49	Independent Clinic	A location, not part of a hospital and not described by any other Place of Service code, that is organized and operated to provide preventive, diagnostic, therapeutic, rehabilitative, or palliative services to outpatients only. (effective 10/1/03)
50	Federally Qualified Health Center	A facility located in a medically underserved area that provides Medicare beneficiaries preventive primary medical care under the general direction of a physician.
51	Inpatient Psychiatric Facility	A facility that provides inpatient psychiatric services for the diagnosis and treatment of mental illness on a 24-hour basis, by or under the supervision of a physician.
52	Psychiatric Facility—Partial Hospitalization	A facility for the diagnosis and treatment of mental illness that provides a planned therapeutic program for patients who do not require full-time hospitalization, but who need broader programs than are possible from outpatient visits to a hospital-based or hospital-affiliated facility.
53	Community Mental Health Center (CMHC)	A facility that provides the following services: outpatient services, including specialized outpatient services for children, the elderly, individuals who are chronically ill, and residents of the CMHC's mental health services area who have been discharged from inpatient treatment at a mental health facility; 24 hour a day emergency care services; day treatment, other partial hospitalization services, or psychosocial rehabilitation services; screening for patients being considered for admission to state mental health facilities to determine the appropriateness of such admission; and consultation and education services.
54	Intermediate Care Facility/Mentally Retarded	A facility that primarily provides health-related care and services above the level of custodial care to mentally retarded individuals but does not provide the level of care or treatment available in a hospital or SNF.

(continued)

TABLE 3-1 *(continued)*

Code(s)	Place of Service	Place of Service Description
55	Residential Substance Abuse Treatment Facility	A facility that provides treatment for substance (alcohol and drug) abuse to live-in residents who do not require acute medical care. Services include individual and group therapy and counseling, family counseling, laboratory tests, drugs and supplies, psychological testing, and room and board.
56	Psychiatric Residential Treatment Center	A facility or distinct part of a facility for psychiatric care that provides a total 24-hour therapeutically planned and professionally staffed group living and learning environment.
57	Nonresidential Substance Abuse Treatment Facility	A location that provides treatment for substance (alcohol and drug) abuse on an ambulatory basis. Services include individual and group therapy and counseling, family counseling, laboratory tests, drugs and supplies, and psychological testing. (effective 10/1/03)
58-59	Unassigned	N/A
60	Mass Immunization Center	A location where providers administer pneumococcal pneumonia and influenza virus vaccinations and submit these services as electronic media claims, paper claims, or using the roster billing method. This generally takes place in a mass immunization setting, such as a public health center, pharmacy, or mall, but may include a physician office setting.
61	Comprehensive Inpatient Rehabilitation Facility	A facility that provides comprehensive rehabilitation services under the supervision of a physician to inpatients with physical disabilities. Services include physical therapy, occupational therapy, speech pathology, social or psychological services, and orthotics and prosthetics services.
62	Comprehensive Outpatient Rehabilitation Facility	A facility that provides comprehensive rehabilitation services under the supervision of a physician to outpatients with physical disabilities. Services include physical therapy, occupational therapy, and speech pathology services.
63-64	Unassigned	N/A
65	End-Stage Renal Disease Treatment Facility	A facility other than a hospital, which provides dialysis treatment, maintenance, and/or training to patients or caregivers on an ambulatory or home-care basis.
66-70	Unassigned	N/A
71	Public Health Clinic	A facility maintained by either state or local health departments that provides ambulatory primary medical care under the general direction of a physician. (effective 10/1/03)
72	Rural Health Clinic	A certified facility that is located in a rural medically underserved area that provides ambulatory primary medical care under the general direction of a physician.
73-80	Unassigned	N/A
81	Independent Laboratory	A laboratory certified to perform diagnostic and/or clinical tests independent of an institution or a physician's office.
82-98	Unassigned	N/A
99	Other Place of Service	Other place of service not identified above.

Source: National Uniform Claim Committee. www.nucc.org/.

***Tip:** It is vital to code the place of service correctly. Because physicians have overhead costs (rent, staff, and so forth) that they must pay when providing care in their freestanding clinics, physicians have to pay more out-of-pocket expenses for these services as opposed to services that are rendered in a facility. When care is provided in a facility, the facility is responsible for the costs of the overhead, and they are responsible for all billings incurred on their facility. For this reason, payment is affected by the accuracy of the coding for place of service. A mistake here could cause an underpayment or an overpayment.*

Item 24C is not currently required by most payers.

Item 24D uses the CPT/HCPCS coding system to indicate the procedures, services, or supplies being billed. On occasion, modifiers may be needed. Modifiers are two-digit codes appended to a CPT/HCPCS code to further explain a service or supply. Detailed information on CPT/HCPCS will be discussed in Chapter 9.

Item 24E is where the provider links the diagnosis code (item 21) to the procedures performed or services provided. If, for example, an A1C lab test were performed and billed for the diabetic patient shown in Figure 3-5, item 24E would have a "2" on the line for the A1C to link that test with the appropriate diagnosis.

Item 24F is where a charge is entered for each service line item. Item 24G captures the number of days or units. Item 24H is currently not required and may be left blank. For item 24I, enter the ID qualifier (see the list of ID qualifiers provided).

Item 24J is where the provider's NPI number is entered in the lower unshaded portion. If services provided are incident to the services of a physician and/or nonphysician practitioner, ie, when the person who ordered the service is not supervising, enter the NPI of the supervisor in the *lower unshaded* portion

Two-Digit Qualifiers

These two-digit qualifiers should be used as appropriate in fields 17a and 24I of the CMS-1500 claim form.

0B State license number

1B Blue Shield provider number

1C Medicare provider number

1D Medicaid provider number

1G Provider unique provider identification number (UPIN)

1H Civilian Health and Medical Program of the Uniformed Services (CHAMPUS) identification number

EI Employer's identification number

G2 Provider commercial number

LU Location number

N5 Provider plan network identification number

SY Social Security number (This may not be used for Medicare.)

X5 State industrial accident provider number

ZZ Provider taxonomy

Note: *In Version 5010, the revised standards that must be used beginning January 1, 2012, the qualifiers change to just 0B, 1G, G2, and LU.*

The following qualifiers can be used in 32b.

0B State license number

1A Blue Cross provider number

(continued)

1B Blue Shield provider number

1C Medicare provider number

1D Medicaid provider number

1G Provider UPIN

1H CHAMPUS identification number

G2 Provider commercial number

LU Location number

N5 Provider plan network identification number

TJ Federal taxpayer's identification number

X4 Clinical Laboratory Improvement Amendment Number

X5 State industrial accident provider number

ZZ Provider taxonomy
Note: *In Version 5010, the revised standards that must be used beginning January 1, 2012, the qualifiers change to just 0B, G2, and LU.*

The following qualifiers can be used in 33b.

0B State license number

1A Blue Cross provider number

1B Blue Shield provider number

1C Medicare provider number

1D Medicaid provider number

1G Provider UPIN

1H CHAMPUS identification number

(continued)

1J Facility ID number

B3 Preferred provider organization number

BQ Health maintenance organization code number

FH Clinic number

G2 Provider commercial number

G5 Provider site number

LU Location number

U3 Unique supplier identification number (USIN)

X5 State industrial accident provider number

ZZ Provider taxonomy
Note: *In Version 5010, the revised standards that must be used beginning January 1, 2012, the qualifiers change to just 0B and 1G.*

The following identifiers are to be used when reporting services related to them.

ZZ Narrative description of unspecified code

N4 National Drug Codes (NDC)

VP Vendor product number Health Industry Business Communications Council (HIBCC) labeling standard

OZ Product number Health Care Uniform Code Council – Global Trade Item Number (GTIN)

CTR Contract rate

of item 24J. ***The shaded portion of item 24J is not to be reported.***

The shaded portion of 24J is strictly to be used for the NPI of the ordering provider and should only be used when the ordering provider is **present and/or supervising** the services. Figure 3-7 shows a completed section of items 24A-J in which a midlevel established patient office visit (code 99213) and an A1C lab test are billed.

Billing Provider's Information

To finish up the claim form, item 25 is for the federal tax ID number (Employer Identification Number or Social Security Number) of the provider. Item 26 shows where the patient's account number assigned by the service provider's or supplier's accounting system is entered. To indicate whether assignment is accepted for benefits, item 27 is completed. For items 23 to 33, see Figure 3-8.

> **Learning Break**
>
> Accepting assignment essentially means physicians accept the allowed charge as payment in full. Not accepting assignment means the physician may bill the patient for more than the allowance for unassigned claims. Participating physicians agree to accept assignment on all patients. Nonparticipating physicians can choose whether to accept assignment on a claim by claim basis.

Lastly, there is some important wording on the reverse side of the CMS-1500 form. Be sure to read the entire document. Figure 3-9 shows what the provider's signature agrees to when completing and submitting the form. This shows the provider is taking responsibility for the medical necessity of the services and that they were provided under the provider's direct care or oversight.

FIGURE 3-7 *Example of Items 24A-J in CMS 1500*

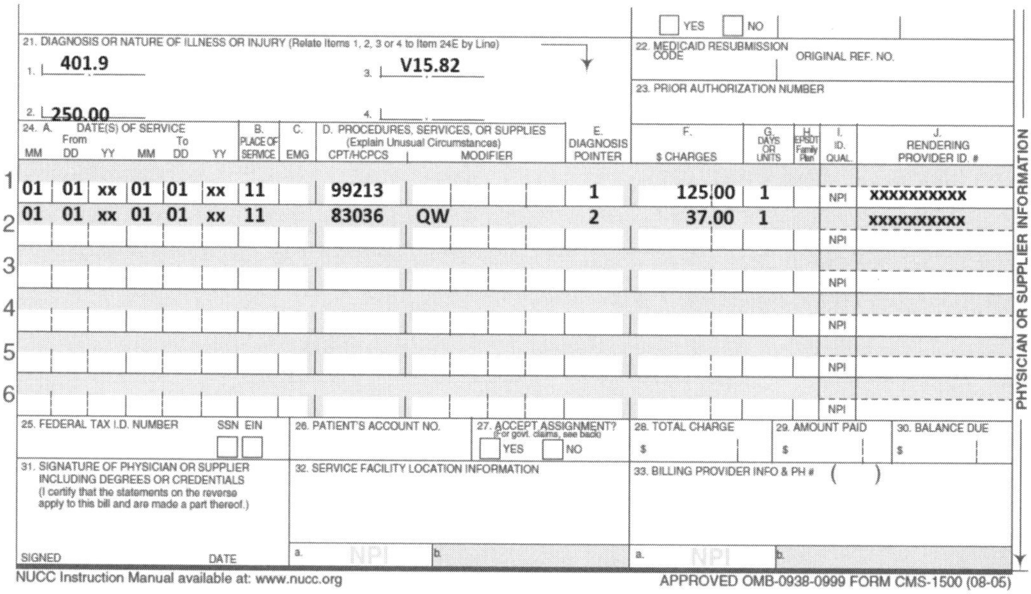
YES NO

21. DIAGNOSIS OR NATURE OF ILLNESS OR INJURY (Relate Items 1, 2, 3 or 4 to Item 24E by Line)

1. 401.9
2. 250.00
3. V15.82
4.

22. MEDICAID RESUBMISSION CODE ORIGINAL REF. NO.

23. PRIOR AUTHORIZATION NUMBER

	24. A. DATE(S) OF SERVICE From MM DD YY	To MM DD YY	B. PLACE OF SERVICE	C. EMG	D. PROCEDURES, SERVICES, OR SUPPLIES (Explain Unusual Circumstances) CPT/HCPCS	MODIFIER	E. DIAGNOSIS POINTER	F. $ CHARGES	G. DAYS OR UNITS	H. EPSDT Family Plan	I. ID. QUAL.	J. RENDERING PROVIDER ID. #
1	01 01 xx	01 01 xx	11		99213		1	125.00	1		NPI	XXXXXXXXXX
2	01 01 xx	01 01 xx	11		83036	QW	2	37.00	1		NPI	XXXXXXXXXX
3											NPI	
4											NPI	
5											NPI	
6											NPI	

25. FEDERAL TAX I.D. NUMBER SSN EIN

26. PATIENT'S ACCOUNT NO.

27. ACCEPT ASSIGNMENT? (For govt. claims, see back) YES NO

28. TOTAL CHARGE $

29. AMOUNT PAID $

30. BALANCE DUE $

31. SIGNATURE OF PHYSICIAN OR SUPPLIER INCLUDING DEGREES OR CREDENTIALS (I certify that the statements on the reverse apply to this bill and are made a part thereof.)

SIGNED DATE

32. SERVICE FACILITY LOCATION INFORMATION

a. NPI b.

33. BILLING PROVIDER INFO & PH # ( )

a. NPI b.

PHYSICIAN OR SUPPLIER INFORMATION

NUCC Instruction Manual available at: www.nucc.org

APPROVED OMB-0938-0999 FORM CMS-1500 (08-05)

FIGURE 3-8 *CMS 1500 Items 25-33*

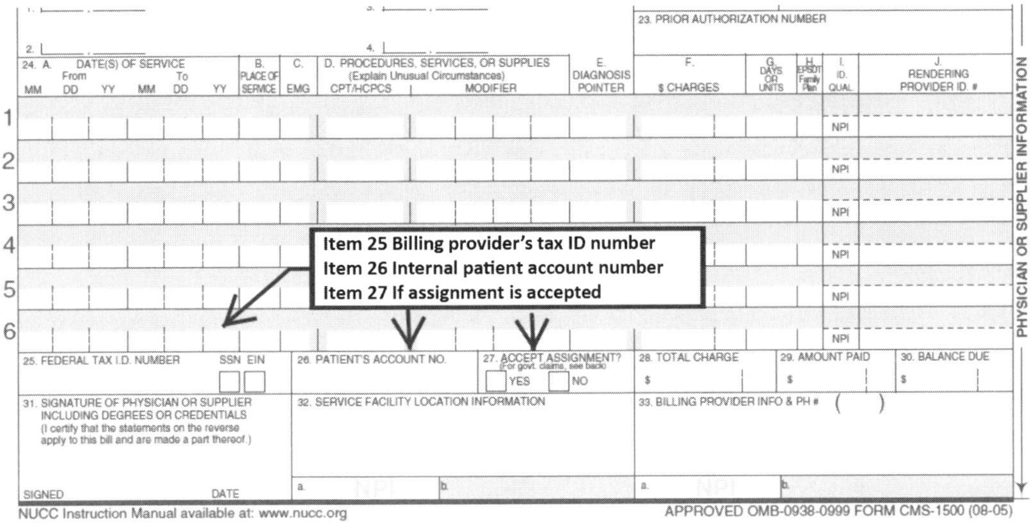

FIGURE 3-9 *CMS 1500 Signature Agreement*

BLACK LUNG AND FECA CLAIMS

The provider agrees to accept the amount paid by the Government as payment in full. See Black Lung and FECA instructions regarding required procedure and diagnosis coding systems.

SIGNATURE OF PHYSICIAN OR SUPPLIER (MEDICARE, CHAMPUS, FECA AND BLACK LUNG)

I certify that the services shown on this form were medically indicated and necessary for the health of the patient and were personally furnished by me or were furnished incident to my professional service by my employee under my immediate personal supervision, except as otherwise expressly permitted by Medicare or CHAMPUS regulations.

For services to be considered as "incident" to a physician's professional service, 1) they must be rendered under the physician's immediate personal supervision by his/her employee, 2) they must be an integral, although incidental part of a covered physician's service, 3) they must be of kinds commonly furnished in physician's offices, and 4) the services of nonphysicians must be included on the physician's bills.

For CHAMPUS claims, I further certify that I (or any employee) who rendered services am not an active duty member of the Uniformed Services or a civilian employee of the United States Government or a contract employee of the United States Government, either civilian or military (refer to 5 USC 5536). For Black-Lung claims, I further certify that the services performed were for a Black Lung-related disorder.

No Part B Medicare benefits may be paid unless this form is received as required by existing law and regulations (42 CFR 424.32).

NOTICE: Any one who misrepresents or falsifies essential information to receive payment from Federal funds requested by this form may upon conviction be subject to fine and imprisonment under applicable Federal laws.

NOTICE TO PATIENT ABOUT THE COLLECTION AND USE OF MEDICARE, CHAMPUS, FECA, AND BLACK LUNG INFORMATION
(PRIVACY ACT STATEMENT)

We are authorized by CMS, CHAMPUS and OWCP to ask you for information needed in the administration of the Medicare, CHAMPUS, FECA, and Black Lung

Source: www.cms.gov/cmsforms/downloads/CMS1500805.pdf.

Example of Completed 1500 Claim Form

Figure 3-10 illustrates a completed CMS-1500 form.

UB-04 Claim Form

The UB-04 (also known as CMS 1450) form is the standard claim form used by institutional providers (eg, hospitals) to bill insurance companies (see Figure 3-11 and 3-17). The National Uniform Billing Committee (NUBC) is responsible for maintaining the UB-04 form. CMS provides detailed instructions on completing the claim form,[2] so this chapter will review only the highlights of the claim form. Several of the items on the claim form are self-explanatory and will not be reviewed. Most payers follow the same instructions as CMS, so these will hold true across the patient population.

FIGURE 3-10 *Sample of Completed CMS 1500 Form*

PLEASE DO NOT STAPLE IN THIS AREA

CARRIER

PICA **HEALTH INSURANCE CLAIM FORM** PICA

1. MEDICARE (Medicare #) MEDICAID (Medicaid #) CHAMPUS (Sponsor's SSN) CHAMPVA (VA File #) GROUP HEALTH PLAN (SSN or ID) FECA BLK LUNG (SSN) OTHER (ID)
1a. INSURED'S I.D. NUMBER (FOR PROGRAM IN ITEM 1)

2. PATIENT'S NAME (Last Name, First Name, Middle Initial): **Doe, John**
3. PATIENT'S BIRTH DATE MM DD YY: **03 22 63** SEX M [X] F [ ]
4. INSURED'S NAME (Last Name, First Name, Middle Initial)

5. PATIENT'S ADDRESS (No., Street): **123 Any Street**
6. PATIENT RELATIONSHIP TO INSURED: Self [ ] Spouse [ ] Child [ ] Other [ ]
7. INSURED'S ADDRESS (No., Street)

CITY: **Cambridge** STATE: **MA**
8. PATIENT STATUS: Single [ ] Married [X] Other [ ]; Employed [ ] Full-Time Student [ ] Part-Time Student [ ]
CITY STATE

ZIP CODE: **01239** TELEPHONE (Include Area Code): **(617) 555-5555**
ZIP CODE TELEPHONE (INCLUDE AREA CODE) ( )

9. OTHER INSURED'S NAME (Last Name, First Name, Middle Initial)
10. IS PATIENT'S CONDITION RELATED TO:
11. INSURED'S POLICY GROUP OR FECA NUMBER

a. OTHER INSURED'S POLICY OR GROUP NUMBER
a. EMPLOYMENT? (CURRENT OR PREVIOUS) [ ] YES [ ] NO
a. INSURED'S DATE OF BIRTH MM DD YY SEX M [ ] F [ ]

b. OTHER INSURED'S DATE OF BIRTH MM DD YY SEX M [ ] F [ ]
b. AUTO ACCIDENT? PLACE (State) [ ] YES [ ] NO
b. EMPLOYER'S NAME OR SCHOOL NAME

c. EMPLOYER'S NAME OR SCHOOL NAME
c. OTHER ACCIDENT? [ ] YES [ ] NO
c. INSURANCE PLAN NAME OR PROGRAM NAME

d. INSURANCE PLAN NAME OR PROGRAM NAME
10d. RESERVED FOR LOCAL USE
d. IS THERE ANOTHER HEALTH BENEFIT PLAN? [ ] YES [ ] NO *If yes,* return to and complete item 9 a-d.

READ BACK OF FORM BEFORE COMPLETING & SIGNING THIS FORM.

12. PATIENT'S OR AUTHORIZED PERSON'S SIGNATURE I authorize the release of any medical or other information necessary to process this claim. I also request payment of government benefits either to myself or to the party who accepts assignment below.

SIGNED ____ DATE ____

13. INSURED'S OR AUTHORIZED PERSON'S SIGNATURE I authorize payment of medical benefits to the undersigned physician or supplier for services described below.

SIGNED ____

PATIENT AND INSURED INFORMATION

14. DATE OF CURRENT: MM DD YY ILLNESS (First symptom) OR INJURY (Accident) OR PREGNANCY(LMP)
15. IF PATIENT HAS HAD SAME OR SIMILAR ILLNESS. GIVE FIRST DATE MM DD YY
16. DATES PATIENT UNABLE TO WORK IN CURRENT OCCUPATION FROM MM DD YY TO MM DD YY

17. NAME OF REFERRING PHYSICIAN OR OTHER SOURCE: **Name of MD**
17a. I.D. NUMBER OF REFERRING PHYSICIAN
18. HOSPITALIZATION DATES RELATED TO CURRENT SERVICES FROM MM DD YY TO MM DD YY

19. RESERVED FOR LOCAL USE
20. OUTSIDE LAB? [ ] YES [ ] NO $ CHARGES

21. DIAGNOSIS OR NATURE OF ILLNESS OR INJURY. (RELATE ITEMS 1,2,3 OR 4 TO ITEM 24E BY LINE)
1. **715 . 16** — Enter the ICD-9-CM code for the patients' diagnosis/condition.
2. ___ . ___
3. ___ . ___
4. ___ . ___

22. MEDICAID RESUBMISSION CODE ORIGINAL REF. NO.
23. PRIOR AUTHORIZATION NUMBER

24.	A DATE(S) OF SERVICE From MM DD YY	To MM DD YY	B Place of Service	C Type of Service	D PROCEDURES, SERVICES, OR SUPPLIES (Explain Unusual Circumstances) CPT/HCPCS	MODIFIER	E DIAGNOSIS CODE	F $ CHARGES	G DAYS OR UNITS	H EPSDT Family Plan	I EMG	J COB	K RESERVED FOR LOCAL USE
1	01 01 08	01 01 08			J7322	LT	1	XXX	1				
2	01 01 08	01 01 08			20610	LT	1	XXX	1				
3													
4													
5													
6													

List the HCPCS Code, J7322, to represent the SYN VISC® injection.

Enter the CPT procedure code to denote the arthrocentesis association with SYN VISC®.

Enter the appropriate modifier -LT, -RT, or -50 to denote the specific knee injected or a bilateral injection.

25. FEDERAL TAX I.D. NUMBER: **000000000** SSN [ ] EIN [ ]
26. PATIENT'S ACCOUNT NO.
27. ACCEPT ASSIGNMENT? (For govt. claims, see back) [ ] YES [ ] NO
28. TOTAL CHARGE: $ **XXX**
29. AMOUNT PAID: $ **00**
30. BALANCE DUE: $

31. SIGNATURE OF PHYSICIAN OR SUPPLIER INCLUDING DEGREES OR CREDENTIALS (I certify that the statements on the reverse apply to this bill and are made a part thereof.)
SIGNED ____ DATE ____
32. NAME AND ADDRESS OF FACILITY WHERE SERVICES WERE RENDERED (If other than home or office)
33. PHYSICIAN'S, SUPPLIER'S BILLING NAME, ADDRESS, ZIP CODE & PHONE #: **00 XXX XX**
PIN# GRP#

PHYSICIAN OR SUPPLIER INFORMATION

(APPROVED BY AMA COUNCIL ON MEDICAL SERVICE 8/88) ***PLEASE PRINT OR TYPE*** APPROVED OMB-0938-0008 FORM CMS-1500 (12-90), FORM RRB-1500, APPROVED OMB-1215-0055 FORM OWCP-1500, APPROVED OMB-0720-0001 (CHAMPUS)

FIGURE 3-11 *UB-04 Health Insurance Claim Form*

1 | 2 | 3a PAT. CNTL # | b. MED. REC. # | 4 TYPE OF BILL

5 FED. TAX NO. | 6 STATEMENT COVERS PERIOD FROM THROUGH | 7

8 PATIENT NAME a | b | 9 PATIENT ADDRESS a | b | c | d | e

10 BIRTHDATE | 11 SEX | ADMISSION 12 DATE 13 HR 14 TYPE 15 SRC | 16 DHR | 17 STAT | CONDITION CODES 18 19 20 21 22 23 24 25 26 27 28 | 29 ACDT STATE | 30

31 OCCURRENCE CODE DATE | 32 OCCURRENCE CODE DATE | 33 OCCURRENCE CODE DATE | 34 OCCURRENCE CODE DATE | 35 OCCURRENCE SPAN CODE FROM THROUGH | 36 OCCURRENCE SPAN CODE FROM THROUGH | 37

38 | 39 VALUE CODES CODE AMOUNT | 40 VALUE CODES CODE AMOUNT | 41 VALUE CODES CODE AMOUNT | a b c d

42 REV. CD.	43 DESCRIPTION	44 HCPCS / RATE / HIPPS CODE	45 SERV. DATE	46 SERV. UNITS	47 TOTAL CHARGES	48 NON-COVERED CHARGES	49
1							1
2							2
3							3
4							4
5							5
6							6
7							7
8							8
9							9
10							10
11							11
12							12
13							13
14							14
15							15
16							16
17							17
18							18
19							19
20							20
21							21
22							22
23	PAGE ____ OF ____	CREATION DATE		TOTALS ➡			23

50 PAYER NAME | 51 HEALTH PLAN ID | 52 REL. INFO | 53 ASG. BEN. | 54 PRIOR PAYMENTS | 55 EST. AMOUNT DUE | 56 NPI | 57 OTHER PRV ID — A B C

58 INSURED'S NAME | 59 P. REL | 60 INSURED'S UNIQUE ID | 61 GROUP NAME | 62 INSURANCE GROUP NO. — A B C

63 TREATMENT AUTHORIZATION CODES | 64 DOCUMENT CONTROL NUMBER | 65 EMPLOYER NAME — A B C

66 DX | 67 A B C D E F G H I J K L M N O P Q | 68

69 ADMIT DX | 70 PATIENT REASON DX a b c | 71 PPS CODE | 72 ECI | 73

74 PRINCIPAL PROCEDURE CODE DATE | a. OTHER PROCEDURE CODE DATE | b. OTHER PROCEDURE CODE DATE | 75 | 76 ATTENDING NPI QUAL LAST FIRST

c. OTHER PROCEDURE CODE DATE | d. OTHER PROCEDURE CODE DATE | e. OTHER PROCEDURE CODE DATE | 77 OPERATING NPI QUAL LAST FIRST

80 REMARKS | 81CC a b c d | 78 OTHER NPI QUAL LAST FIRST | 79 OTHER NPI QUAL LAST FIRST

UB-04 CMS-1450 APPROVED OMB NO. THE CERTIFICATIONS ON THE REVERSE APPLY TO THIS BILL AND ARE MADE A PART HEREOF.

NUBC National Uniform Billing Committee LIC9213257

Source: www.cms.gov/Transmittals/downloads/R1104CP.pdf (page 18).

Provider and Patient Information

The first section of the UB-04 (form locators [FLs] or items [as they will be referred to throughout this chapter] 1-17) as shown in Figure 3-12 is for provider and patient information. Some of the fields are self-explanatory (item 1, provider name, address), and others need some instruction (item 2, pay-to name, address, and secondary identification fields).

Item 2 is required when the pay-to name and address information is different from the billing provider (item 1).

Item 4 is a required field to indicate the type of bill (TOB). The TOB is a four-digit alphanumeric code that gives three specific pieces of information.

- The first digit is a zero.
- The second digit in the code identifies the type of facility, for example, a hospital.
- The third digit classifies the type of care, for example, outpatient care versus inpatient care.
- The fourth code may be a letter or number that indicates the sequence of the bill within a particular episode of care. It is referred to as a "frequency" code.

Table 3-2 provides a sample list of the TOBs.

Item 6 is another required field for the beginning and ending dates of the period included on the bill, and item 12 is required only for inpatient and home health services showing the date the patient was admitted to the hospital or home health agency.

Condition, Occurrence, and Value Codes

This section focuses on items 18-41 (see Figure 3-13) and gives a brief description of condition, occurrence, and value codes.

FIGURE 3-12 *Provider and Patient Information Items*

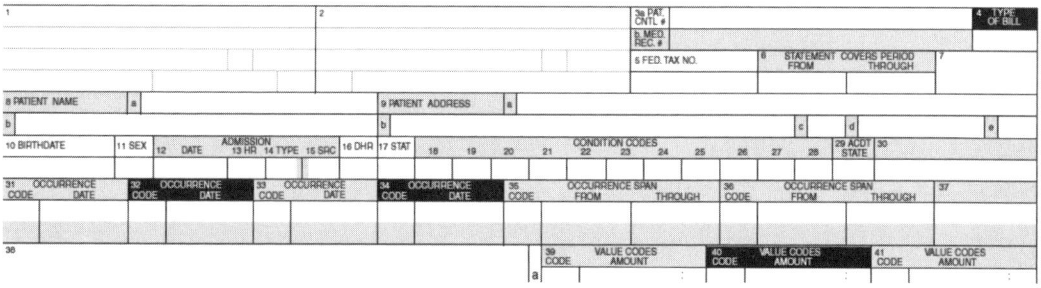

FIGURE 3-13 *Condition, Occurrence, and Value Codes Items*

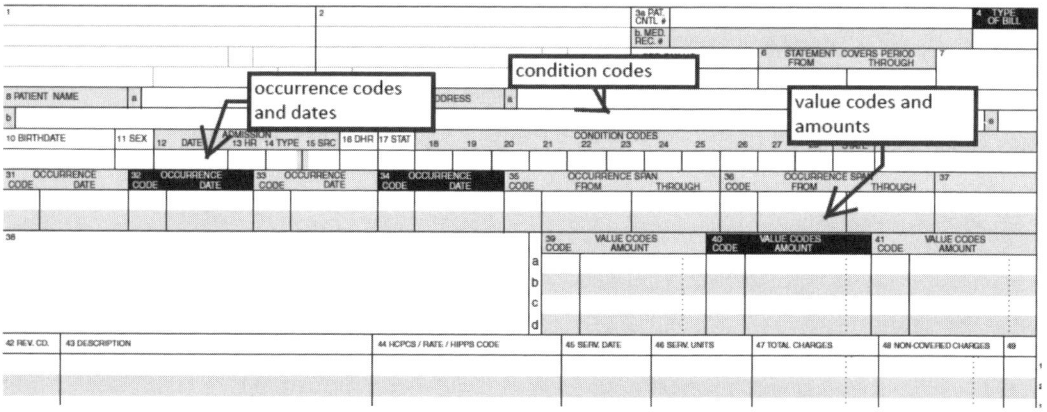

TABLE 3-2 *Sample Type of Bills for UB-04 Billing*

UB-04 JOB AID C **2007**

Type of Bill (TOB) Code Structure (FL 4)

2nd Digit-Type of Facility (CMS will process this as the 1st digit)
1. Hospital
2. Skilled Nursing
3. Home Health (Includes Home Health PPS claims, for which CMS determines whether the services are paid from the Part A Trust Fund or the Part B Trust Fund.)
4. Religious Non-medical (Hospital)
5. Reserved for National Assignment (discontinued effective 10/1/05).
6. Intermediate Care
7. Clinic or Hospital Based Renal Dialysis Facility (requires special information in second digit below).
8. Special facility or hospital ASC surgery (requires special information in second digit below).
9. Reserved for National Assignment

3rd Digit-Bill Classification (Except Clinics and Special Facilities) (CMS will process this as the 2nd digit)
1. Inpatient (Part A)
2. Inpatient (Part B) - (For HHA non PPS claims, Includes HHA visits under a Part B plan of treatment, for HHA PPS claims, indicates a Request for Anticipated Payment - RAP.) Note: For HHA PPS claims, CMS determines from which Trust Fund payment is made. Therefore, there is no need to indicate Part A or Part B on the bill.
3. Outpatient (For non-PPS HHAs, includes HHA visits under a Part A plan of treatment and use of HHA DME under a Part A plan of treatment). For home health agencies paid under PPS, CMS determines from which Trust Fund, Part A or Part B. Therefore, there is no need to indicate Part A or Part B on the bill.
4. Other (Part B) - Includes HHA medical and other health services not under a plan of treatment, hospital and SNF for diagnostic clinical laboratory services for "nonpatients " and referenced diagnostic services. For HHAs under PPS indicates an osteoporosis claim. **NOTE: 24X is discontinued effective 10/1/05.**
5. Intermediate Care - Level I
6. Intermediate Care - Level II
7. Reserved for National Assignment (discontinued effective 10/1/05).
8. Swing Bed (may be used to indicate billing for SNF level of care in a hospital with an approved swing bed agreement).
9. Reserved for National Assignment

3rd Digit-Classification (Clinics Only) (CMS will process this as the 2nd digit)
1. Rural Health Clinic (RHC)
2. Hospital Based or Independent Renal Dialysis Facility
3. Free Standing Provider Based Federally Qualified Health Center (FQHC)
4. Other Rehabilitation Facility (ORF)
5. Comprehensive Outpatient Rehabilitation Facility (CORF)
6. Community Mental Health Center (CMHC)

7-8. Reserved for National Assignment
9. OTHER

3rd Digit-Classification (Special Facilities Only) (CMS will process this as the 2nd digit)
1. Hospice (Nonhospital Based)
2. Hospice (Hospital Based)
3. Ambulatory Surgical Center Services to Hospital Outpatients
4. Free Standing Birthing Center
5. Critical Access Hospital

6-8. Reserved for National Assignment
9. OTHER

Source: http://cms.meridianksi.com/kc/content/ilc/courses/28C2EE19DB8A4789BE6F5EE3D5A575A1/html/PDFs/JobAid_C.pdf.

Items 18-28, Condition Codes

These fields contain codes identifying patient or payer conditions that may affect the processing of a bill. The codes help determine beneficiary eligibility and benefits and are used to administer primary or secondary insurance coverage. Some examples of condition codes are as follows:

- Condition code 02 represents that the treated condition is related to employment.
- Condition code 03 represents that the patient is covered by insurance not reflected on the claim.

- Condition code 21 represents that the facility is billing for a denial (denial is expected but facility wants or needs the remittance advice to show denial).
- Condition code 38 indicates that a semi-private room was not available for the patient's accommodations.

Items 31-34, Occurrence Codes

Occurrence codes and associated dates define specific events relating to a bill that might affect the payer's processing of the claims. Some examples of occurrence codes are as follows:

- Occurrence code 01 indicates an accident-related injury for which there is medical payment coverage.
- Occurrence code 04 indicates an accident that relates to the patient's employment.
- Occurrence code 09 is used to indicate the start of infertility treatment.
- Occurrence code 11 is used to indicate the date the patient first became aware of symptoms/illness.

For example, a Medicare beneficiary was in the hospital from January 1, XXXX, to January 10, XXXX; however, her Medicare Part A benefits were exhausted January 8, XXXX, and she was not entitled to Part B benefits. Therefore, item 31 should contain occurrence code A3 and 0108XX in the date field. See Figure 3-14 for illustration.

Items 39-41, Value Codes

Codes and related dollar or unit amounts that identify monetary-related data are necessary for the processing of this claim. Some examples of value codes are as follows:

- Value code 31. Patient liability amount is where the fiscal intermediary (FI) approves the provider, who charges the beneficiary the listed amount for noncovered accommodations, diagnostic procedures, or treatments.
- Value code 32. Multiple patient ambulance transport is when more than one patient is transported in a single ambulance trip; report the total number of patients transported.

Revenue Codes, HCPCS Codes, Service Dates, Units of Service, and Charges (Items 42-49)

Item 42, Revenue Code

A revenue code identifies the specific type of service being billed by line item (eg, accommodation, laboratory test, emergency department service). Every line item charged requires a revenue code, but not every revenue code (or bill) requires a CPT/HCPCS code. For example, inpatient services being billed to Medicare are not paid by CPT/HCPCS code. They are paid by MS-DRG (see Chapter 6), which is driven by the ICD-9-CM coding, and therefore, no CPT/HCPCS codes are necessary. See Figure 3-15 for items 42 to 49.

However, outpatient Medicare claims are paid by CPT/HCPCS code and would require CPT/HCPCS codes on most line items. Some examples of revenue codes are as follows:

FIGURE 3-14 *Occurrence Code Example*

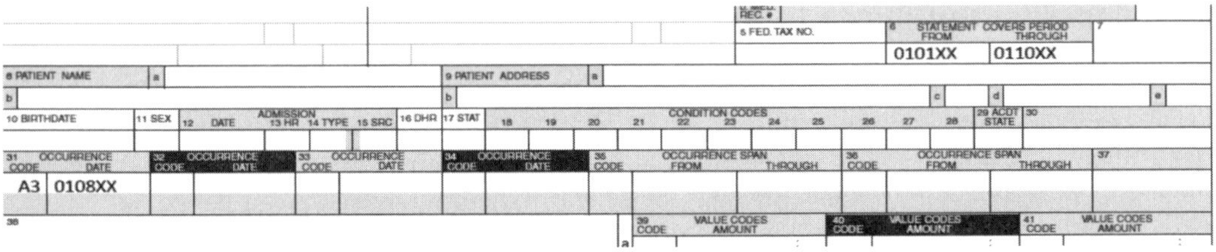

Revenue Code	Service
012X	Room & Board - general
0122	OB/two beds
0123	Pediatric/two beds
0350	CT Scan General
0351	Head CT Scan
0360	Operating Room Services—General
0361	Minor Operating Room Services

CT indicates computed tomography; OB, obstetrics.

Item 44, HCPCS Codes/Rates/HIPPS Codes

The CPT/HCPCS code and modifiers describing the procedure are entered here. On inpatient hospital bills the accommodation rate is shown here. The UB-04 accommodates up to four modifiers for each HCPCS code.

Again, not every line item requires a HCPCS code. For example, in Medicare billing, only outpatient hospital services are reimbursed by the HCPCS code (see Chapter 6); therefore, inpatient bills do not require HCPCS coding as a rule. Even in outpatient billing, not every charge requires a HCPCS code because the charges may be bundled into another service.

Item 46, Units of Service

Generally, the entries in this item quantify services by revenue code category, eg, number of days in a particular type of accommodation, pints of blood, and so forth. However, when HCPCS codes are required for services, the units are equal to the number of times the procedure/service being reported was performed.

Diagnosis, Procedure Codes, Physician Information, and Remarks

Items 66-81 are used to report ICD-9-CM diagnosis codes and procedure codes, provider NPIs, and additional information that may be required to adjudicate the claim. See Figure 3-16 for items 66 to 81.

FIGURE 3-15 *UB-04 Items 42-49*

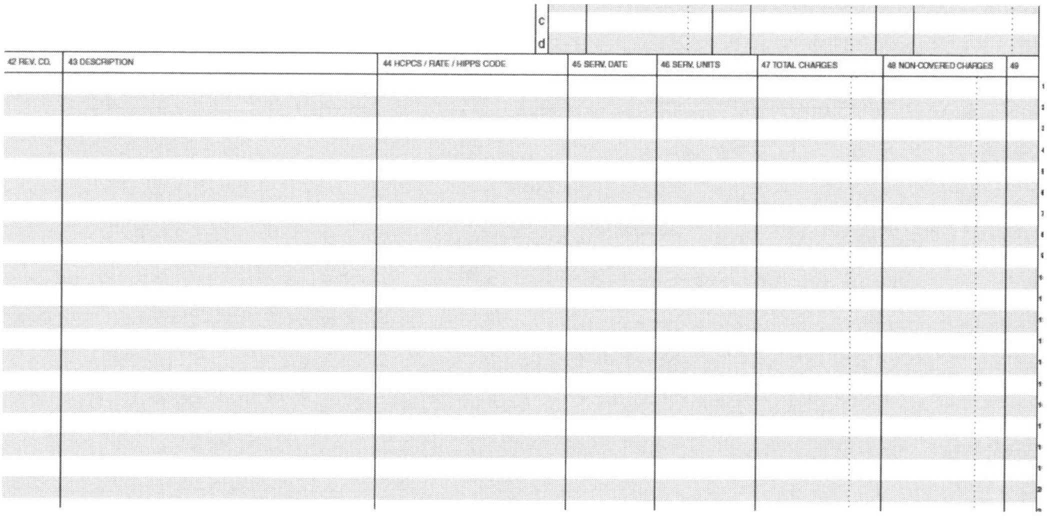

42 REV. CD.	43 DESCRIPTION	44 HCPCS / RATE / HIPPS CODE	45 SERV. DATE	46 SERV. UNITS	47 TOTAL CHARGES	48 NON-COVERED CHARGES	49

FIGURE 3-16 *UB-04 Items 66-81*

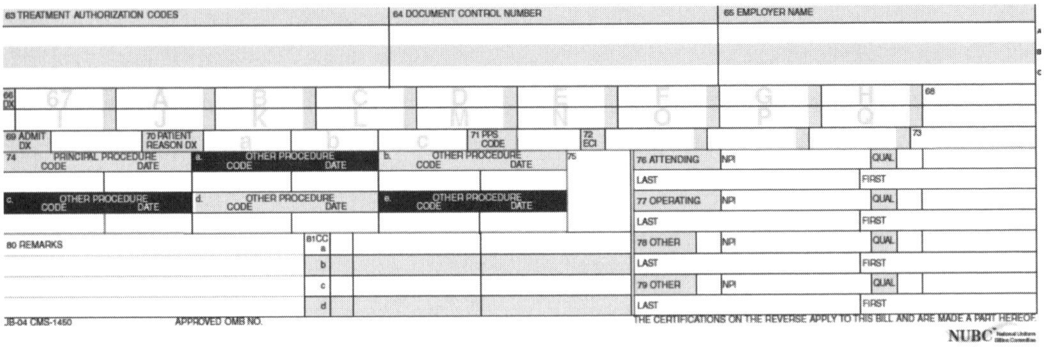
63 TREATMENT AUTHORIZATION CODES | 64 DOCUMENT CONTROL NUMBER | 65 EMPLOYER NAME

66 DX | 67 | A | B | C | D | E | F | G | H | 68

I | J | K | L | M | N | O | P | Q

69 ADMIT DX | 70 PATIENT REASON DX | a | b | c | 71 PPS CODE | 72 ECI | 73

74 PRINCIPAL PROCEDURE CODE DATE | a. OTHER PROCEDURE CODE DATE | b. OTHER PROCEDURE CODE DATE | 75 | 76 ATTENDING NPI QUAL LAST FIRST

c. OTHER PROCEDURE CODE DATE | d. OTHER PROCEDURE CODE DATE | e. OTHER PROCEDURE CODE DATE | 77 OPERATING NPI QUAL LAST FIRST

80 REMARKS | 81CC a b c d | 78 OTHER NPI QUAL LAST FIRST | 79 OTHER NPI QUAL LAST FIRST

UB-04 CMS-1450 APPROVED OMB NO. THE CERTIFICATIONS ON THE REVERSE APPLY TO THIS BILL AND ARE MADE A PART HEREOF. NUBC

Item 66, Diagnosis and Procedure Code Qualifier (ICD Version Indicator)

Medicare does not accept ICD-10 codes at this time. Medicare processes only ICD-9 codes.

This qualifier field is used to report the version of ICD used for the diagnosis codes listed on the claim. Medicare will ignore this data.

The following qualifier codes reflect the edition of the ICD:

- 9 - Ninth Revision
- 0 - Tenth Revision

Item 67, Principal Diagnosis

The hospital enters the ICD-9-CM code for the principal diagnosis. The principal diagnosis is the condition established after study to be principally responsible for an admission.

Items 67A-Q, Other Diagnosis Codes

This field is used to report all of a beneficiary's medical conditions that coexist at the time of the admission or visit, or develop subsequently, or affect the treatment received and/or the length of stay.

Item 69, Admitting Diagnosis

Admitting diagnosis is the condition requiring hospitalization identified by the physician at the time of the beneficiary's admission.

Item 74, Principal Procedure Code and Date

This field contains the ICD-9-CM procedure code for the principal procedure performed during the inpatient stay and the date on which the procedure was performed.

Items 74a-74e, Other Procedure Codes and Dates

This field allows reporting of up to five ICD-9-CM procedure codes to identify the significant procedures performed during the billing period, other than the principal procedure, and the corresponding dates on which the procedures were performed.

> **Note**
>
> ICD-9-CM procedure codes apply only to inpatient hospital claims. Do not report these procedure codes on outpatient claims.

Electronic Data Interchange

The Administrative Simplification Compliance Act (ASCA) requires that all initial Medicare claims for payment be submitted electronically. This requirement is for all Medicare providers except for small providers. Initial claims are those claims submitted for fee-for-service payment for the first time.

Paper Claim Submission

There are some circumstances where the electronic billing requirement could be waived. A provider must obtain preapproval to submit paper claims in:

- Any situation where a provider can demonstrate that the applicable HIPAA claim standard does not permit submission of a claim electronically;
- Any situation where the disability of all staff of a provider prevents use of a computer for electronic submission of claims; and
- Other cases where a provider can establish that due to conditions outside the provider's control, electronic claims cannot be submitted.

Electronic Claim Submission

Claims are electronically transmitted from the provider to the Medicare contractor. Medicare contractors perform a series of edits. Providers billing electronic claims must comply with the ASC X12N 837 Professional or Institutional Guides.[3]

Each provider must complete an EDI Enrollment form prior to starting to exchange any EDI transactions directly with the payer or through a billing service or clearinghouse. In that agreement, the provider agrees to accept responsibility for safeguarding beneficiary data and assuring billing services.

Definitions and Acronyms

clearinghouse. A company that receives electronic medical claims information from providers, analyzes the claims for errors, edits the information into a standardized format, and then transmits the information to the insurance company.

CMS 1500 claim form. Standard paper claim form for submitting requests for payment to insurance companies for professional services.

Electronic data interchange (EDI). The electronic transmitting of claims, other administrative transactions, and other data.

National provider identifier (NPI). The NPI is an identification number for HIPAA-covered health care providers, which must be used with health plans and clearinghouses.

National Uniform Billing Committee (NUBC).[4] The NUBC is responsible for maintaining a single billing form and standard data set that could be used nationwide by institutional providers and payers for health care claims.

National Uniform Claim Committee (NUCC).[5] The NUCC was created to develop a standardized data set for use by the noninstitutional health care community to transmit claim and encounter information to and from all third-party payers.

ordering physician. A provider who orders nonphysician services for the patient.

UB-04 claim form. Standard paper claim form for submitting requests for payment to insurance companies for facility (hospital) charges.

FIGURE 3-17 *Sample UB-04 Form*

1 Provider Name	2 Pay-to-Name	3a PAT. CNTL # Required	4 TYPE OF BILL
Street Address	Street Address or Post Office Box	b. MED. REC. # Recommended	0131
City, State, ZIP Code	City, State, ZIP Code	5 FED. TAX NO. ## ########	6 STATEMENT COVERS PERIOD FROM MMDDYY THROUGH MMDDYY; 7
Telephone; Fax; Country Code			
8 PATIENT NAME a		9 PATIENT ADDRESS a Patient Street Address or Post Office Box	
b Patient Last, First, Middle Initial		b City c State d ZIP Code	e Country Code
10 BIRTHDATE MMDDCCYY	11 SEX X	ADMISSION 12 DATE 13 HR 14 TYPE 15 SRC # 16 DHR 17 STAT ##	CONDITION CODES 18 19 20 21 22 23 24 25 26 27 28; 29 ACDT STATE; 30
31 OCCURRENCE CODE DATE	32 OCCURRENCE CODE DATE	33 OCCURRENCE CODE DATE; 34 OCCURRENCE CODE DATE	35 OCCURRENCE SPAN CODE FROM THROUGH; 36 OCCURRENCE SPAN CODE FROM THROUGH; 37
38		39 VALUE CODES CODE AMOUNT a b c d	40 VALUE CODES CODE AMOUNT; 41 VALUE CODES CODE AMOUNT

42 REV. CD.	43 DESCRIPTION	44 HCPCS / RATE / HIPPS CODE	45 SERV. DATE	46 SERV. UNITS	47 TOTAL CHARGES	48 NON-COVERED CHARGES	49
1 0###	Revenue Code Description	####	MMDDYY	#	$$$ $$		
23 0001	PAGE _#_ OF _#_	CREATION DATE		TOTALS	$$$ $$		

50 PAYER NAME	51 HEALTH PLAN ID	52 REL INFO	53 ASG BEN	54 PRIOR PAYMENTS	55 EST. AMOUNT DUE	56 NPI ##########
A Medicare		X				57 OTHER PRV ID
58 INSURED'S NAME	59 P. REL	60 INSURED'S UNIQUE ID	61 GROUP NAME	62 INSURANCE GROUP NO.		
A Beneficiary Last, First Name	##	###-##-####X				
63 TREATMENT AUTHORIZATION CODES	64 DOCUMENT CONTROL NUMBER	65 EMPLOYER NAME				
66 DX ##### 9	A B C D E F G H	I J K L M N O P Q	68			
69 ADMIT DX	70 PATIENT REASON DX a b c	71 PPS CODE	72 ECI	73		
74 PRINCIPAL PROCEDURE CODE DATE	a. OTHER PROCEDURE CODE DATE	b. OTHER PROCEDURE CODE DATE	75	76 ATTENDING NPI ########## QUAL		
c. OTHER PROCEDURE CODE DATE	d. OTHER PROCEDURE CODE DATE	e. OTHER PROCEDURE CODE DATE		LAST Physician Last Name FIRST First Name		
				77 OPERATING NPI QUAL LAST FIRST		
80 REMARKS	81CC a B3 ###XX####X			78 OTHER NPI QUAL LAST FIRST		
Add any additional information here.	b c d			79 OTHER NPI QUAL LAST FIRST		

UB-04 CMS-1450 APPROVED OMB NO.

THE CERTIFICATIONS ON THE REVERSE APPLY TO THIS BILL AND ARE MADE A PART HEREOF.

NUBC National Uniform Billing Committee LIC9213257

REFERENCES

1. Centers for Medicare and Medicaid Services. Medicare Claims Processing Manual 100-04. Chapter 26: Completing and Processing Form CMS 1500. Available at: www.cms.gov/manuals/downloads/clm104c26.pdf. Accessed January 5, 2011.
2. Centers for Medicare and Medicaid Services. Medicare Claims Processing Manual 100-04. Chapter 25: Completing and Processing Form CMS 1450. Available at: www.cms.gov/manuals/downloads/clm104c25.pdf. Accessed January 5, 2011.
3. Centers for Medicare and Medicaid Services. National Provider Identification. Available at: www.cms.gov/NationalProvIdentStand/. Accessed January 6, 2011.
4. National Uniform Billing Committee. Available at: www.nubc.org/. Accessed January 5, 2011.
5. Centers for Medicare and Medicaid Services. Electronic Billing & EDI Transactions www.cms.gov/ElectronicBillingEDITrans/08_HealthCareClaims.asp. Accessed January 5, 2011.

Chapter 4

Medicare Payment Systems Overview

Medicare Overview

This chapter will address specific Medicare payment mechanisms. Although these are Medicare-specific methodologies, many non-Medicare payers use similar systems when processing claims.

Medicare is the federal health insurance benefit plan for the aged and disabled, enacted under the Social Security Act (Title XVIII). The Centers for Medicare and Medicaid Services (CMS) oversee administration of the Medicare program and fall within the Department of Health and Human Services (HHS).

Medicare provides health insurance for:

- individuals age 65 or older,
- individuals (regardless of age) with certain disabilities, and
- individuals (regardless of age) with end-stage renal disease.

The four distinct parts of the Medicare program are:

Part A Medicare. Medicare Part A is hospital insurance that covers inpatient care in hospitals.

Part B Medicare. Medicare Part B is medical insurance that covers physician or nonphysician providers' services and outpatient care in addition to other medical services that Part A doesn't cover.

Part C Medicare. Medicare Part C is a Medicare advantage insurance in which beneficiaries can choose a private payer's managed care type of insurance. Medicare pays the private health plan a capitated rate and beneficiaries usually pay an additional monthly premium to cover items not covered by traditional Medicare (Parts A and B), such as prescription drugs, dental care, and vision care.

Part D Medicare. Medicare Part D is medical insurance that covers prescription drugs.

Medicare issues a health insurance card (see Figure 4-1) that indicates the patient's coverage.

Medicare Payment Systems Overview

Medicare payment is determined by several factors including the type of provider and the type of medical service, supply, or pharmaceutical provided. Table 4-1 illustrates the driving factors for payment.

Medicare's payment has changed substantially since inception. Years ago, most services were paid by reasonable cost, which meant providers would bill charges for services and Medicare would reimburse a percentage of those charges. There are a few payers who still follow a similar system, but not Medicare. One obvious point when paying based on the charge is that the higher the charge, the higher the payment; there is no incentive for the provider to manage resources efficiently. With skyrocketing payments by Medicare and limited funds available, methods were sought to control payments while incentivizing providers to control costs—supposedly a win-win situation.

FIGURE 4-1 *Sample Medicare Health Insurance Card*

TABLE 4-1 *Factors Determining Primary[a] Medicare Payment System*

Provider Type[b]	Payment System[c]	Coding System
Physician and nonphysician providers	RBRVS	• HCPCS for services, supplies • ICD-9-CM for diagnoses
Hospital inpatient services	MS-DRGs	• ICD-9-CM
Hospital outpatient services	APCs	• HCPCS for services, supplies • ICD-9-CM for diagnoses
Ambulatory surgery centers	APCs	• HCPCS for services, supplies • ICD-9-CM for diagnoses
Durable medical equipment (DME) centers	HCPCS	• HCPCS for services, supplies • ICD-9-CM for diagnoses

[a] Not all-inclusive list.
[b] There are many other provider types (eg, skilled nursing facilities, ambulance providers, Federally Qualified Health Centers, Critical Access Hospitals).
[c] All of these are prospective payment systems.

This search for a different payment mechanism to control costs was the impetus for the current payment structures for Medicare patients. Medicare now uses prospective payment systems (PPSs) and fee schedules to pay claims as are summarized in Table 4-1.

A PPS is a method of payment in which payment is made based on a predetermined amount. Payment is based on specific coding and classification systems. See Table 4-2 for examples of coding and classification systems.

Although all Medicare payment schemes are not called prospective payment systems, fee schedules are prospectively determined amounts based on care provided and are not based on charges submitted. A fee schedule is a listing of allowable amounts payers agree to for paying claims. As shown in Table 4-3, CMS has fee schedules for physicians and nonphysician providers, ambulance services, clinical laboratory services, and durable medical equipment/prosthetic and orthotic supplies (DMEPOS).

Medicare determines prospectively what will be paid using different systems, some of which are shown in Table 4-3.

The Resource Based Relative Value Scale (RBRVS), ambulatory payment classifications (APCs), and Diagnosis Related Groups (DRGs) will be explained

TABLE 4-2 *Coding and Classification Systems**

Coding System	Classification System
HCPCS	Ambulatory Payment Classification (APC)
HCPCS	Medicare Physician Fee Schedule (MPFS)
HCPCS	Ambulance Fee Schedule
HCPCS	Clinical Laboratory Fee Schedule
HCPCS	Durable Medical Equipment, Prosthetic and Orthotic Supplies Fee Schedule
ICD-9-CM	Medicare Severity Diagnosis Related Groups
HIPPS codes	Home Health Prospective Payment System

* Not all-inclusive list.

TABLE 4-3 *Examples of Medicare Prospective Payment Systems (PPS)*

Service	Prospective Payment System
Physician/nonphysician medical services	RBRVS/Medicare Fee Schedule
Hospital inpatient facility services	MS-DRGs (IPPS)
Hospital inpatient psychiatric facility services	IPF PPS
Hospital inpatient rehabilitation facility services	IRF PPS
Hospital outpatient facility services	APCs (OPPS)
Long-term hospital facility services	LTCH PPS
Ambulatory surgery center facility services	APCs (OPPS)
Durable medical equipment/prosthetic and orthotic supplies	DMEPOS Fee Schedule
Home health services	HH PPS
Ambulance services	Ambulance Fee Schedule
End-stage renal disease care	Composite Rate Payment
Skilled nursing facility services	Prospective Payment System (SNF PPS)

more completely in later chapters, but first there are some other payment implications that impact all Medicare claims. These include Medicare secondary payer (MSP), coverage criteria, and resources on the CMS Web site at www.cms.gov.

Filing claims with Medicare is complicated and carries some risks, which are attributed to two factors: revenue risks and compliance risks. If Medicare claims are not filed correctly, if the documentation does not support the appropriate level of care provided, or if the person assigning codes to the care is not accurate, the provider's payment can be less than is deserved. Also, these same issues can cause an overpayment from Medicare. For example, if a complicated surgery was billed instead of the minor procedure that was actually performed, the payment would be based on what was billed (complicated surgery), which would be inaccurate and erroneous. This overpayment could cause an audit by the payer and could result in many problems for the provider (see Chapter 12 on compliance). Remember, accuracy in billing is paramount.

Medicare as Secondary Payer

Medicare secondary payer (MSP) simply means Medicare is not responsible for paying first on a claim, ie, another payer should pay as the primary insurer and Medicare will pay as the secondary insurer. Since Medicare is a federal program, federal laws have authority over local laws or private contracts. Medicare would be the secondary payer regardless of state law or plan provisions based on the following categories:

- Medicare pays secondary to group health coverage plans for individuals age 65 or over if the group plan is by the individual's current employer or the current employment status of the individual's spouse.
- Medicare is secondary payer to plans for individuals eligible for, or entitled to, Medicare benefits based on end-stage renal disease (ESRD) during a coordination period.
- Medicare is secondary payer to large group health plans (LGHPs) for individuals under age 65 entitled to Medicare on the basis of disability and whose LGHP coverage is based on the individual's (or family member's) current employment status.
- Medicare does not make payment for items or services when payment is made by a liability policy.
- Medicare does not pay items and services paid by workers' compensation.
- Medicare does pay for services that are paid under no-fault insurance.

Refer to the CMS Web site, which has extensive information on MSP.[1]

Medicare Coverage Criteria

Coverage criteria are key elements of Medicare claims, and several methods for deciding coverage are built within Medicare claims processing. The majority of coverage criteria are developed at a local level by the Medicare payer clinicians. There are also circumstances where Medicare will develop a national coverage determination (NCD) for an item or service that applies to all Medicare beneficiaries nationwide. Furthermore, some services and items are statutorily excluded from coverage and will not be paid regardless of circumstance. Some of the coverage limitations include:

- General exclusions from coverage
- Services not reasonable and necessary
- Foot care
- Items and services furnished, paid for, or authorized by governmental entities—federal, state, or local governments
- Services not provided within the United States
- Services resulting from war
- Personal comfort items
- Routine services and appliances
- Hearing aids and auditory implants
- Custodial care
- Cosmetic surgery
- Charges imposed by immediate relatives of the patient or members of the patient's household

- Dental services
- Services reimbursable under automobile, no-fault, or any liability insurance or workers' compensation
- Services related to and required as a result of services that are not covered under Medicare

Services that are statutorily covered can still be denied due to specific medical necessity issues for a single claim. In order to be paid, all services must be determined to be reasonable and necessary for the specific patient and the specific medical encounter. Medicare provides (as mentioned above) both local and national coverage determinations (LCDs and NCDs), which serve to inform physicians of the gauge for covering specific services.

Figures 4-2 to 4-5 illustrate sample LCDs and NCDs that providers can access from the CMS or local Medicare contractor Web sites.

Patients should be aware of those services and supplies that are statutorily excluded (eg, cosmetic surgery, acupuncture) from coverage. When a service or supply is noncovered by law, the patient should be aware of the noncoverage as Medicare provides notification to beneficiaries of the benefits to which they are entitled. Should the patient decide to receive the service or supply that is known to be noncovered, the patient will bear responsibility for paying the provider. However, for services and supplies that are conditionally covered (eg, bariatric treatment), the provider may bill the patient only if the patient is made aware before treatment of the potential for the service to be denied **and** the provider obtains patient acknowledgement of the potential for denial as well as patient consent to provide the treatment with the patient taking on the responsibility for payment. This consent can be obtained through the advanced beneficiary notification (ABN) document. See Figure 4-6 for an example of an ABN. Note that there are very specific guidelines on the CMS Web site on how to properly obtain an ABN in order to bill a patient.

***Tip:** Explain to a patient the services that are statutorily excluded and request a signed ABN to avoid the patient being upset when he or she is later billed for these services.*

FIGURE 4-2 *Local Coverage Determination (LCD) Categories for Indiana*[2]

Local Coverage Determinations by Title

The following table lists local coverage determinations (LCDs) that are currently active for National Government Services Medicare Part A and Part B providers. To search for and access LCDs, please use the Medical Policy Center.

LCD ID	LCD TITLE
L28539	Abdominal and Pelvic Ultrasound
L25879	Acid Phosphatase
L28451	Allergy Immunotherapy
L26375	B-type Natriuretic Peptide (BNP) Testing
L28482	Bariatric Surgery
L28192	Beta2-Microglobulin Testing
L26003	Biologic Products for Wound Treatment and Surgical Interventions
L26448	Blepharoplasty

Source: www.ngsmedicare.com/wps/portal/ngsmedicare/mpc www.ngsmedicare.com/wps/portal/ngsmedicare.

FIGURE 4-3 *Specific Example of LCD Guidelines in Indiana: Bariatric Surgery (L28482)*[2]*

Revision Ending Date

Indications and Limitations of Coverage and/or Medical Necessity

Abstract:

This local coverage determination (LCD) addresses both local and national coverage and noncoverage treatment options which include supplemented fasting and various bariatric surgical interventions such as Roux-en-Y Gastric Bypass (RYGBP), Biliopancreatic Diversion with Duodenal Switch (BPD/DS), sleeve gastrectomy , etc. used to treat comorbid conditions associated with morbid obesity. The LCD also contains the ICD-9-CM codes for the comorbid conditions which are not defined in the national coverage determination (NCD).

Indications and Limitations:

Obesity is an increase in body weight beyond the limitation of skeletal and physical requirements, as a result of an excessive accumulation of fat in the body. In general, 20% to 30% above "ideal" body weight, according to standard life insurance tables, constitutes obesity. Morbid obesity is further defined as a condition of consistent and uncontrollable weight gain. Individuals who may be considered as candidates for gastrointestinal surgery include those with a body mass index (BMI) equal to or above 35 who suffer from Type II diabetes or life-threatening cardiopulmonary problems such as severe sleep apnea or obesity -related heart disease.

BMI is a method used to quantitatively evaluate body fat by reflecting the presence of excess adipose tissue.

---

* Partial view

Source: www.ngsmedicare.com/wps/portal/ngsmedicare/mpc www.ngsmedicare.com/wps/portal/ngsmedicare.

FIGURE 4-4 *Examples of National Coverage Determination (NCD) Categories*

Closed NCAs Alphabetical Index Results **[180 Records]**

Select a link: 0-9 A B C D E F G H I J K L M N O P Q R S T U V W X Y Z

Note: Only displaying linked letters for which there are records.

Page 1 of 8 | Enter Page # | Go to page | First Prev 1 2 3 4 5 6 7 ... Next Last | View Items Per Page: 25

	NCA TITLE	SELECT ALL
A	Abarelix for the Treatment of Prostate Cancer	
	Actinic Keratoses	
	Acupuncture for Fibromyalgia	
	Acupuncture for Nausea after Chemotherapy and Post-operative Pain	
	Acupuncture for Osteoarthritis	
	Air-Fluidized Beds for Pressure Ulcers	
	Air-Fluidized Beds for Pressure Ulcers (1st Recon)	

Source: www.ngsmedicare.com/wps/portal/ngsmedicare/mpc www.ngsmedicare.com/wps/portal/ngsmedicare.

FIGURE 4-5 *Specific Example of NCD Guidelines: Acupuncture**

Benefit Category
Incident to a physician's professional Service
Inpatient Hospital Services
Outpatient Hospital Services Incident to a Physician's Service
Physicians' Services
Note: This may not be an exhaustive list of all applicable Medicare benefit categories for this item or service.

Indications and Limitations of Coverage

Although acupuncture has been used for thousands of years in China and for decades in parts of Europe, it is a new agent of unknown use and efficacy in the United States. Even in those areas of the world where it has been widely used, its mechanism is not known. Three units of the National Institutes of Health, the National Institute of General Medical Sciences, National Institute of Neurological Diseases and Stroke, and Fogarty International Center have been designed to assess and identify specific opportunities and needs for research attending the use of acupuncture for surgical anesthesia and relief of chronic pain. Until the pending scientific assessment of the technique has been completed and its efficacy has been established, Medicare reimbursement for acupuncture, as an anesthetic or as an analgesic or for other therapeutic purposes, may not be made. Accordingly, acupuncture is not considered reasonable and necessary within the meaning of §1862(a)(1) of the Act.

* Partial view

Source: www.ngsmedicare.com/wps/portal/ngsmedicare/mpc www.ngsmedicare.com/wps/portal/ngsmedicare.

Medicare Payment Systems Resources

When billing Medicare, providers should access as many official resources as possible. Because this book does not include every aspect of billing Medicare, the resources listed in this book should be considered integral to effectively finding and understanding the guidelines.

As with seemingly everything in health care, guidelines for billing change continuously. Current and official resources are critical. In addition to accessing resources, there are ways to have payers notify you of updates when they occur. This can be achieved by accessing the national CMS Web site or the Web sites of specific Medicare Administrative Contractors' (MACs) and requesting e-mailed updates. In addition, the Office of Inspector General (OIG) will provide update notifications by e-mail as well. Figure 4-7 illustrates the CMS Web page for requesting such information.

CMS (Medicare) Resources

CMS, the official overseer for Medicare payment, has a wealth of information on its Web site. The following steps explain how to access necessary billing and payment guidelines on the CMS Web site:

Step 1: Go to www.cms.gov and select the Medicare category.

Step 2: Scroll down to the Provider Type category and select the appropriate provider type (either Physician Center for physician/nonphysician providers or Hospital for hospital providers).

Step 3: Within the appropriate provider category (either physician or hospital), choose the type of guidance or guidelines from the various available resources on this Web page. You should access the information that is applicable to your provider type. Some examples of the different options that are available on the Web page are:
- Internet manuals
- Coding guidelines
- Fee schedules
- Coverage criteria

Figures 4-8a–4-8d highlight the three-step process to access billing and payment guidelines from the CMS Web site.

There are many resources on the CMS Web site, which include the following:
- Frequently asked questions (FAQs) with Medicare responses (see Figure 4-9)
- Memorandums
- Transmittals
- Articles
- Links

FIGURE 4-6 *Advanced Beneficiary Notification (ABN)*

(A) **Notifier(s):**
(B) **Patient Name:** ***(C)*** **Identification Number:**

ADVANCE BENEFICIARY NOTICE OF NONCOVERAGE (ABN)

NOTE: If Medicare doesn't pay for ***(D)***_____________ below, you may have to pay.

Medicare does not pay for everything, even some care that you or your health care provider have good reason to think you need. We expect Medicare may not pay for the ***(D)***_____________ below.

(D)_______________	***(E)*** **Reason Medicare May Not Pay:**	***(F)*** **Estimated Cost:**

WHAT YOU NEED TO DO NOW:

- Read this notice, so you can make an informed decision about your care.
- Ask us any questions that you may have after you finish reading.
- Choose an option below about whether to receive the ***(D)***_____________ listed above.
  Note: If you choose Option 1 or 2, we may help you to use any other insurance that you might have, but Medicare cannot require us to do this.

(G) **OPTIONS:** **Check only one box. We cannot choose a box for you.**

❑ **OPTION 1.** I want the ***(D)***__________ listed above. You may ask to be paid now, but I also want Medicare billed for an official decision on payment, which is sent to me on a Medicare Summary Notice (MSN). I understand that if Medicare doesn't pay, I am responsible for payment, but **I can appeal to Medicare** by following the directions on the MSN. If Medicare does pay, you will refund any payments I made to you, less co-pays or deductibles.

❑ **OPTION 2.** I want the ***(D)***__________ listed above, but do not bill Medicare. You may ask to be paid now as I am responsible for payment. **I cannot appeal if Medicare is not billed**.

❑ **OPTION 3.** I don't want the ***(D)***__________listed above. I understand with this choice I am **not** responsible for payment, and **I cannot appeal to see if Medicare would pay.**

(H) **Additional Information:**

This notice gives our opinion, not an official Medicare decision. If you have other questions on this notice or Medicare billing, call **1-800-MEDICARE** (1-800-633-4227/**TTY**: 1-877-486-2048).

Signing below means that you have received and understand this notice. You also receive a copy.

(I) **Signature:**	***(J)*** **Date:**

According to the Paperwork Reduction Act of 1995, no persons are required to respond to a collection of information unless it displays a valid OMB control number. The valid OMB control number for this information collection is 0938-0566. The time required to complete this information collection is estimated to average 7 minutes per response, including the time to review instructions, search existing data resources, gather the data needed, and complete and review the information collection. If you have comments concerning the accuracy of the time estimate or suggestions for improving this form, please write to: CMS, 7500 Security Boulevard, Attn: PRA Reports Clearance Officer, Baltimore, Maryland 21244-1850.

Form CMS-R-131 (03/08) Form Approved OMB No. 0938-0566

FIGURE 4-7 *Request for Updates via E-mail Notification at CMS Web Site*

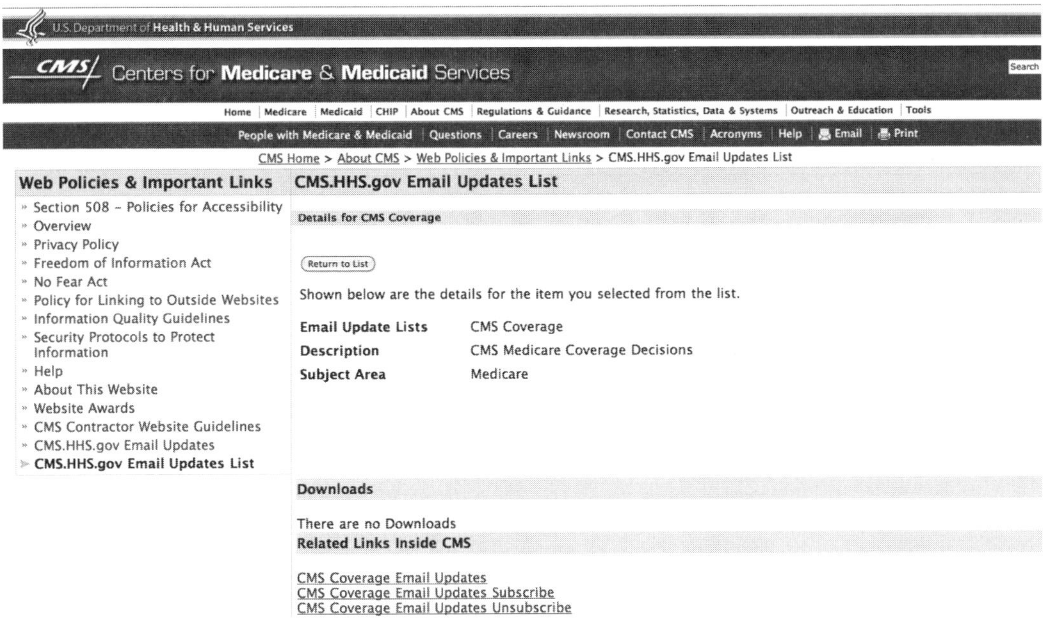

Learning Opportunity

The frequently asked questions (FAQs) option on the CMS Web site is key to a better understanding of how to appropriately complete CMS forms. Also, the FAQs are updated on an as-needed basis (there is no regularly scheduled update), which means users should check the site on at least a quarterly basis for new information.

Medicare Administrative Contractor Resources

In addition to the CMS Web site, each Medicare Administrative Contractor (MAC) has a Web site devoted to local guidelines, educational opportunities, and updates. These MACs also offer electronic notification of changes when made. Figures 4-10a and 4-10b illustrate a MAC (ie, TrailBlazer) Web site and the information it provides. Each MAC Web site will have a different look and flow, but all provide the same overall information.

Tip: *Do not rely solely on your MAC for information. Often, when one payer does not have the information to answer a specific question, another MAC might. Although guidelines can vary from one MAC to another, understanding how any Medicare payer addresses an issue can at the very least provide insight into how your payer may handle the issue. It does not hurt to use one payer's guideline to query another for confirmation.*

The next chapters will briefly review the most common Medicare payment systems for physicians (RBRVS), hospitals (MS-DRGs), and ambulatory surgery centers (APCs).

FIGURE 4-8a *Online Access of CMS Billing and Payment Guidelines*
Step 1. Go to www.cms.gov and select Medicare.

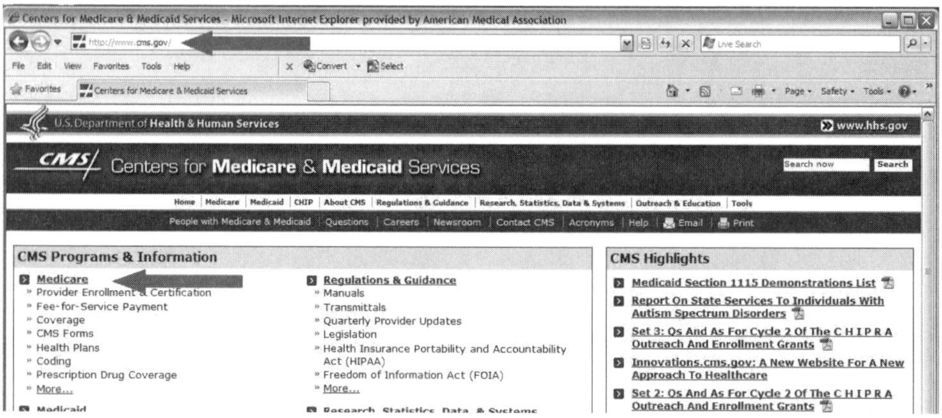

FIGURE 4-8b *Online Access of CMS Billing and Payment Guidelines*
Step 2. Scroll down and select the appropriate provider type.

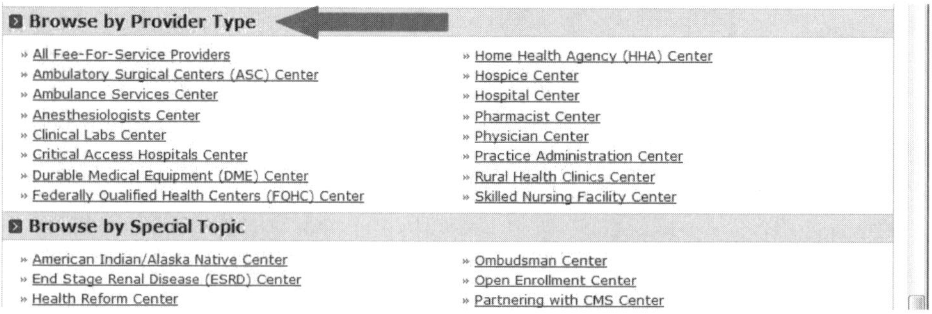

FIGURE 4-8c *Online Access of CMS Billing and Payment Guidelines: Physician*
Step 3a. Select the applicable resource for guidance (in this figure, "Physician Center" has been selected).

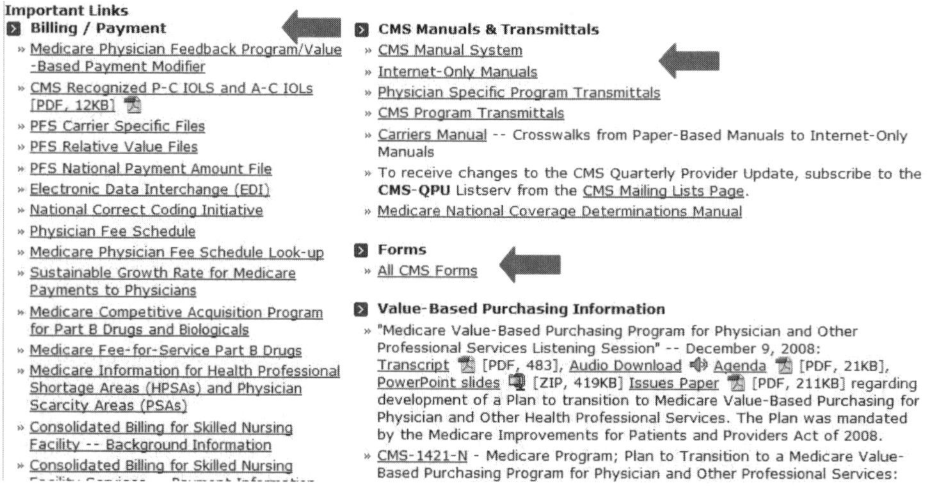

FIGURE 4-8d *Online Access of CMS Billing and Payment Guidelines: Hospital*

Step 3. Select the applicable resource for guidance (in this figure, "Hospital Center" has been selected).

Important Links

Payment
- » Acute Inpatient Prospective Payment System (PPS) -- New Medical Services and New Technologies and Hospital Acquired Conditions
- » Critical Access Hospitals
- » Hospital Outpatient PPS
- » Long-Term Care Hospital (LTCH)
- » Inpatient Rehabilitation Facility (IRF) PPS
- » Inpatient Psychiatric Facility (IPF) PPS
- » Electronic Data Interchange (EDI)(Billing): Medicare information on electronic transactions under HIPAA
- » Medicare Fee-for-Service Part B Drugs
- » Transplant Centers
- » Section 1011, Federal Reimbursement of Emergency Health Services Furnished to Undocumented Aliens

Enrollment, Participation & Certification
- » Provider Enrollment Information
- » CMS 855 Enrollment Applications
- » Conditions of Participation: Hospitals
- » Conditions of Participation: Critical Access Hospitals
- » Conditions of Participation: Psychiatric Hospitals
- » Survey & Certification

Policies & Regulations
- » Inpatient PPS Regulations & Notices

CMS Manuals & Transmittals
- » CMS Manuals
- » CMS Internet-Only Manuals
- » Program Transmittals
- » Medicare National Coverage Determinations Manual

National Provider Identifier (NPI)
- » Information for Medicare Fee-for-Service Providers about the NPI

Cost Reporting
- » Provider Reimbursement Manual (Pub 15)
- » Provider Reimbursement Review Board

Forms
- » Hospital Advanced Beneficiary Notice
- » CMS 855 Enrollment Applications
- » Form 1450 (UB-04)
- » Form 1500
- » All CMS Forms

Hospital Value-Based Purchasing
- » Report to Congress: Plan to Implement a Medicare Hospital Value-Based Purchasing Program
- » Agenda - April 12, 2007 Listening Session
- » Slide Presentations - April 12, 2007 Listening Session

FIGURE 4-9 *FAQs on the CMS Web Site*

59 Answers Available

	ID	Summary
1	3373	What is the column 1/column 2 correct coding edit table?
2	3517	How should modifier -59 be reported under the CCI?
3	3510	What modifiers are allowed with the CCI edits?
4	2435	How often will the Correct Coding Initiative (CCI) edits be updated for FIs?
5	3365	If I want to determine what codes/procedures are paired with a certain code, how can I find this out?
6	2392	Do the critical care Correct Coding Initiative (CCI) edits apply to hospitals?
7	3356	How do I obtain the CCI Edits Manual?
8	3367	What are Correct Coding Initiative (CCI) edits?
9	3369	What exactly does "column 1" mean in the column 1/column 2 correct coding edits table and in the mutually exclusive edits table?
10	3366	If I receive a denial for a procedure bundled into another service, and I cannot find this code pair in the column 1/column 2 correct coding list of edits, where else should I look?
11	3372	What is the mutually exclusive edit table?
12	3368	What does it mean when codes are considered "mutually exclusive" of each other?
13	3516	How should modifier "-25" be reported under the CCI?

FIGURE 4-10a *TrailBlazer Medicare Web Site: Quick Links and E-mail Lists*[3]

Note that the main page includes many links for additional information and an area to join e-mail lists (to have access to additional information).

FIGURE 4-10b *TrailBlazer Medicare Web Site: Publications*[3]

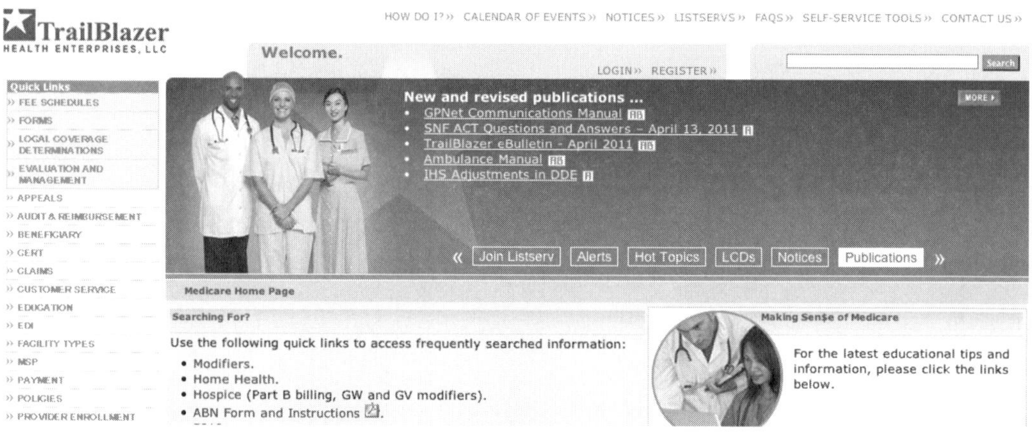

Note the links to payer-specific manuals and education.

Definitions and Acronyms

advanced beneficiary notification (ABN). ABN is the official CMS form used to notify beneficiaries or patients of their potential liability for payment of services when the physician expects that a Medicare *covered* service may be denied because of coverage criteria (eg, frequency of coverage, diagnosis restrictions, or other payment limitations), as required by Medicare statute. If the physician practice fails to get a signed ABN, the patient cannot be held financially liable for the service in the event of a denial due to coverage limitations.

ambulatory payment classifications (APCs). Outpatient services grouped by similar resources, costs, and clinical characteristics.

Centers for Medicare and Medicaid Services (CMS). This is a branch of the Department of Health and Human Services (HHS) responsible for overseeing the Medicare and Medicaid federal health care programs.

durable medical equipment/prosthetic and orthotic supplies (DMEPOS). Durable medical equipment is equipment and supplies that can withstand repeated use. Prosthetics and orthotics replace all or part of an internal body organ or a part's functionality.

Inpatient Prospective Payment System (IPPS). PPS used for inpatient hospital claims.

inpatient services. Medical services provided to a patient admitted to an acute inpatient hospital.

outpatient hospital services. Medical services provided to a patient in a hospital outpatient department (eg, emergency services, diagnostic services, day surgeries).

Outpatient Prospective Payment System (OPPS). PPS used for outpatient hospital claims.

Medicare Administrative Contractors (MACs). Insurance companies responsible for processing Medicare claims replacing fiscal intermediaries and carriers.

Medicare Physician Fee Schedule (MFS). Medicare's physician fee schedule used to determine payment levels for covered physician professional services.

Medicare secondary payer (MSP). When Medicare is the second payer for claims.

Medicare Severity Diagnosis Related Groups (MS-DRGs). Patients with similar characteristics and costs are assigned to these groups.

Part A Medicare. Medicare Part A is hospital insurance that covers inpatient care in hospitals.

Part B Medicare. Medicare Part B is medical insurance that covers physician/nonphysician providers' services and outpatient care in addition to other medical services that Part A doesn't cover.

Part C Medicare. Medicare Part C is a Medicare advantage insurance where beneficiaries can choose a private payer's managed care type of insurance.

Part D Medicare. Medicare Part D is medical insurance that covers prescription drugs.

prospective payment system (PPS). Medicare payment methodologies based on a prospectively determined allowable amount.

Resource Based Relative Value Scale (RBRVS). Measurement of the relative resource cost of providing individual physician services. Used as a component in the MFS.

skilled nursing facility prospective payment system (SNF PPS). PPS used for skilled nursing facility claims.

REFERENCES

1. Centers for Medicare and Medicaid Services. *Medicare Secondary Payer Manual.* Available at: www.cms.gov/Manuals/IOM/itemdetail.asp?filterType=none&filterByDID=-99&sortByDID=1&sortOrder=ascending&itemID=CMS019017. Accessed January 11, 2011.
2. National Government Services: Indiana Medicare Payer. Medical Policy Center/LCD Search. Available at: http://apps.ngsmedicare.com/applications/MedicalPolicyCenter.aspx?CatID=2. Accessed January 11, 2011.
3. TrailBlazer Health Enterprises, LLC. Available at: www.trailblazerhealth.com/Medicare.aspx. Accessed January 11, 2011.

Chapter 5

Medicare Physician Payment: Medicare Physician Fee Schedule (MFS)

Physician Services Overview

Physicians can provide care in many different settings, for example:

- Physicians' offices;
- Ambulatory surgical centers;
- Hospitals;
- Skilled nursing facilities;
- Other post-acute care settings;
- Hospices;
- Clinical laboratories; and
- Patients' homes.

There are many different types of physician care, which include:

- Office visits;
- Surgical procedures;
- Injections;
- Supplies; and
- Other diagnostic or therapeutic services.

Patient care drives documentation. Documentation drives HCPCS and ICD-9-CM coding. Correct coding is required for payment. Each link or step of the process is important to ensure payment. Figure 5-1 shows the link between patient care, documentation, coding, and payment.

Medicare Physician Payment

Medicare Part B pays for physician services based on the Medicare Physician Fee Schedule (MFS). The MFS determines how much to pay medical professionals for Medicare services. Also, almost every HMO and many other payers follow a similar system for determining payment amounts. The MFS is categorized by HCPCS codes (see Figure 5-2).

FIGURE 5-1 *Link Between Patient Care, Documentation, Coding, and Payment*

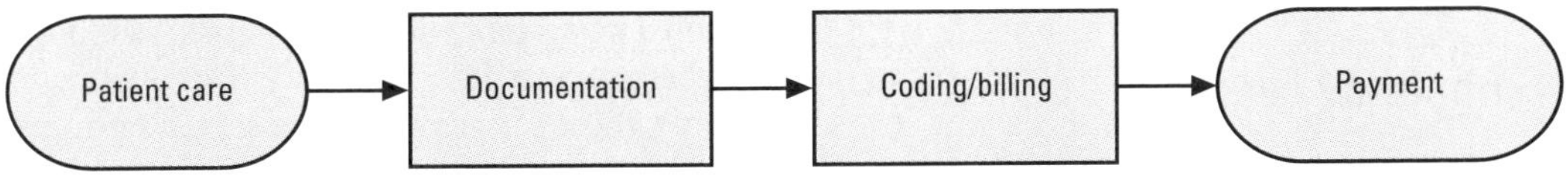

FIGURE 5-2 *Example of HCPCS Procedural Codes in Medicare Physician Fee Schedule (MFS)*

HCPCS	MOD	DESCRIPTION	STATUS CODE	GLOB DAYS	MULT PROC	BILAT SURG	ASST SURG	CO-SURG	TEAM SURG	ENDO BASE	CONV FACTOR
15788		Chemical peel face epiderm	R	090	2	0	1	0	0		33.976
15789		Chemical peel face dermal	R	090	2	0	1	0	0		33.976
15792		Chemical peel nonfacial	R	090	2	0	0	0	0		33.976
15793		Chemical peel nonfacial	A	090	2	0	0	0	0		33.976
15819		Plastic surgery neck	A	090	2	0	0	0	0		33.976

In addition to the MFS, physician services and supplies might be reimbursed through other fee schedules (eg, clinical laboratory fee schedule, Durable Medical Equipment, Prosthetic and Orthotic Supplies [DMEPOS] fee schedule).

Physician Payment Limitations

As the HCPCS code drives the payment level, accuracy in coding is extremely important. If the HCPCS codes are incorrect, the payment is also likely to be wrong. In essence, every individual service is billed by using a HCPCS code and paid separately by Medicare for physician services. HCPCS codes include all services, equipments, and supplies that might be provided during a patient's visit (see Chapter 9 for more comprehensive description of HCPCS), but remember that the mere presence or availability of a code does not automatically guarantee payment.

Coverage

As mentioned before, Medicare may deny payment because the service is not a covered Medicare benefit (eg, acupuncture) or the service is not covered under the circumstances presented on a claim (eg, a fracture repair when there is no diagnosis or ICD-9-CM code for a fracture injury on the claim). In the latter situation, the diagnosis coding can support (or not support) the service provided. Therefore, accuracy of ICD-9-CM is just as important as the HCPCS coding.

Frequency Limits

There are also limitations as to how often services might be covered. This means that Medicare would not pay a professional for an unreasonable number of services (eg, three cataract extractions on one service date when normal anatomy dictates that there are only two eyes, and even then it's unusual to treat more than one cataract at a time).

Discounting of Multiple Procedures

When multiple procedures (surgery and diagnostics) are performed during a single medical encounter, Medicare will discount (pay less for) the secondary procedures. It is believed that there are efficiencies with overlapping portions of procedures, and as a result, those efficiencies will result in cost savings for the provider. As there are costs savings for the professional, Medicare will discount multiple procedures or at least portions of the secondary procedures.

Bundling

Another type of limitation in paying physicians is related to coding guidelines and bundling issues. There are tens of thousands of HCPCS codes, and some have overlapping care; therefore, coding guidelines and bundling restrictions serve to ensure accurate coding to reflect the care provided, and to avoid overstating services provided. For example, Medicare does not pay a professional for an abdominal hysterectomy (removing the uterus through an opening in the abdomen) and a laparotomy (opening the abdomen). Therefore, coding and payment guidelines limit those services from being paid separately when they are billed together. The rationale for not paying these two procedures separately is because the surgeon has to open the abdomen in order to remove the uterus, and therefore, the laparotomy is an integral part of the abdominal hysterectomy. Chapter 9 on HCPCS will cover this in more details.

Global Surgical Package

"A global surgical package for major surgical procedures refers to a payment policy of bundling payment for the various services associated with an operation into a single payment covering the operation and these other services, such as postoperative hospital visits. It is common practice among surgeons to bill for such global surgical packages, which generally include the immediate preoperative care, the operation itself, and the normal, uncomplicated follow-up care."[1]

For certain HCPCS codes, Medicare has built global surgery days into its payment schedule. Clinically, global surgery defines which services are considered to be a part of the overall surgical care for a procedure, ie, what the surgeon believes to be appropriate pre- or postprocedure necessary care.

CMS has established global periods in the form of follow-up days for certain surgical procedure codes. The global periods are published in the Medicare Physician Fee Schedule. The assigned global periods can be 0 days, 10 days, or 90 days. Global period is defined as the number of days during which all necessary services normally furnished by a physician (before, during, and after the procedure) are included in the payment for the procedure performed. Codes that have global days include payment for the surgery itself as well as the patient follow-up care after the surgery to ensure suitable recovery. Therefore, there should be no additional payment made for surgical follow-up care falling within the global period. To make the distinction between global surgery days and global period clearer, consider the following scenarios that illustrate the differences and circumstances to use the appropriate code for reporting and billing.

Understandably, not all surgeries are serious or major surgeries. Some are small procedures that can have zero global surgery days. For example, if a small procedure that has zero global surgery days is performed, the patient is seen by the physician in a follow-up visit. Because the small procedure has zero global surgery days, the follow-up visit can be reported with an Evaluation and Management (E/M) code instead. In another scenario, if a minor but larger procedure is performed, the procedure can be assigned 10 global surgery days. And, within the immediate 10 days following the operation, no E/M codes can be reported because the care provided during the 10 days is valued, ie, already included in the payment for the procedure. Finally, major surgical procedures are assigned 90 global surgery days, and therefore, if a patient is seen over the next 90 days relative to that particular major operation, the physician may **not** report an E/M-related code for that procedure.

To help clarify and distinguish between the two terms, it helps to remember that *global period* refers to the entire surgical timeframe, ie, from the day before surgery to the day of the procedure and to the assigned number of global surgery days for that particular procedure. When we discuss global surgery from a payment perspective, we focus on:

1. What services are included within the surgery's payment?
2. What services may be billed in addition to the surgery's payment?

Medicare has established a national policy on what is and is not included in the surgery's payment, and this should be consulted for accurate billing and proper payment.

Figure 5-3 indicates how surgery care extends beyond what happens during the procedure itself. Services in each phase either

FIGURE 5-3 *Global Period Surgery Care*

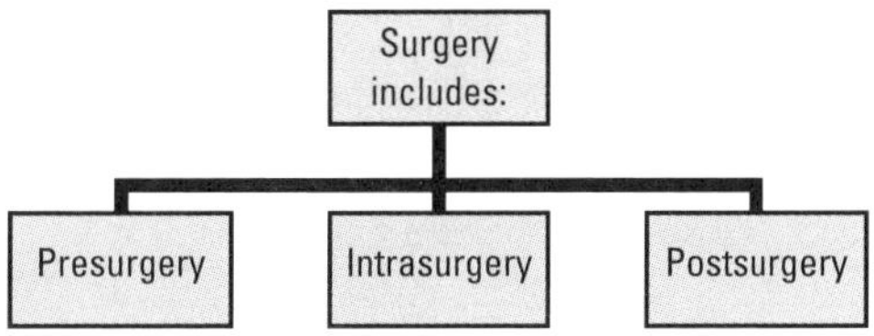

are included in the surgery payment or are paid separately.

A global surgical fee includes all necessary services performed by the physician before, during, and after a surgical procedure. Medicare payment for a given surgical procedure includes applicable preoperative and intraoperative services, complications, and postoperative care.

Therefore, when a practice is paid for the surgery, it is also receiving payment for any preoperative care, the surgery itself, and all appropriate and normal follow-up care. See the section on modifiers in Chapter 9 for more detailed discussion about this.

Medicare Physician Fee Schedule (MFS) Database

All physician practices should access the fee schedules each year to understand how they will be paid by Medicare. Figure 5-4 shows an example of the MFS. Built within the MFS are indicators as to how Medicare will process the service. The following explains some of the different columns within Figure 5-4. Refer to the Medicare Web site for more complete descriptions.

Status Code. The status code indicates how a code is processed if submitted to Medicare. Within the MFS each HCPCS code is assigned a status code, and only relative value units (RVUs) associated with status codes of "A", "R", or "T" are used for Medicare payment. The definitions of status codes "A", "R", and "T" are as follows:

Active (A) = **Active Code.** These codes are paid using the MFS. Note that none of the "A" codes have a national noncoverage policy. However, be aware that there may be local coverage decisions regarding these codes.

Restricted (R) = **Restricted Coverage.** Special coverage instructions apply, and coverage is priced by the individual carrier/MAC.

Injections (T) = **Injections.** There are RVUs and payment amounts for these services, but they are paid only if there are no other payable services on the same service date by the same provider.

FIGURE 5-4 *Snapshot of Medicare Physician Fee Schedule (MFS) Database*[1]

HCPCS	MOD	DESCRIPTION	STATUS CODE	GLOB DAYS	MULT PROC	BILAT SURG	ASST SURG	CO-SURG	TEAM SURG	ENDO BASE	CONV FACTOR
A0021		Outside state ambulance serv	I	XXX	9	9	9	9	9		33.976
A0080		Noninterest escort in non er	I	XXX	9	9	9	9	9		33.976
A0090		Interest escort in non er	I	XXX	9	9	9	9	9		33.976
A0100		Nonemergency transport taxi	I	XXX	9	9	9	9	9		33.976

HCPCS	MOD	DESCRIPTION	STATUS CODE	GLOB DAYS	MULT PROC	BILAT SURG	ASST SURG	CO-SURG	TEAM SURG	ENDO BASE	CONV FACTOR
G8459		Doc pt rec antivir treat	M	XXX	9	9	9	9	9		33.976
G8460		Pt inelig RNA no antvir tx	M	XXX	9	9	9	9	9		33.976

HCPCS	MOD	DESCRIPTION	STATUS CODE	GLOB DAYS	MULT PROC	BILAT SURG	ASST SURG	CO-SURG	TEAM SURG	ENDO BASE	CONV FACTOR
G8459		Doc pt rec antivir treat	M	XXX	9	9	9	9	9		33.976
G8460		Pt inelig RNA no antvir tx	M	XXX	9	9	9	9	9		33.976
0048T		Implant ventricular device	C	XXX	0	0	0	0	0		33.976
0050T		Removal circulation assist	C	XXX	0	0	0	0	0		33.976
00500		Anesth esophageal surgery	J	XXX	9	9	9	9	9		33.976
0051T		Implant total heart system	C	XXX	0	0	0	0	0		33.976

(continued)

FIGURE 5-4 *(continued)*

HCPCS	MOD	DESCRIPTION	STATUS CODE	GLOB DAYS	MULT PROC	BILAT SURG	ASST SURG	CO-SURG	TEAM SURG	ENDO BASE	CONV FACTOR
15788		Chemical peel face epiderm	R	090	2	0	1	0	0		33.976
15789		Chemical peel face dermal	R	090	2	0	1	0	0		33.976
15792		Chemical peel nonfacial	R	090	2	0	0	0	0		33.976
15793		Chemical peel nonfacial	A	090	2	0	0	0	0		33.976
15819		Plastic surgery neck	A	090	2	0	0	0	0		33.976

HCPCS	MOD	DESCRIPTION	STATUS CODE	GLOB DAYS	MULT PROC	BILAT SURG	ASST SURG	CO-SURG	TEAM SURG	ENDO BASE	CONV FACTOR
27604		Drain lower leg bursa	A	090	2	1	0	0	0		33.976
27605		Incision of achilles tendon	A	010	2	1	0	0	0		33.976
27606		Incision of achilles tendon	A	010	2	1	1	1	0		33.976

HCPCS	MOD	DESCRIPTION	STATUS CODE	GLOB DAYS	MULT PROC	BILAT SURG	ASST SURG	CO-SURG	TEAM SURG	ENDO BASE	CONV FACTOR
70330		X-ray exam of jaw joints	A	XXX	0	2	0	0	0		33.976
70330	TC	X-ray exam of jaw joints	A	XXX	0	2	0	0	0		33.976
70330	26	X-ray exam of jaw joints	A	XXX	0	2	0	0	0		33.976
70332		X-ray exam of jaw joint	A	XXX	0	3	0	0	0		33.976
70332	TC	X-ray exam of jaw joint	A	XXX	0	3	0	0	0		33.976
70332	26	X-ray exam of jaw joint	A	XXX	0	3	0	0	0		33.976
70336		Magnetic image jaw joint	A	XXX	4	0	0	0	0		33.976
70336	TC	Magnetic image jaw joint	A	XXX	4	0	0	0	0		33.976

There are also other status codes, for example:

Bundled (B) = **Bundled Code.** Payment is bundled into another service.

Deleted (D) = **Deleted Codes.** These codes are deleted as of January 1.

Exclude Statute (X) = **Statutory Exclusion.** These codes are for services that are not in the statutory definition of "physician services" for fee schedule payment purposes.

Noncovered (N) = **Noncovered code.** Medicare has established a national noncoverage policy.

Global Surgery. As mentioned, there are global surgery days affiliated with certain surgical procedures. The MFS provides the number of postoperative days for each surgical procedure where applicable. When payment is made for a surgery that includes the postoperative care, the postoperative care should not be charged separately.

The following are the MFS indications for the application of global surgery days. The numbers (eg, 000) indicate how many postoperative care days are included in the surgery's payment.

000 = Procedures where related pre- or postoperative care is included in the procedure payment only when provided on the same calendar date.

010 = Procedures where related preoperative care is included in the payment of the procedure when provided on the same date and postoperative care during a 10-day postoperative period is included in the procedure's payment.

090 = Major surgeries with a one-day preoperative period and 90-day postoperative period included in the fee schedule payment amount of the surgery.

MMM = Maternity codes where the usual global period does not apply.

XXX = Global concept does not apply for this type of service.

YYY = The local Medicare payer determines the global concept for the procedure.

ZZZ = Code for procedure is always related to another procedure and follows the global period of the other service.

Some additional columns in the MFS are for when multiple or bilateral procedures are billed together.

Multiple Procedure. This column indicates if adjustments will be made to payment when multiple procedures are billed.

0 = No adjustment will be made when more than one procedure are billed on the same patient's single-date claim.

2 = There will be a 50% reduction in secondary (or lesser) procedures when multiple procedures are performed on the same date. In order to have the 50% reduction, both procedures would need this indicator in the MFS.

3 = There are special rules for multiple endoscopic procedures billed together.

4 = When a technical component (TC) is billed for diagnostic imaging and the MFS has indicator 4, there will be a 25% reduction of the TC's payment.

5 = For certain therapy services with an indicator of 5, a 20% reduction of the practice expense is applied.

9 = A 9 indicator simply means the concept doesn't apply.

Bilateral Surgery. The following are MFS indicators when billing bilateral surgery codes.

0 = No adjustment made for bilateral procedures

1 = 150% adjustment made for bilateral procedures (100% for one side and 50% for the second side)

2 = No adjustment made for bilateral procedures because the HCPCS code is inherently bilateral

3 = No adjustment made for bilateral procedures but both services will be allowed at 100% (no 50% discounting)

9 = Concept does not apply

Medicare Physician Fee Schedule (MFS) Payment Calculation

Figure 5-5 illustrates the MFS payment processes. The MFS consists of three elements:

- Relative Value Unit (RVU)
- Geographic Practice Cost Indices (GPCIs)
- Conversion Factor (CF)

Relative Value Unit. The RVU essentially rates the HCPCS code relative to all other HCPCS codes allowed by Medicare. An injection HCPCS code would have a substantially lower RVU than an open heart surgery HCPCS code.

The total RVU is composed of three elements based on: (1) the physician's effort based on work, time, and intensity to provide the service, (2) a practice expense that is the cost of the physician's direct costs (clinical staff, supplies, and equipments) and overhead (rent, administrative staff) used to provide the service, and (3) a malpractice component to acknowledge the cost of malpractice insurance needed in order to perform the service.

Geographic Practice Cost Indices. GPCIs adjust the nationally derived RVUs to account for geographic variations in costs. Given that the cost to provide care in New York City is higher than the cost in Tupelo, Mississippi, the GPCIs adjust the RVUs for the area where services are provided. The RVU components (work, practice expense [PE], and malpractice [MP]) are multiplied by the corresponding GPCI (work, practice expense, and malpractice) to determine the physician's RVU for each code.

Conversion Factor. The CF is a national rate determined by Medicare at the beginning of each calendar year. The total adjusted RVUs are multiplied by the dollar CF to determine the national allowance for any HCPCS code. The CF is updated on an annual basis.

See the MFS calculation example below. HCPCS codes 99212, 99213, and 99214 represent examples of established patient visits (low, medium, and high respectively).

HCPCS 99212

	Nonfacility	Facility
Work	0.48	0.48
Practice Expense	0.70	0.22
Malpractice	<u>0.04</u>	<u>0.04</u>
Total	1.22 (or $41.45)	0.74 (or $25.14)

FIGURE 5-5 *Medicare Physician Fee Schedule (MFS) Process for Payment*

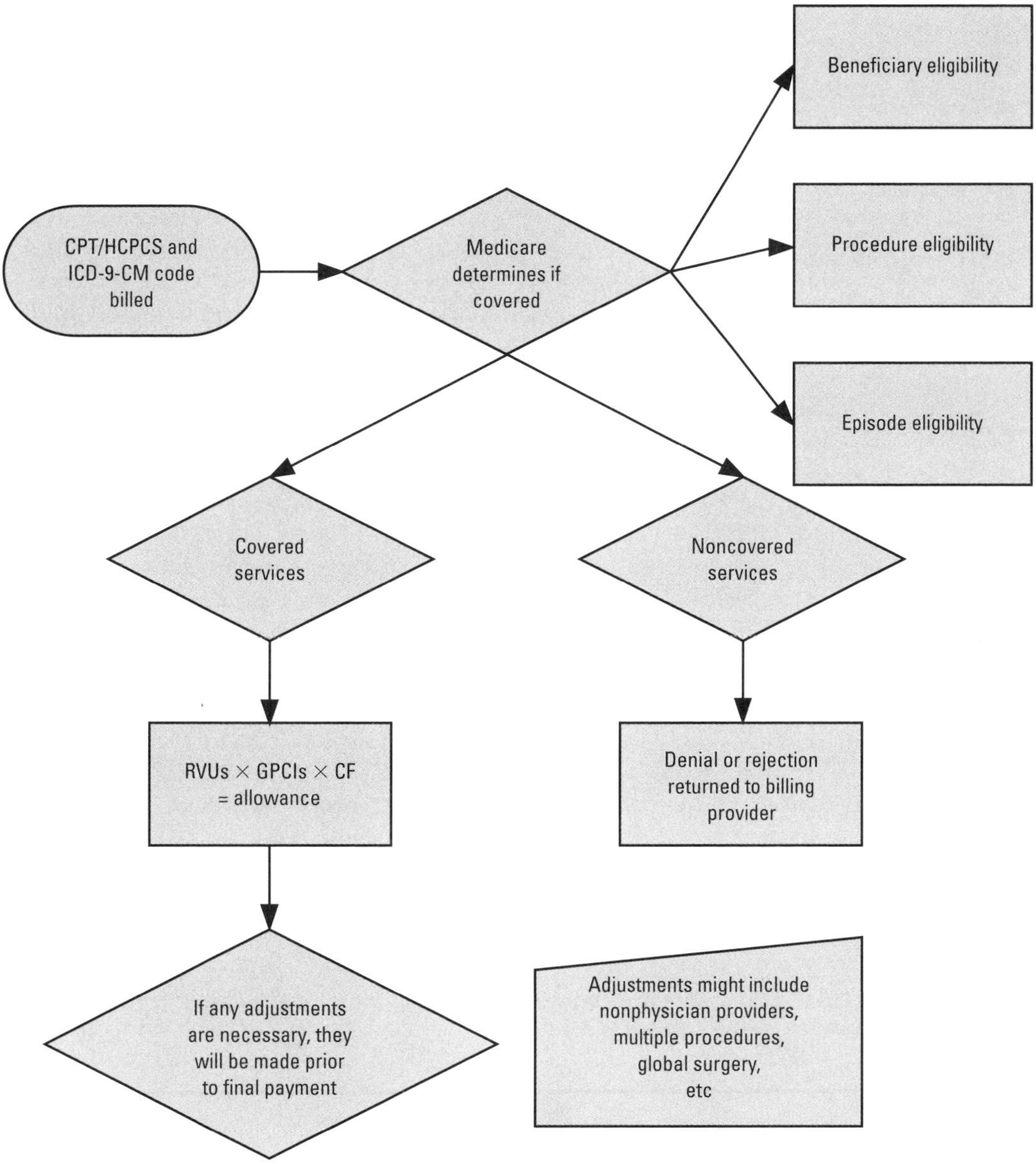

HCPCS 99213

	Nonfacility	Facility
Work	0.97	0.97
Practice Expense	0.99	0.41
Malpractice	0.07	0.07
Total	2.03 (or $68.97)	1.45 (or $49.27)

HCPCS 99214

	Nonfacility	Facility
Work	1.50	1.50
Practice Expense	1.41	0.63
Malpractice	0.10	0.10
Total	3.01 (or $102.27)	2.23 (or $75.77)

Note

Different levels of service (eg, CPT codes 99212, 99213, 99214) have different payment levels, ie, more complex services have higher payments.

MFS Payment Rate Formula

[(Work RVU × Work GPCI) + (PE RVU × PE GPCI) + (MP RVU × MP GPCI)] × CF

See Figure 5-6 for a visual illustration of this calculation example.

One other aspect of the RVUs is that there are facility and nonfacility RVUs. The difference between these is based on the site of service (where the service was provided) because a physician's costs vary relative to where the care is provided. If the service was performed in the physician's independent office, the nonfacility RVU would be used because the professional bears the entire cost of the overhead (staff, equipment, etc). If the service was performed in a facility-owned setting (eg, hospital, ASC), the physician would receive a reduced practice expense RVU (see the Facility columns above) because the physician did not have the costs for the overhead. In this case, the facility where the service was performed bears that cost and will bill separately for that part of the care.

Alternate Method to Show MFS Calculation

If physicians billed for CPT code 99213 in their office, then the RVUs for that service are 0.97 (work), 0.99 (practice expense), and 0.07 (malpractice). These RVUs are multiplied by the GPCIs for the physician's geographic location. For example purposes, we will use a work GPCI of 1.00, a practice expense GPCI of 0.928, a malpractice GPCI of 0.484, and a CF of $33.9764.

<u>[(Work RVU × Work GPCI) + (Practice Expense RVU × Practice Expense GPCI) + (Malpractice RVU × Malpractice GPCI)] × CF</u> = <u>(Allowance RVU × Allowance GPCI)</u>

[(0.97 × 1.00) + (0.99 × 0.928) + (0.07 × 0.484)] → [(0.9700) + (0.9187) + (0.0339)] × $33.9764 = $65.32

Or, to break down the calculation formula item by item, this is what it looks like:

0.97 (Work RVU)	× 1.00 (Work GPCI)	=	0.9700 (Adjusted Work RVU)
0.99 (Prac Exp RVU)	× 0.928 (Prac Exp GPCI)	=	0.9187 (Adjusted Prac Exp RVU)
0.07 (Malprac RVU)	× 0.484 (Malprac GPCI)	=	<u>0.0339</u> (Adjusted Malprac RVU)
	Total adjusted RVU	=	1.9226

The total adjusted RVU is then multiplied by the national conversion factor ($33.9764 in this example) to give the total allowance for the HCPCS code.

1.9226 (Adjusted RVU)	× $33.9764 (CF)	=	$65.32 (Allowance for CPT 99213)

FIGURE 5-6 *Sample Medicare Physician Fee Schedule (MFS) Calculation*

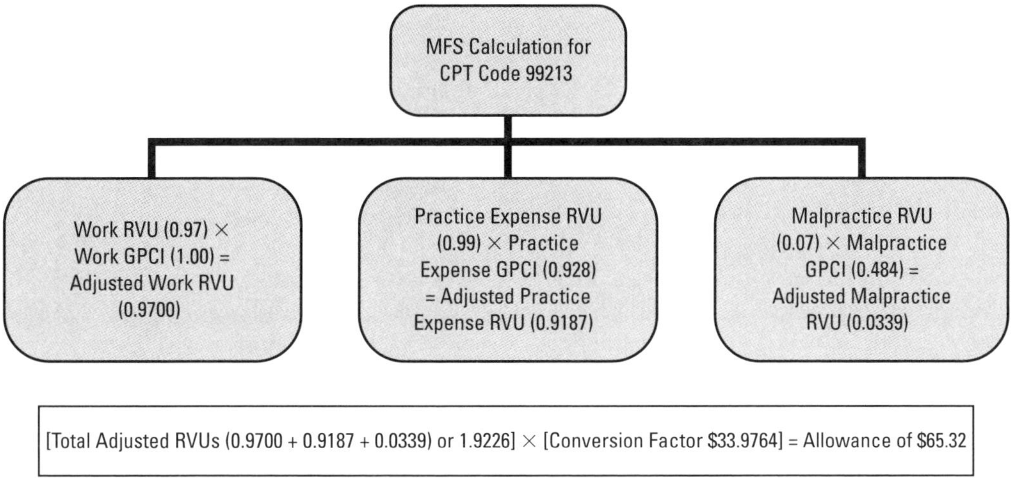

Example

A physician performs a colonoscopy (CPT 45378) in an outpatient hospital setting. When billing Medicare, the physician will bill for the work in performing the colonoscopy and the hospital will bill for the use of the facility, staff, equipment, etc. If the practice expense RVU for the colonoscopy is 7.37 when performed in the physician's office and 2.22 when performed in a facility, then there is a difference of 5.15 in RVUs between the two sites of service (office versus hospital). The hospital will also submit a bill for payment, and the reduction in the physician's payment helps cover the additional costs from a second bill for the hospital while also recognizing the reduced cost for the physician. The work and malpractice RVUs are the same regardless of service site. See Figure 5-5.

Medicare Physician Payment for Nonphysician Professionals (NPPs)

The MFS is focused on payment information for physicians; however, nonphysician practitioners (NPPs) can also be paid by Medicare. NPPs are those midlevel professionals whose services are covered under Medicare payment policies with some limitations in coverage and payment. NPPs also have special regulations that must be followed. The most common NPPs to bill Medicare are advanced practice nurses (APNs) and physician assistants (PAs). APNs include certified registered nurse anesthetists (CRNAs), anesthesiologist assistants (AAs), nurse practitioners (NPs), certified nurse midwives (CNMs), and clinical nurse specialists (CNSs).

For NPPs to be paid by Medicare, they must meet the required qualifications (licensure, certification, and education) and coverage criteria for the services.

Note

Many non-Medicare payers are less restrictive than Medicare when covering NPP services. Check with your local payers to see their requirements for billing these providers.

Each NPP has licensure-specific qualifications and coverage restrictions for services. As an example, the following will highlight those for physician assistants (PAs), but NPs, CNMs, etc, will have their own qualifications, coverage, and payment regulations. If billing for an NPP, research the coverage for the specific licensure.

To bill Medicare, PAs must meet these qualifications:

- They must be licensed by the state to practice as a PA, and either:
  - have graduated from a PA educational program accredited by the Accreditation Review Commission on Education for the Physician Assistant (or its predecessor agencies, the Commission on Accreditation of Allied Health Education Programs and the Committee on Allied Health Education and Accreditation); or
  - have passed the national certification examination administered by the National Commission on Certification of Physician Assistants.

For Medicare payment, PAs must meet the following coverage standards:

- Services or supplies must be medically reasonable and necessary (same as with any service to be covered by Medicare);
- Services are the type considered physician's services if furnished by an MD or a DO;
- Services are performed by an individual who meets all PA qualifications;
- Services are performed under the general supervision of an MD or a DO;
- Services are not otherwise precluded from coverage because of statutory exclusion;
- The PA is legally authorized to furnish the services in the state in which they are performed;
- The physician supervisor or designee need not be physically present when a service is being furnished unless state law or regulations require otherwise; and
- "Incident to" services and supplies may be covered.

"Incident to" services:

- Are paid as if the physician provided the care (no reduction in allowance);
- Must be an integral part of the patient's normal course of treatment during which the physician has personally performed an initial service and remains actively involved in the course of treatment;
- Are commonly furnished without charge (included in the physician's bill);
- Are an expense to the physician;
- Are commonly furnished in the physician's office or clinic; and
- The physician provides direct supervision, which means that he or she is present in the office suite and immediately available if needed.

When billing the Medicare program for PA services, the PA's employer must bill under the PA's NPI, or the employer may bill under the physician's NPI only if the physician in the group practice/employer has performed a visit that assesses the patient and establishes a plan of care (see "incident to" above).

PA services are only paid as assigned (they must accept assignment) and are allowed at 85% of the physician's allowance unless paid as "incident to." Consequently, a PA's payment is lower than that for the physician. Because the MFS is based on physician payment, an additional calculation is made when the service is billed by a PA to reduce the allowance to 85% of that for a physician. If the services are paid as "incident to," there is no reduction in the allowance from the physician's fee schedule, and the payment is made as if billed by the physician.

FIGURE 5-7 *Nonphysician Practitioner (NPP) Billing Options for Medicare*

"Incident to" Services

- Must be an integral, although incidental part of the physician's personal professional service
- NP or PA may be an employee, independent contractor, or a contractor under an indirect contractual arrangement
- Physician must first see patient and develop the plan of care the NP or PA will carry out
- Physician must remain active in patient's ongoing treatment
- Direct physician supervision is required (physician is on site)
- Bill service under physician's name and number with reimbursement 100% of MFS amount

or

- Bill service under NP's or PA's name and number with reimbursement 85% of MFS amount

"Incident to" not applicable to:

- consultation services
- new patient office services (physician has not seen patient and established plan of care)
- established patient office services with a new problem (physician has not seen patient for presenting condition and established plan of care)

Split/Shared Services

Applies only to selected E/M visits and locations

- Not applicable to new patient visits, consultations, procedures and critical care services
- Not applicable to services in the skilled nursing facility or nursing facility setting
- Both a physician and NP or PA provide services in the office setting for the same encounter
- "Incident to" criteria must be met
- Bill service under physician's name and number with reimbursement 100% of MFS amount

or

- Bill service under NP's or PA's name and number with reimbursement 85% of MFS amount
- Both a physician and NP or PA provide services in the hospital inpatient, hospital outpatient, observation, or emergency department on the same day
- "Incident to" not applicable in an institutional setting
- Bill service under physician's name and number with reimbursement 100% of MFS amount

Direct Billing

Service performed by NP or PA

- Consultation services
- New patient services
- Established patient services
- Hospital outpatient services
- Hospital inpatient services
- Emergency department services
- Other services

Bill service under NP's or PA's name and number

Medicare reimbursement 85% of MFS amount

Figure 5-7 illustrates the billing options for NPPs.

Medicare Physician Fee Schedule (MFS) Resources

There are many resources for looking up individual codes on the MFS, various payment policy indicators, RVUs, and GPCIs. CMS has a Physician Fee Schedule look-up tool.[2]

Definitions and Acronyms

Medicare physician fee schedule (MFS). Medicare's physician fee schedule used to determine payment levels for covered physician professional services.

nonphysician professionals (NPPs). Midlevel professionals whose services are covered under Medicare payment policies with certain limitations.

Part B Medicare. Medicare Part B is medical insurance that covers physician/nonphysician providers' services and outpatient care in addition to other medical services that Part A doesn't cover.

Resource Based Relative Value Scale (RBRVS). Measurement of the relative resource cost of providing individual physician services. Used as a component of the MFS.

REFERENCES

1. Centers for Medicare and Medicaid Services. Medicare Fee Schedule Database. www.cms.gov/PhysicianFeeSched/. Accessed January 10, 2011.
2. Centers for Medicare and Medicaid Services. Medicare Physician Fee Schedule look-up. www.cms.gov/apps/physician-fee-schedule/overview.aspx. Accessed January 10, 2011.

Chapter 6

Medicare Hospital Payment: Outpatient Prospective Payment System (OPPS) and Inpatient Prospective Payment System (IPPS)

Hospital Services Overview

Hospital facility services include services provided by the hospital using the hospital's resources to inpatients, outpatients, and nonpatients of the hospital. **Inpatient** refers to patients admitted to the hospital on the order of a licensed practitioner permitted by the state to admit patients to a hospital. A patient who has not been admitted as an inpatient but who is registered on the hospital records as an outpatient and receives services directly from the hospital is considered an **outpatient**. *This includes those patients from whom a specimen was taken and sent to the hospital.* **Nonpatient** refers to people who are neither inpatients nor outpatients (eg, visitors, hospital employees, clergy). Although physicians, anesthesiologists, radiologists, etc, see and treat patients in hospital settings, the professional services of these clinicians (and others) are not included in the hospital's payment system. Those services are billed as professional services separately. See Chapters 5 and 7 for additional information on these payment systems.

Hospital Payment Systems Overview

Medicare has different payment systems for hospitals depending on whether the services were provided as inpatient or outpatient; however, both are paid using prospective payment systems (PPSs). See Chapter 4 for further explanation of PPS payments.

The Inpatient Prospective Payment System (IPPS) is also known as Diagnosis Related Groups (DRGs) or Medicare Severity

Diagnosis Related Groups (MS-DRGs). The Outpatient Prospective Payment System (OPPS) is known as Ambulatory Payment Classifications (APCs). Both will be discussed in depth in this chapter.

Remember that other payers may choose to adopt similar payment systems and many do, but they are not obligated to do so. Every facility should know what mechanism each payer uses to process claims.

As a reminder from Chapter 4, prospective payment systems are payment instruments where payment is predetermined based on a classification system of services rendered, patients' diagnoses, or a combination of both. Prior to the use of a PPS, most Medicare payments were made on charges or costs that a provider incurred. A PPS is used to incentivize health care providers to efficiently manage costs. The better providers manage the resources used to provide care, the better they will fare financially.

One concern with a PPS-type payment is the thought that providers might make decisions that negatively impact quality of care in order to lower their costs; however, Medicare has built in review methods that will reduce payment or somehow penalize providers if poor quality is discovered.

Outpatient Prospective Payment System (OPPS)

CMS implemented the OPPS in August 2000 to pay for:

- hospital outpatient services,
- certain Part B services furnished to hospital inpatients who have no Part A coverage, and
- partial hospitalization services furnished by community mental health centers.

The OPPS applies to designated hospital outpatient services furnished in all hospitals, except:

- hospitals that only provide Part B services to inpatients;
- Critical Access Hospitals (CAHs);
- Indian Health Service (IHS) and tribal hospitals, including IHS tribal CAHs;
- Hospitals located in American Samoa, Guam, Commonwealth of the Northern Mariana Islands, and the Virgin Islands; and
- Hospitals in Maryland (that are paid under that state's waiver provisions).

Ambulatory Payment Classification

All services paid under the OPPS are classified into groups called Ambulatory Payment Classifications (APCs). *OPPS* and *APCs* are terms that are often used interchangeably. APC groupings are determined by HCPCS code. See Figure 6-1 for an example of an APC grouping. CMS developed this grouping classification system as set forth in §419.31 of the regulations. CMS uses Level I and Level II HCPCS codes and descriptors to identify and group the services within each APC. The APCs are organized such that each group is homogeneous both clinically and in terms of resource use. Using this classification system, CMS has established distinct groups of surgical services, diagnostic services, partial hospitalization services, and medical visits. CMS has also developed separate APC groups for certain medical devices, drugs, biologicals, radiopharmaceuticals, and brachytherapy devices. CMS has packaged into each procedure or service within an APC group the cost associated with those items or services that are directly related and integral to performing a procedure or furnishing a service.

Each CPT or HCPCS code that is assigned to an APC has the same status indicator as the APC to which it is assigned. The software that controls Medicare payment looks to the status indicators attached to the HCPCS codes and APCs for direction in the processing of the claim; therefore, the assignment of the status indicators has significance for the payment of services.

Codes that are similar in type of service and resources consumed group to the same APC.

For example, APC 260 is for all level I plain film X rays except teeth. So every HCPCS

FIGURE 6-1 *Ambulatory Payment Classifications (APC) Driven by CPT® Codes*

HCPCS Code	Short Descriptor	APC
72010	X-ray exam of spine	0261
72020	X-ray exam of spine	0260
72040	X-ray exam of neck spine	0260
72050	X-ray exam of neck spine	0261
72052	X-ray exam of neck spine	0261
72069	X-ray exam of trunk spine	0260
72070	X-ray exam of thoracic spine	0260
72072	X-ray exam of thoracic spine	0260
72074	X-ray exam of thoracic spine	0260
72080	X-ray exam of trunk spine	0260
72090	X-ray exam of trunk spine	0261
72100	X-ray exam of lower spine	0260
72110	X-ray exam of lower spine	0261
72114	X-ray exam of lower spine	0261
72120	X-ray exam of lower spine	0261
72125	Ct neck spine w/o dye	0332

HCPCS codes determine APC category.

HCPCS codes that are similar in type and resource consumption group to the same APC.

code that means a level I plain film (excluding teeth) would be linked to this APC grouping because they all are the same type of X ray and require comparable resources to perform. See Table 6-1 for examples of this process.

CMS uses the following criteria when reviewing procedures to determine whether they should be moved from the inpatient list and assigned to an APC group for payment under the OPPS:

- Most outpatient departments are equipped to provide the services to the Medicare population.
- The simplest procedure described by the code may be performed in most outpatient departments.
- The procedure is related to codes moved off the inpatient list.

Since 2003, CMS has reviewed procedures to determine whether they should be removed from the inpatient list and assigned to an APC group for payment under the OPPS:

- The procedure is being performed in numerous hospitals on an outpatient basis.
- The procedure can be appropriately and safely performed in an ambulatory surgical center (ASC) and is on the list of approved ASC procedures or proposed by CMS for addition to the ASC list.

TABLE 6-1 *Example of Similar Services Grouped by APC*

APC 260: Level I Plain Film Except Teeth	APC 261: Level II Plain Film Except Teeth Including Bone Density Measurement
Examples of codes in this APC group:	Examples of codes in this APC group:
70030 – eye xray for foreign body	70134 – xray internal auditory meati
70100 – mandible xray (4 views)	70260 – complete skull xray
70110 – mandible xray (4 views or more)	71111 – xray of ribs and PA chest
70120 – mastoids xray	73520 – bilateral hip xray
70350 – orthodontic cephalogram	74022 – complete abdomen series xray
70355 – orthopantogram	74710 – pelvimetry

Outpatient Payment Limitations

As the HCPCS code drives the payment level, accuracy in coding is extremely important. If the HCPCS codes are incorrect, the payment is also likely to be wrong. Basically, every individual service is billed by HCPCS code and separately paid by Medicare for outpatient services. HCPCS codes include all services, equipment, and supplies that might be provided during a patient's outpatient hospital encounter (see Chapter 9 for a more comprehensive description of HCPCS). However, having a code does not guarantee payment.

Coverage

As mentioned before, Medicare may deny payment because the service is not a covered Medicare benefit (eg, acupuncture) or the service is not covered under the circumstances presented on a claim (eg, a fracture repair when there is no diagnosis, or ICD-9-CM code, for a fracture injury on the claim). In the latter situation, the diagnosis coding can support (or not support) the service provided; therefore, accuracy of ICD-9-CM coding is just as important as accuracy of HCPCS coding.

Frequency limits

There are also limitations regarding how often services might be covered. This means that Medicare would not pay a provider for an unreasonable number of services (eg, three cataract extractions on one service date when normal anatomy dictates that there are only two eyes, and even then it's unusual to treat more than one cataract at a time).

Discounting of Multiple Procedures

There are discounted payments that occur in the following circumstances:

1. When multiple significant procedure APCs are furnished during the same session, the highest payment is allowed at 100% and the lesser procedures are allowed at 50% of their value. There are efficiencies with overlapping portions of procedures, resulting in cost savings for the payer. Therefore, Medicare discounts multiple procedures, or at least portions of secondary procedures.
2. For certain imaging services, Medicare will pay for only one imaging service when two or more are performed in the same family of codes. For example, if a computed tomography of the chest was performed during the same session as a computed tomography of the abdomen, only one APC would be paid.
3. Surgical procedures that are terminated after a patient is prepared for surgery but before anesthesia is given are paid at 50% of the APC payment. Medicare discounts these because there was no anesthesia provided and the surgery was not started, as well as because of the likelihood that the patient will have to present for the procedure to be completed successfully. HCPCS modifiers that apply in these circumstances will be discussed in Chapter 9.

Packaging

CMS has packaged into each procedure or service within an APC group the cost associated with those items or services that are directly related and integral to performing a procedure or furnishing a service. CMS does not make separate payment for packaged items or services. For example, packaged items and services for a surgical procedure include use of an operating, treatment, or procedure room; use of a recovery room; use of an observation bed; anesthesia; medical or surgical supplies; certain pharmaceuticals (other than those for which separate payment may be allowed under the provisions discussed in the final rule preamble); and incidental services such as venipuncture.

The unit of payment under APCs is the individual service. For example, if a patient had two level I plain films performed during the same encounter both of which group to APC 260, two APC 260s would be allowed. Payments for packaged services under the OPPS are bundled into the payments providers receive for separately payable services provided on the same day. Hospitals include charges for packaged services on their claims, and the costs associated with these packaged services are then bundled into the costs for separately payable procedures on the claims for purposes of median cost calculations.

Some examples of usually packaged services are:

- Routine supplies;
- Anesthesia;
- Operating and recovery room use;
- Implantable medical devices such as pacemakers;
- Inexpensive drugs;
- Imaging supervision and interpretation services; and
- Observation services.

These will not be reimbursed separately from the primary service being paid.

New Technology

Sometimes new services are discovered and are used in health care. These are assigned to new technology APCs, which are based on similarity of resource use only, until clinical and cost data are available to permit assignment to a clinical APC. In the April 7, 2000, final rule (68 FR 18477), CMS created a set of new technology APCs to pay for certain new technology services under OPPS. CMS proposed to limit eligibility for placement in new technology APCs only to comprehensive services or procedures. New technology APCs are reported using certain CPT Category I and Category III codes or HCPCS Level II codes and represent technology services not addressed by the transitional pass-through provisions (see page 85).

Twice each year, the AMA issues CPT Category III codes, which the AMA defines as temporary codes for emerging technology, services, and procedures. In addition, AMA issues midyear CPT Category I codes for vaccines for which FDA approval is imminent, to ensure timely availability of a code. CMS modified its process for implementing the Category III codes that the AMA releases each January for implementation in July to ensure timely collection of data pertinent to services described by the codes; to ensure patient access to the services the codes describe; and to eliminate potential redundancy between CPT Category III codes and some of the "C" codes (see page 85), which are payable under the OPPS and created by CMS in response to applications for new technology services.

Some of the new CPT Category III codes describe services that CMS determines to be similar in clinical characteristics and resource use to HCPCS codes in an existing APC. In these instances, CMS may assign the CPT Category III code to the appropriate clinical APC. Other CPT Category III codes describe services that CMS has determined are not compatible with an existing clinical APC, yet are appropriately provided in the hospital outpatient setting. In these cases, CMS may assign the CPT Category III code to what it estimates is an appropriately priced new technology APC. In other cases, CMS may assign a CPT Category III code one of several nonseparately payable status indicators.

APC Database

Figure 6-2 illustrates an expanded view of the APC database (expanded from Figure 6-1). As previously discussed, the first column represents the HCPCS code and is followed by a short descriptor of what that code represents. The third column is a status indicator (SI). The SI designates how a particular code is processed when billed on an outpatient hospital claim to Medicare. Packaged services are identified by the status indicator "N."

FIGURE 6-2 *APC Classification Database Example*

	Addendum B.-OPPS Payment by							
HCPCS Code	Short Descriptor	SI	APC	Relative Weight	Payment Rate	National Unadjusted Copayment	Minimum Unadjusted Copayment	* Indicates a Change
10021	Fna w/o image	T	0002	1.5703	$108.16	.	$21.64	
10022	Fna w/image	T	0004	4.5843	$315.75	.	$63.15	
10040	Acne surgery	T	0013	0.9103	$62.70	.	$12.54	
10060	Drainage of skin abscess	T	0006	1.4906	$102.67	.	$20.54	
10061	Drainage of skin abscess	T	0006	1.4906	$102.67	.	$20.54	
10080	Drainage of pilonidal cyst	T	0006	1.4906	$102.67	.	$20.54	
10081	Drainage of pilonidal cyst	T	0007	13.0129	$896.28	.	$179.26	
10120	Remove foreign body	T	0016	2.7318	$188.16	.	$37.64	
10121	Remove foreign body	T	0021	18.0784	$1,245.17	.	$249.04	
10140	Drainage of hematoma/fluid	T	0007	13.0129	$896.28	.	$179.26	
10160	Puncture drainage of lesion	T	0006	1.4906	$102.67	.	$20.54	
10180	Complex drainage wound	T	0008	20.1996	$1,391.27	.	$278.26	
11000	Debride infected skin	T	0016	2.7318	$188.16	.	$37.64	
11001	Debride infected skin add-on	T	0013	0.9103	$62.70	.	$12.54	
11004	Debride genitalia & perineum	C						
11005	Debride abdom wall	C						
11006	Debride genit/per/abdom wall	C						
11008	Remove mesh from abd wall	C						
11010	Debride skin at fx site	T	0019	5.0887	$350.49	.	$70.10	
11011	Debride skin musc at fx site	T	0019	5.0887	$350.49	.	$70.10	
11012	Deb skin bone at fx site	T	0019	5.0887	$350.49	.	$70.10	
11042	Deb subq tissue 20 sq cm/<	T	0016	2.7318	$188.16	.	$37.64	
11043	Deb musc/fascia 20 sq cm/<	T	0016	2.7318	$188.16	.	$37.64	
11044	Deb bone 20 sq cm/<	T	0020	8.4929	$584.96	.	$117.00	
11045	Deb subq tissue add-on	T	0016	2.7318	$188.16	.	$37.64	
11046	Deb musc/fascia add-on	T	0016	2.7318	$188.16	.	$37.64	
11047	Deb bone add-on	T	0020	8.4929	$584.96	.	$117.00	
11055	Trim skin lesion	T	0013	0.9103	$62.70	.	$12.54	
11056	Trim skin lesions 2 to 4	T	0013	0.9103	$62.70	.	$12.54	
11057	Trim skin lesions over 4	T	0013	0.9103	$62.70	.	$12.54	
11100	Biopsy skin lesion	T	0015	1.4975	$103.14	.	$20.63	
11101	Biopsy skin add-on	T	0013	0.9103	$62.70	.	$12.54	
11200	Removal of skin tags	T	0013	0.9103	$62.70	.	$12.54	
11201	Remove skin tags add-on	T	0013	0.9103	$62.70	.	$12.54	
11300	Shave skin lesion	T	0013	0.9103	$62.70	.	$12.54	
11301	Shave skin lesion	T	0013	0.9103	$62.70	.	$12.54	
11302	Shave skin lesion	T	0013	0.9103	$62.70	.	$12.54	
11303	Shave skin lesion	T	0015	1.4975	$103.14	.	$20.63	
11305	Shave skin lesion	T	0013	0.9103	$62.70	.	$12.54	
11306	Shave skin lesion	T	0013	0.9103	$62.70	.	$12.54	
11307	Shave skin lesion	T	0013	0.9103	$62.70	.	$12.54	
11308	Shave skin lesion	T	0013	0.9103	$62.70	.	$12.54	
11310	Shave skin lesion	T	0013	0.9103	$62.70	.	$12.54	
11311	Shave skin lesion	T	0013	0.9103	$62.70	.	$12.54	
11312	Shave skin lesion	T	0013	0.9103	$62.70	.	$12.54	

Table 6-2 is a complete listing of the status indicators and their meanings. An OPPS payment status indicator is assigned to every HCPCS code and defines how a service is processed.

The column after the status indicator is the APC to which the HCPCS is grouped. There will not be an APC if the HCPCS is not paid under an APC system. This could be because the service is excluded from payment altogether or because the service is paid under a different mechanism (fee schedules, for example). The next columns show the RVU and national payment amounts. We have omitted some of the columns to simplify the explanation.

APC Payment Rates

The components of APC payment are:

- Relative Weight (RW) for the APC
- National Conversion Factor (CF)
- National Payment Rate
- Geographic Wage Index (WI)

The Relative Weight (RW) prospectively establishes weights for each APC group relative to all other APCs allowed by Medicare. A less resource consuming APC would have a lower RW than a high resource consuming APC. For example, a chest X-ray APC will have a lower RW than a cholecystectomy APC. (*Continued on page 83*)

TABLE 6-2 *Status Indicators and Their Meanings*

Indicator	Item/Code/Service	OPPS Payment Status
A	Services furnished to a hospital outpatient that are paid under a fee schedule or payment system other than OPPS, for example: • Ambulance services • Clinical diagnostic laboratory services • Nonimplantable prosthetic and orthotic devices • Epoetin alfa (EPO) for end-stage renal disease (ESRD) patients • Physical, occupational, and speech therapy • Routine dialysis services for ESRD patients provided in a certified dialysis unit of a hospital • Diagnostic mammography • Screening mammography	Not paid under OPPS. Paid by fiscal intermediaries under a fee schedule or payment system other than OPPS.
B	Codes that are not recognized by OPPS when submitted on an outpatient hospital Part B bill type (12x and 13x)	Not paid under OPPS. • May be paid by intermediaries when submitted on a different bill type, for example, 75x (comprehensive outpatient rehabilitation facility [CORF]), but not paid under OPPS. • An alternate code that is recognized by OPPS when submitted on an outpatient hospital Part B bill type (12x and 13x) may be available.
C	Inpatient procedures	Not paid under OPPS. Admit patient. Bill as inpatient.
D	Discontinued codes	Not paid under OPPS or any other Medicare payment system.
E	Items, codes, and services: • That are not covered by Medicare based on statutory exclusion. • That are not covered by Medicare for reasons other than statutory exclusion. • That are not recognized by Medicare but for which an alternate code for the same item or service may be available. • For which separate payment is not provided by Medicare.	Not paid under OPPS or any other Medicare payment system.

(continued)

TABLE 6-2 *(continued)*

Indicator	Item/Code/Service	OPPS Payment Status
F	Corneal tissue acquisition; certain certified registered nurse anesthetist (CRNA) services and hepatitis B vaccines	Not paid under OPPS. Paid at reasonable cost.
G	Pass-through drugs and biologicals	Paid under OPPS; separate APC payment includes pass-through* amount.
H	(1) Pass-through device categories (2) Radiopharmaceutical agents	(1) Separate cost-based pass-through payment; not subject to coinsurance. (2) Separate cost-based non-pass-through payment.
K	(1) Non-pass-through drugs, Biologicals, and	(1) Paid under OPPS; separate APC payment.
	(2) Brachytherapy sources	(2) Paid under OPPS; separate APC payment.
	(3) Blood and blood products	(3) Paid under OPPS; separate APC payment.
L	Influenza vaccine; pneumococcal pneumonia vaccine	Not paid under OPPS. Paid at reasonable cost; not subject to deductible or coinsurance.
M	Items and services not billable to the fiscal intermediary	Not paid under OPPS.
N	Items and services packaged into APC rates	Paid under OPPS; Payment is packaged into payment for other services, including outliers. Therefore, there is no separate APC payment.
P	Partial hospitalization	Paid under OPPS; Per diem APC payment.
Q	Packaged services subject to separate payment under OPPS payment criteria.	Paid under OPPS; Addendum B** displays APC assignments when services are separately payable. (1) Separate APC payment based on OPPS payment criteria. (2) If criteria are not met, payment is packaged into payment for other services, including outliers. Therefore, there is no separate APC payment.
S	Significant procedure, not discounted when multiple	Paid under OPPS; separate APC payment.
T	Significant procedure, multiple reduction applies	Paid under OPPS; separate APC payment.
V	Clinic or emergency department visit	Paid under OPPS; separate APC payment.
Y	Nonimplantable durable medical equipment	Not paid under OPPS. All institutional providers other than home health agencies bill to durable medical equipment regional carrier (DMERC).
X	Ancillary services	Paid under OPPS; separate APC payment.

* See pages 83-85.
** See page 85.

APC Payment Rate Formula

[(National Payment Rate × 60% labor portion) × wage index] + [(National Payment Rate × 40% nonlabor portion)]

Example of APC calculation for APC 0021 for a hospital with a wage index of 0.8377:

[(payment rate × 60%) × wage index]	+ [non-wage-adjusted portion] = total allowance
[(1,176.55 × 60%) × 0.8377]	+ [1,176.55 × 40%]
[(705.93 × 0.8377)]	+ [470.62]
591.36	+ 470.62 = $1,061.98 total allowance

(*continued from page 80*) **The Conversion Factor (CF)** is a national rate determined by Medicare at the beginning of each calendar year. This converts the RW to the national payment rate for a specific APC.

The National Payment Rate is the national allowance for each APC group resulting from multiplying the RW by the CF. The database provides the national payment rate; consequently there is no need for facilities to calculate the national rate. However, the wage index element is not included in the national payment rate and must be calculated on an individual facility basis.

The Geographic Wage Index (WI) is specific to a geographic location and is used to adjust a portion of the national payment rate to account for geographic variations in labor costs. Sixty percent of the national payment amount is multiplied by the WI to determine an individual hospital's allowance for an APC.

CMS publishes the APC groupings and their national payment rates and copayments in Addendum B of the Calendar Year Hospital Outpatient Prospective Payment System/ Ambulatory Surgical Center Payment System Final Rule and on their Web site.[1] These are updated annually.

In Chapter 3 (UB-04) it was mentioned that not every charge for outpatient hospital services requires a HCPCS code because certain charges are bundled into another service's payment. An example of this would be for anesthesia services. The revenue code for anesthesia is 0370. Medicare instructions state not to use a HCPCS code for these charges because they will not be assigned an APC group. The payment for the procedure in which anesthesia was employed includes the payment for the anesthesia as well. Figure 6-3 illustrates UB-04 items 42 and 44-47 completed correctly for an outpatient surgery case utilizing anesthesia.

This example is for a surgery (revenue code 0360, *operating room*, with HCPCS code 26117, *Radical resection of tumor*), the tissue exam for the removed tumor (revenue code 0310, *pathology*, with HCPCS code 88309), and the supplies, pharmaceuticals, and anesthesia (these revenue codes do not require HCPCS coding).

HCPCS code 26117 groups to APC 0021 with a payment rate of $1,176.55.

HCPCS code 88309 groups to APC 0344 with a payment rate of $53.98.

The total allowance is $1,230.53 for this claim. This amount will be adjusted for coinsurance (the patient's or the secondary insurance company's responsible portion of the allowance). See Figure 6-4.

The other (supplies, pharmaceuticals, and anesthesia) are not charges paid separately from the surgery because the surgery's payment includes the other services and supplies.

Additional Comments

Hospitals may also receive the following payments in addition to standard OPPS payments:

- Fee schedule payments that are paid under a different system than APCs (eg, clinical laboratory services, mammographies).

FIGURE 6-3 *UB-04 Billing Example*

42 REV. CD.	43 DESCRIPTION	44 HCPCS / RATE / HIPPS CODE	45 SERV. DATE	46 SERV. UNITS	47 TOTAL CHARGES	48 NON-COVERED CHARGES	49
0250	pharmaceuticals		0101xx	15	172 49		
0272	sterile supplies		0101xx	3	147 00		
0310	pathology	88309	0101xx	1	97 00		
0360	operating room	26117	0101xx	1	2185 00		
0370	anesthesia		0101xx	1	347 00		
0001	Total Charges				2948 49		

PAGE ____ OF ____ CREATION DATE TOTALS

50 PAYER NAME | 51 HEALTH PLAN ID | 52 REL. INFO | 53 ASG. BEN. | 54 PRIOR PAYMENTS | 55 EST. AMOUNT DUE | 56 NPI | 57 OTHER

FIGURE 6-4 *Payment Examples for UB-04*

42 REV. CD.	43 DESCRIPTION	44 HCPCS / RATE / HIPPS CODE	45 SERV. DATE	46 SERV. UNITS	47 TOTAL CHARGES	48 NON-COVERED CHARGES	49
0250	pharmaceuticals		0101xx	15	172 49		
0272	sterile supplies		0101xx	3	147 00		
0310	pathology	88309	0101xx	1	97 00		
0360	operating room	26117	0101xx	1	2185 00		
0370	anesthesia		0101xx	1	347 00		
0001	Total Charges				2948 49		

1. Revenue codes 250, 272, and 370 package into the payment for the surgery.
2. HCPCS 88309 groups to APC 0344 with a national payment of $53.98.
3. HCPCS 26117 groups to APC 0021 with a national payment of $1,176.55.
4. $53.98 + $1,176.55 = $1,230.53 for a national payment level on this claim.

PAGE ____ OF ____ CREATION DATE TOTALS

50 PAYER NAME | 51 HEALTH PLAN ID | 52 REL. INFO | 53 ASG. BEN. | 54 PRIOR PAYMENTS | 55 EST. AMOUNT DUE | 56 NPI | 57 OTHER

Note that this example illustrates how the codes group, ie, the purple text shows an example of manual grouping. In the provider's office, this might be performed either using grouping software or manually.

- Pass-through payments for specific drugs, biologicals, and devices used in the delivery of services. Pass-through payments are made for a period of time, and then the supplies are included in the usual APC payment system and removed from pass-through status.
- Outlier payments for individual services that cost hospitals much more than the payment rates for the services' APC groups.
- Transitional outpatient payments for cancer hospitals and children's hospitals.

The CF is reduced by 2% for hospitals that fail to meet the requirements of the hospital outpatient quality data reporting program, which will result in reduced payment for most of the facility's services.

Annual updates are made final through the publication of proposed and final rules in the *Federal Register*. Each year's proposed and final rules and all supporting files and documentation can be accessed on the CMS Web site.[1]

Figure 6-5 illustrates the claims payment process for payment under the Outpatient Prospective Payment System.

FIGURE 6-5 *Outpatient Prospective Payment System (OPPS) Payment Flow*

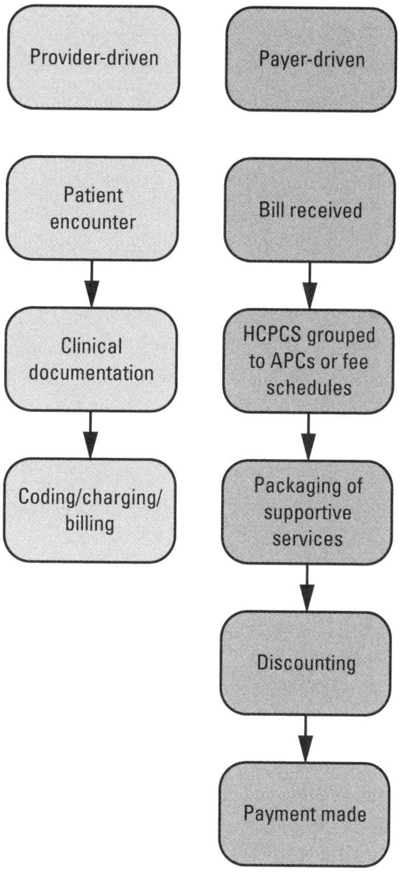

Inpatient Prospective Payment System (IPPS)

A hospital is an institution that is primarily engaged in providing medical services to inpatients. Procedures that are not payable under OPPS but are paid under the Inpatient Prospective Payment System (IPPS) are procedures that the CMS has identified as typically provided only in an inpatient setting. These procedures make up what is referred to as the *inpatient list*, representing services that require inpatient care because of the nature of the procedure, the need for at least 24 hours of postoperative recovery time or monitoring before the patient can be safely discharged, or the underlying physical condition of the patient. CMS assigns status indicator "C" to delineate which procedures are performed on an inpatient basis. CMS updates the inpatient list as often as quarterly through program memoranda to reflect current advances in medical practice.

The IPPS was developed in the early 1980s to move from a charge-based payment model to paying a predetermined (prospective) rate for each type of hospital stay. These rates represent payment in full to the hospital for the inpatient costs.

Medicare Part A coverage is available for each day of inpatient hospital care up to a maximum of 90 days in any single episode of illness plus 60 Lifetime Reserve (LTR) days. The payment for the inpatient stay is subject to a hospital deductible as well as a coinsurance applied during the 61st through the 90th days of the inpatient stay.

Medicare pays for inpatient hospital care if all the following conditions are met:

- The hospital is participating in the Medicare program.
- A physician orders inpatient hospital care.
- The patient requires care that only a hospital can provide.
- The care the patient receives is medically necessary according to CMS regulations.

The following services or supplies provided while the beneficiary is an inpatient in the hospital are covered:

- Semiprivate accommodations unless private accommodations are medically necessary or where semiprivate accommodations are unavailable
- Nursing services (other than a private duty nurse) and other related services that are ordinarily furnished by the hospital for the care and treatment of inpatients
- The use of hospital facilities (ie, endoscopy suite, radiology) and medical social services customarily furnished by the hospital for inpatients
- Drugs and biologicals, supplies, appliances, and equipment for use in the hospital that are ordinarily furnished by the hospital
- Other diagnostic or therapeutic items or services furnished by the hospital

Inpatient hospital services do not include extended care services furnished by the hospital. Those are considered extended care services.

The patient's responsibility is limited to deductibles, coinsurance, and noncovered items. IPPS uses DRGs as the classification system to determine the payment for an inpatient stay. The DRGs are classified "per discharge" based on the:

- Patient diagnosis
- Treatment procedure
- Discharge status
- Sex

Primarily, the DRG is determined by the patient's principal diagnosis (based on ICD-9-CM coding) and up to eight secondary diagnoses (ICD-9-CM codes). Also, the DRG can be impacted by procedures (based on ICD-9-CM coding) furnished during the stay. The DRGs include cases with clinically similar conditions that require comparable amounts of inpatient resources. Each DRG has a payment weight assigned to it, based on the average resources used to treat Medicare patients in that DRG.

All covered inpatient hospital services furnished to patients are paid for under DRGs except:

- Services that are excluded from IPPS (psychiatric, rehabilitation, or long-term care, for example)
- Clinical laboratory services
- Pacemakers and other prosthetic devices including lenses, and artificial limbs, knees, and hips
- Radiology services furnished by a physician's office, other hospital, or radiology clinic
- Total parenteral nutrition (TPN) services
- Transportation

DRGs cover patients for 90 days of inpatient care per episode of illness. An episode of illness begins when the patient is admitted to an inpatient stay and ends after the patient has been out of the hospital for 60 consecutive days. Given that payment is made per discharge, the entire inpatient stay is paid as a single DRG. This is different than both OPPS and MFS, in which individual services were reimbursed. The hospital's payment is not affected by the patient's length of stay unless the patient is transferred or has an unusually short length of stay.

In the late 2000s, Medicare developed and implemented a Medicare severity DRG system (MS-DRG) to better account for severity of illness and resource consumption for inpatient stays. There are three levels of severity in the MS-DRGs based on secondary diagnosis codes:

- Major complication/comorbidity (MCC) for the highest level of severity.
- Complication/comorbidity (CC) for the next level of severity.
- Noncomplication/comorbidity (NonCC), which does not significantly affect severity of illness.

Note

An MCC or CC is defined as a secondary diagnosis that increases the length of stay and resources consumed. CMS is responsible for developing the list of recognized MCC and CC diagnoses.

In the MS-DRG system, many DRGs are split into one, two, or three MS-DRGs based on whether any of the secondary diagnoses has been categorized as an MCC, a CC, or no CC.

Examples of MS-DRGs with a three-way split include:

DRG 20 Intracranial vascular procedures with PDX hemorrhage w/MCC
DRG 21 Intracranial vascular procedures with PDX hemorrhage w/CC
DRG 22 Intracranial vascular procedures with PDX hemorrhage w/o MCC/CC

The MS-DRG system consists of hundreds of groupings. MS-DRGs are assigned as follows:

1. All principal diagnoses are divided into major diagnostic categories (MDCs) that correspond to single organ systems.

   Examples of MDCs include:
   - MDC 01 Diseases and Disorders of the Nervous System
   - MDC 02 Diseases and Disorders of the Eye
   - MDC 03 Diseases and Disorders of the Ear, Nose, Mouth, and Throat
   - MDC 04 Diseases and Disorders of the Respiratory System
   - MDC 05 Diseases and Disorders of the Circulatory System
2. Pre-MDC MS-DRG. Because some patient groups are enormously resource intensive, they are put into a separate DRG group before MDC assignment based on the surgical procedure rather than the principal diagnosis. This group is called pre-MDC DRGs. Pre-MDC DRGs include organ transplants, bone marrow transplants, and tracheostomy cases. If a procedure places a case into a pre-MDC DRG, the DRG is assigned outside of the MDC.

For example, DRG 006 Liver transplant w/o MCC is assigned based on the procedure performed pre-MDC. The principal diagnosis is not taken into consideration.

Table 6-3 includes all MDCs for the MS-DRG system.

TABLE 6-3 ***MS-DRG Major Diagnostic Categories***

Major Diagnostic Category (MDC)	Description
01	Diseases and Disorders of the Nervous System
02	Diseases and Disorders of the Eye
03	Diseases and Disorders of the Ear, Nose, Mouth, and Throat
04	Diseases and Disorders of the Respiratory System
05	Diseases and Disorders of the Circulatory System
06	Diseases and Disorders of the Digestive System

(continued)

TABLE 6-3 *(continued)*

Major Diagnostic Category (MDC)	Description
07	Diseases and Disorders of the Hepatobiliary System and Pancreas
08	Diseases and Disorders of the Musculoskeletal System and Connective Tissue
09	Diseases and Disorders of the Skin, Subcutaneous Tissue, and Breast
10	Endocrine, Nutritional, and Metabolic Diseases and Disorders
11	Diseases and Disorders of the Kidney and Urinary Tract
12	Diseases and Disorders of the Male Reproductive System
13	Diseases and Disorders of the Female Reproductive System
14	Pregnancy, Childbirth, and the Puerperium
15	Newborns and Other Neonates with Conditions Originating in the Perinatal Period
16	Diseases and Disorders of the Blood and Blood Forming Organs and Immunological Disorders
17	Myeloproliferative Diseases and Disorders and Poorly Differentiated Neoplasms
18	Infectious and Parasitic Diseases (Systemic or Unspecified Sites)
19	Mental Diseases and Disorders
20	Alcohol/Drug Use and Alcohol/Drug Induced Organic Mental Disorders
21	Injuries, Poisonings, and Toxic Effects of Drugs
22	Burns
23	Factors Influencing Health Status and Other Contacts with Health Services
24	Multiple Significant Trauma
25	Human Immunodeficiency Virus Infections

The following are MDC-assignment procedures:

1. Operating room (OR) procedures: If a discharge is not assigned to a pre-MDC DRG, patients are then classified by whether they had an operating room procedure within each MDC. It is important to note that in some instances there are also nonoperating room procedures that may affect the DRG assignment. If an operating procedure was performed, the stay is then classified by the type of procedure. There is a surgical hierarchy within each MDC, and usually patients with multiple procedures are assigned to the most resource-intensive DRG.
2. Unrelated OR procedure DRG: Within the Medicare DRG system there are DRGs for unrelated operating room procedures. These DRGs are assigned when the case has no OR procedures related to the principal diagnoses within the MDC for the procedure.
3. Principal diagnosis: If no OR procedure is performed, the case is classified into medical categories by the principal diagnosis. Medical categories include neoplasms, specific conditions related to

TABLE 6-4 *Sample Principal Diagnoses from ICD-9-CM to Major Diagnostic Categories*

DRG 309 Cardiac arrhythmia & conduction disorders w/Complication or Comorbidity							
Groups to MDC 05							
Principal ICD-9-CM diagnoses that group to this Diagnosis Related Group (DRG)							
426.0	426.10	426.11	426.12	426.13	426.2	426.3	426.4
426.50	426.51	426.52	426.53	426.54	426.6	426.7	426.81
426.82	426.89	426.9	427.0	427.1	427.2	427.31	427.32
427.41	427.42	427.60	427.61	427.69	427.81	427.89	427.9
746.86	785.0	785.1	996.01	996.04			

the anatomical site, symptoms, and other diagnoses.

4. In the DRG system, each case may be further analyzed for sex, discharge disposition, and/or the presence of a CC or MCC, and the MS-DRG is assigned.

Table 6-4 shows an example of how the diagnoses assigned (ICD-9-CM codes) group into Diagnosis Related Groups (DRGs). Remember, DRGs are categorized into Major Diagnostic Categories (MDCs).

DRG Payment

Accurate and complete ICD-9-CM coding is essential for accurate MS-DRG assignment and payment.

Step 1. Hospitals submit a bill for each Medicare patient they treat to their Medicare payer (MAC).

Step 2. Based on the information provided on the bill (patient demographics, pre-MDC screening, principal diagnoses or procedures, complications and comorbidities), the case is categorized into an MS-DRG.

Step 3. The MS-DRG determines how much payment the hospital receives.

Step 4. There is a base payment rate composed of an amount, which is divided into a labor-related and nonlabor share. The labor-related share is adjusted by the wage index applicable to the area where the hospital is located (exception: Alaska or Hawaii have the nonlabor share adjusted by a cost of living adjustment factor).

Step 5. This base payment rate is multiplied by the MS-DRG relative weight.

Step 6. The individual hospital might have special payment adjustments:

- If it has a disproportionate share of low-income patients (DSH), the hospital receives a percentage add-on for each case paid through the PPS.
- If the hospital is an approved teaching hospital, it receives a percentage add-on payment for indirect medical education (IME) for each case paid through the PPS.
- A hospital can receive an additional payment for those cases that include technologies that meet the new technology add-on payment criteria.

Step 7. The costs incurred by the hospital for the case are evaluated to determine whether the case is eligible for an additional payment as an outlier case. This additional payment is designed to protect the hospital from large financial losses due to unusually expensive cases. Any outlier payment due is added onto the MS-DRG-adjusted base payment rate.

TABLE 6-5 *Examples of MS-DRGs, MDCs, and Assigned Weights*

MS-DRG	MDC	Type	MS-DRG title	Weights	Geometric mean LOS	Arithmetic mean LOS
001	PRE	SURG	HEART TRANSPLANT OR IMPLANT OF HEART ASSIST SYSTEM W MCC	26.3441	31.6	41.9
002	PRE	SURG	HEART TRANSPLANT OR IMPLANT OF HEART ASSIST SYSTEM W/O MCC	13.6127	17.6	22.6
003	PRE	SURG	ECMO OR TRACH W MV 96+ HRS OR PDX EXC FACE, MOUTH & NECK W MAJ O.R.	18.1239	30.1	36.6
004	PRE	SURG	TRACH W MV 96+ HRS OR PDX EXC FACE, MOUTH & NECK W/O MAJ O.R.	11.2403	22.2	27.1
005	PRE	SURG	LIVER TRANSPLANT W MCC OR INTESTINAL TRANSPLANT	10.1771	14.9	19.9
117	02	SURG	INTRAOCULAR PROCEDURES W/O CC/MCC	0.7305	1.6	2.0
121	02	MED	ACUTE MAJOR EYE INFECTIONS W CC/MCC	0.9104	4.1	5.1
122	02	MED	ACUTE MAJOR EYE INFECTIONS W/O CC/MCC	0.6522	3.3	4.0
123	02	MED	NEUROLOGICAL EYE DISORDERS	0.7144	2.2	2.7
124	02	MED	OTHER DISORDERS OF THE EYE W MCC	1.1903	3.8	5.3
125	02	MED	OTHER DISORDERS OF THE EYE W/O MCC	0.6859	2.7	3.4
129	03	SURG	MAJOR HEAD & NECK PROCEDURES W CC/MCC OR MAJOR DEVICE	2.2349	3.7	5.2
130	03	SURG	MAJOR HEAD & NECK PROCEDURES W/O CC/MCC	1.2299	2.3	2.9
131	03	SURG	CRANIAL/FACIAL PROCEDURES W CC/MCC	2.0915	4.1	5.6
132	03	SURG	CRANIAL/FACIAL PROCEDURES W/O CC/MCC	1.2447	2.1	2.7
133	03	SURG	OTHER EAR, NOSE, MOUTH & THROAT O.R. PROCEDURES W CC/MCC	1.7000	3.6	5.4
134	03	SURG	OTHER EAR, NOSE, MOUTH & THROAT O.R. PROCEDURES W/O CC/MCC	0.8514	1.7	2.1

(continued)

TABLE 6-5 *(continued)*

MS-DRG	MDC	Type	MS-DRG title	Weights	Geometric mean LOS	Arithmetic mean LOS
135	03	SURG	SINUS & MASTOID PROCEDURES W CC/MCC	1.9082	4.3	6.4
136	03	SURG	SINUS & MASTOID PROCEDURES W/O CC/MCC	0.9751	1.7	2.3
166	04	SURG	OTHER RESP SYSTEM O.R. PROCEDURES W MCC	3.7383	9.5	11.9
167	04	SURG	OTHER RESP SYSTEM O.R. PROCEDURES W CC	2.0567	5.8	7.4

Adjustments to MS-DRG Payments

Patient Transfers

Hospitals receive adjusted payment if Medicare patients are transferred to another acute-care facility or to a post-acute-care facility. For patients transferring from one acute-care facility to another, the hospital that transfers the patient is paid an MS-DRG-based per-diem rate. The receiving facility receives the full MS-DRG payment.

Three-Day Window

Related outpatient services provided within three days prior to admission are included in the payment for the inpatient stay and may not be separately billed.

Definitions and Acronyms

Ambulatory Payment Classifications (APCs). "All services paid under the prospective payment system (PPS) are classified into groups called ambulatory payment classifications (APCs), which contain all outpatient services included in the payment schedule. The services within each group are clinically similar and require comparable resources. The APCs group together services, supplies, drugs, and devices used in a particular procedure. A payment rate is established for each APC."[2]

Diagnosis Related Groups. "The Diagnosis Related Groups (DRG) were developed for the Health Care Financing Administration (HCFA) as a patient classification scheme to relate the type of patients a hospital treats (ie, its case mix) to the costs incurred by the hospital. While all patients are unique, groups of patients have common demographic, diagnostic and therapeutic attributes that determine their resource needs. The DRGs form a manageable, clinically coherent set of patient classes that relate a hospital's case mix to the resource demands and associated costs experienced by the hospital. Each discharge in the uniform hospital discharge data set (UHDDB) was assigned into a DRG based on the principal diagnosis, secondary diagnoses, surgical procedures, age, sex, and discharge status of the patient."[3]

Inpatient Prospective Payment System (IPPS). Prospective payment system used for inpatient hospital claims.

inpatient services. Medical services provided to a patient admitted to an acute inpatient hospital.

Medicare Severity Diagnosis Related Groups (MS-DRGs). Payment groups designed for the Medicare population, in which "patients who have similar clinical characteristics and similar costs are assigned to a MS-DRG. The MS-DRG will be linked to a fixed payment amount based on the average cost of patients in the group. Patients can be assigned to a

MS-DRG based on their diagnosis, surgical procedures, age and other information."[4]

Outpatient hospital services. Medical services provided to a patient in a hospital outpatient department (eg, emergency services, diagnostic services, day surgeries).

Outpatient Prospective Payment System (OPPS). PPS used for outpatient hospital claims.

Prospective Payment System (PPS). "The prospective pricing system (PPS) was introduced in 1983 to pay for Medicare patients' hospital costs, provides a standardized payment for each hospital admission, with variations to reflect geographic differences in wage rates and hospital location (urban or rural)."[5]

Healthcare Common Procedure Coding System (HCPCS). "The CMS developed this system in 1993 to standardize the coding systems used to process Medicare claims on a national basis."[2] The HCPCS coding system comprises two levels: Level I CPT and Level II HCPCS codes, each being a unique code set.

REFERENCES

1. Centers for Medicare and Medicaid Services. Annual Updated OPPS Addendum B. Available at: www.cms.gov/HospitalOutpatientPPS/AU/itemdetail.asp?filterType=none&filterByDID=-99&sortByDID=3&sortOrder=descending&itemID=CMS1243097&intNumPerPage=10. Accessed January 10, 2011.
2. Grider D. *Coding with Modifiers*. Chicago, IL: American Medical Association; 2007: p322.
3. Utah Government Services. Available at: http://health.utah.gov/opha/IBIShelp/codes/DRGCode.htm. Accessed April 15, 2011.
4. U.S. Department of Health and Human Services. Available at: HHS.gov. Accessed April 15, 2011.
5. American Medical Association. *Medicare RBRVS 2011: The Physicians' Guide*. Chicago, IL: 2011.

Chapter 7

Other Medicare Payment Systems

Other Health Care Providers

Physicians and acute care hospitals provide the lion's share of health care. However, there are many other providers who can bill and be paid for services provided. This chapter will take a quick look at some of those providers as well as different payment systems Medicare employs. Naturally, each different system is much more complex than illustrated within this chapter.

Ambulance Services

Ambulance services are those where a patient is transported from one place to another for treatment of an illness or injury. Usually ambulance operators have specialized medical training to give care to the patient during the transportation.

Ambulance services are covered under Medicare Part B only if the following circumstances are met:

- A patient is transported to an appropriate destination;
- The transportation must be medically necessary to be performed by an ambulance. If a cab or car would suffice, the ambulance would not be medically necessary;
- The ambulance provider meets applicable vehicle, staffing, and billing requirements; and
- The transportation is not part of a Part A service, which is often bundled into the Part A allowance.

There are HCPCS codes for ambulance services shown in Table 7-1.

TABLE 7-1 *HCPCS Codes for Ambulance Services*

HCPCS	Description
A0021	Ambulance service, outside state per mile, transport (Medicaid only)
A0080	Non-emergency transportation, per mile - vehicle provided by volunteer (individual or organization), with no vested interest
A0090	Non-emergency transportation, per mile - vehicle provided by individual (family member, self, neighbor) with vested interest
A0100	Non-emergency transportation; taxi
A0110	Non-emergency transportation and bus, intra or interstate carrier
A0120	Non-emergency transportation: mini-bus, mountain area transports, or other transportation systems
A0130	Non-emergency transportation: wheelchair van

(continued)

TABLE 7-1 *(continued)*

HCPCS	Description
A0140	Non-emergency transportation and air travel (private or commercial) intra or inter state
A0160	Non-emergency transportation: per mile - case worker or social worker
A0170	Transportation ancillary: parking fees, tolls, other
A0180	Non-emergency transportation: ancillary: lodging-recipient
A0190	Non-emergency transportation: ancillary: meals-recipient
A0200	Non-emergency transportation: ancillary: lodging escort
A0210	Non-emergency transportation: ancillary: meals-escort
A0225	Ambulance service, neonatal transport, base rate, emergency transport, one way
A0380	BLS mileage (per mile)
A0382	BLS routine disposable supplies
A0384	BLS specialized service disposable supplies; defibrillation (used by ALS ambulances and BLS ambulances in jurisdictions where defibrillation is permitted in BLS ambulances)
A0390	ALS mileage (per mile)
A0392	ALS specialized service disposable supplies; defibrillation (to be used only in jurisdictions where defibrillation cannot be performed in BLS ambulances)
A0394	ALS specialized service disposable supplies; IV drug therapy
A0396	ALS specialized service disposable supplies; esophageal intubation
A0398	ALS routine disposable supplies
A0420	Ambulance waiting time (ALS or BLS), one half (1/2) hour increments
A0422	Ambulance (ALS or BLS) oxygen and oxygen supplies, life sustaining situation
A0424	Extra ambulance attendant, ground (ALS or BLS) or air (fixed or rotary winged); (requires medical review)
A0425	Ground mileage, per statute mile
A0426	Ambulance service, advanced life support, non-emergency transport, level 1 (ALS 1)
A0427	Ambulance service, advanced life support, emergency transport, level 1 (ALS1-emergency)
A0428	Ambulance service, basic life support, non-emergency transport (BLS)
A0429	Ambulance service, basic life support, emergency transport (BLS-emergency)
A0430	Ambulance service, conventional air services, transport, one way (fixed wing)
A0431	Ambulance service, conventional air services, transport, one way (rotary wing)
A0432	Paramedic intercept (PI), rural area, transport furnished by a volunteer ambulance company which is prohibited by state law from billing third party payers
A0433	Advanced life support, level 2 (ALS 2)
A0434	Specialty care transport (SCT)
A0435	Fixed wing air mileage, per statute mile
A0436	Rotary wing air mileage, per statute mile
A0888	Noncovered ambulance mileage, per mile (eg, for miles traveled beyond closest appropriate facility)
A0998	Ambulance response and treatment, no transport
A0999	Unlisted ambulance service

Source: www.cms.gov/HCPCSReleaseCodeSets/ANHCPCS/itemdetail.asp?filterType=none&filterByDID=-99&sortByDID=1&sortOrder=descending&itemID=CMS1240961&intNumPerPage=10ov/center/provider.asp.

Payment under the fee schedule for ambulance services:

- Includes a base rate payment plus a payment for mileage;
- Covers patient transport to the nearest appropriate facility; and
- Covers all items and services associated with approved transport as long as they are medically necessary.

The ground ambulance services fee schedule includes:

- The conversion factor (CF), which is the national uniform base rate;
- A relative value unit (RVU) assigned to each type of ground ambulance service;
- A geographic adjustment factor (GAF) for each locality;
- The national loaded mileage rate; and
- Additional amounts for rural point of pickup mileage.

The air ambulance services fee schedule includes:

- Base rates for fixed wing and rotary wing;
- A geographic adjustment factor (GAF) for each locality;
- The national loaded mileage rate for each type of air service; and
- Additional amounts for rural point of pickup mileage.

Mileage refers to loaded mileage per loaded mile.

In order to determine the payment for an ambulance claim, the ambulance fee schedule (see Figure 7-1) should be used for the locality of the ambulance provider.

Ambulatory Surgery Centers

Ambulatory surgery centers (ASCs) are freestanding or hospital-based centers that provide surgery on an outpatient basis. For those that are hospital-based, the Outpatient Prospective Payment System (OPPS) is used for payment. Refer to Chapter 6 for in-depth information on OPPS. For freestanding centers, the payment is based on OPPS but with a few minor differences. Physicians are still paid for professional services under the Medicare Physician Fee Schedule (MFS) (see Chapter 5).

On January 1, 2008, CMS implemented a revised ASC payment system using the hospital OPPS (see Chapter 6) as a basis. This greatly expanded the procedures eligible

FIGURE 7-1 *Example of Ambulance Fee Schedule*

(1) CONTRACTOR/ CARRIER	(2) LOCAL.	(3) HCPCS	(4) BASE RATE	(5) RVU	(6) GPCI	(7)(a) URBAN BASE RATE / URBAN MILEAGE	(7)(b) RURAL BASE RATE / RURAL MILEAGE	(7)(c) RURAL BASE RATE / LOWEST QUARTILE	(8) RURAL GROUND MILES 1-17*
Mississippi									
00512	00	A0425	6.73	1.00	0.929	$6.86	$6.93	n/a	$10.40
00512	00	A0426	209.44	1.20	0.929	$243.61	$246.00	$301.60	n/a
00512	00	A0427	209.44	1.90	0.929	$385.72	$389.50	$477.53	n/a
00512	00	A0428	209.44	1.00	0.929	$203.01	$205.00	$251.33	n/a
00512	00	A0429	209.44	1.60	0.929	$324.82	$328.00	$402.13	n/a
00512	00	A0430	2842.29	1.00	0.929	$2,741.39	$4,112.08	n/a	$4,112.08
00512	00	A0431	3304.58	1.00	0.929	$3,187.27	$4,780.90	n/a	$4,780.90
00512	00	A0432	209.44	1.75	0.929	$355.27	$358.75	n/a	n/a
00512	00	A0433	209.44	2.75	0.929	$558.28	$563.75	$691.16	n/a
00512	00	A0434	209.44	3.25	0.929	$659.79	$666.26	$816.83	n/a
00512	00	A0435	8.06	1.00	0.929	$8.06	$12.09	n/a	$12.09
00512	00	A0436	21.51	1.00	0.929	$21.51	$32.27	n/a	$32.27
Arkansas									
00520	13	A0425	6.73	1.00	0.923	$6.86	$6.93	n/a	$10.40
00520	13	A0426	209.44	1.20	0.923	$242.54	$244.91	$300.27	n/a
00520	13	A0427	209.44	1.90	0.923	$384.02	$387.78	$475.42	n/a
00520	13	A0428	209.44	1.00	0.923	$202.11	$204.10	$250.22	n/a
00520	13	A0429	209.44	1.60	0.923	$323.38	$326.55	$400.35	n/a
00520	13	A0430	2842.29	1.00	0.923	$2,732.86	$4,099.29	n/a	$4,099.29

Source: www.cms.gov/center/ambulance.asp.

for Medicare payment when performed in an ASC. ASC procedures are those surgical and other medical procedures that are:

- Commonly performed on an inpatient basis but may be safely performed in an ASC;
- Not of a type that are commonly performed or that may be safely performed in physicians' offices;
- Limited to procedures requiring a dedicated operating room or suite and generally requiring a postoperative recovery room or short term (not overnight) convalescent room; and
- Not otherwise excluded from Medicare coverage.

Specific standards in §416.65(b) limit covered ASC procedures to those that do not generally exceed 90 minutes operating time and a total of four hours recovery or convalescent time. If anesthesia is required, the anesthesia must be local or regional anesthesia, or general anesthesia of not more than 90 minutes duration.

Section 416.65(b)(3) of the regulations excludes from the ASC list procedures that generally result in extensive blood loss, that require major or prolonged invasion of body cavities, that directly involve major blood vessels, or that are generally emergency or life-threatening in nature.[1]

Services on ASC List

Statute requires CMS to specify surgical procedures that, although appropriately performed in an inpatient hospital setting, can also be performed safely on an ambulatory basis in an ASC. CMS revises the ASC-approved code listing to be consistent with annual calendar year changes to HCPCS and CPT codes. Inclusion and/or exclusion of a code is predicated on whether the procedure and/or service can be appropriately and safely performed in an ASC and whether it is on the list of approved ASC procedures or proposed by CMS for addition to the ASC list. These annual coding updates are implemented through program instructions issued to carriers that process ASC claims. Therefore, some surgical procedures that may be performed in an ASC are not on the ASC list of covered surgical procedures. The ASC may not bill a facility fee for those services, but they may be billed by the physician who performs the service under the MFS.

Medicare will make an additional payment to ASCs for certain ancillary services provided, which are integral to a covered ASC surgical procedure.

The following services and/or costs are included in the ASC payments and are not paid separately from the surgeries billed.

- Nursing, technician, and related services;
- Use of the facility where the surgical procedures are performed;
- Any laboratory testing performed under a Clinical Laboratory Improvement Amendments of 1988 (CLIA) certificate of waiver;
- Drugs and biologicals for which separate payment is not allowed under the hospital OPPS;
- Medical and surgical supplies not on pass-through status;
- Equipment and surgical dressings;
- Implanted prosthetic devices, including intraocular lenses (IOLs), and related accessories and supplies not on pass-through status;
- Implanted durable medical equipment (DME) and related accessories and supplies not on pass-through status;
- Splints and casts and related devices;
- Radiology services for which separate payment is not allowed under the OPPS, and other diagnostic tests or interpretive services that are integral to a surgical procedure;
- Administrative, recordkeeping, and housekeeping items and services;
- Materials, including supplies and equipment for the administration and monitoring of anesthesia;
- Supervision of the services of an anesthetist by the operating surgeon;

- Blood, blood plasma, platelets, and so forth, except those in which blood deductible applies;
- Materials for anesthesia; and
- IOLs and new technology intraocular lenses (NTIOLs).
  Note: Generally, no separate charges for IOLs are allowed, but approved NTIOLs may be billed separately and an adjustment to the facility payment will be made for eligible lenses.

Payment for the services above is packaged into the ASC payment for the covered surgical procedure. ASCs should incorporate the charges for packaged services into the charges reported for the services that are paid.

Note

Medicare pays the lesser of 80% of actual charges or the ASC payment rate for the procedure. Bcause this is on a line by line basis, ASCs may not be paid appropriately if they unbundle charges and report those charges for packaged codes as separate line items.

Unlike the prior list, the following services may be separately charged and paid.

- Physicians' services (billed by the physician);
- Purchase or rental of nonimplantable DME (billed by the supplier);
- Implantable DME and accessories;
- Nonimplantable prosthetic devices (billed by the supplier);
- Implantable prosthetic other than certain intraocular lenses (IOLs and NTIOLs) and accessories;
- Ambulance services (billed by the ambulance provider);
- Leg, arm, back, and neck braces (billed by the supplier);
- Artificial legs, arms, and eyes (billed by the supplier); and
- Services furnished by an independent laboratory (billed by the certified lab, or the ASC if the ASC has received certification).

The following ancillary items and services are considered for separate payment when performed as an integral procedure to a covered surgical procedure:

- Covered ancillary services;
- Brachytherapy sources;
- Certain implantable items that have pass-through status under the OPPS;
- Certain drugs and biologicals for which separate payment is allowed under the OPPS;
- Certain items that CMS designates as contractor-priced; and
- Certain radiology services for which separate payment is allowed under the OPPS.

ASC Payment

The standard payment for most ASC covered surgical procedures is calculated based on multiplying a conversion factor by the relative weight for the procedure for each separately payable procedure. Payment rates for surgical procedures that are commonly performed in physicians' offices and the technical component of covered ancillary radiology procedures cannot exceed the MFS nonfacility practice expense amount.

ASC facility services are subject to the usual Medicare Part B deductible and coinsurance requirements. The Medicare program pays ASCs 80% of the lesser of the actual charge or the ASC facility payment rate for the covered services performed. The beneficiary is responsible for the 20% coinsurance. See Table 7-2 for the payment indicators listing from the ASC fee schedule.

Table 7-3 illustrates an excerpt from the ASC fee schedule.

See Table 7-4 for an example excerpt from the ASC fee schedule for ancillary services covered if they are integral to covered surgical procedures.

TABLE 7-2 *ASC Fee Schedule Payment Indicators*

Indicator	Definition
A2	Surgical procedure on ASC list in CY 2007; payment based on OPPS relative payment weight.
D5	Deleted/discontinued code; no payment made.
F4	Corneal tissue acquisition, hepatitis B vaccine; paid at reasonable cost.
G2	Non-office-based surgical procedure added in CY 2008 or later; payment based on OPPS relative payment weight.
H2	Brachytherapy source paid separately when provided integral to a surgical procedure on ASC list; payment based on OPPS rate.
H8	Device-intensive procedure on ASC list in CY 2007; paid at adjusted rate.
J7	OPPS pass-through device paid separately when provided integral to a surgical procedure on ASC list; payment contractor-priced.
J8	Device-intensive procedure added to ASC list in CY 2008 or later; paid at adjusted rate.
K2	Drugs and biologicals paid separately when provided integral to a surgical procedure on ASC list; payment based on OPPS rate.
K7	Unclassified drugs and biologicals; payment contractor-priced.
L1	Influenza vaccine; pneumococcal vaccine. Packaged item/service; no separate payment made.
L6	New Technology Intraocular Lens (NTIOL); special payment.
N1	Packaged service/item; no separate payment made.
P2	Office-based surgical procedure added to ASC list in CY 2008 or later with MPFS nonfacility PE RVUs; payment based on OPPS relative payment weight.
P3	Office-based surgical procedure added to ASC list in CY 2008 or later with MPFS nonfacility PE RVUs; payment based on MPFS nonfacility PE RVUs.
R2	Office-based surgical procedure added to ASC list in CY 2008 or later without MPFS nonfacility PE RVUs; payment based on OPPS relative payment weight.
Z2	Radiology service paid separately when provided integral to a surgical procedure on ASC list; payment based on OPPS relative payment weight.
Z3	Radiology service paid separately when provided integral to a surgical procedure on ASC list; payment based on MPFS nonfacility PE RVUs.

Source: www.cms.gov/apps/ama/license.asp?file=/ascpayment/downloads/CMS_1414_P_2010_ASC _NPRM_Addenda_AA_BB_DD1_DD2.zip.

TABLE 7-3 *Example of ASC Fee Schedule*

HCPCS Code	Short Descriptor	Subject To Multiple Procedure Discounting	Final CY 2011 Comment Indicator	Final CY 2011 Payment Indicator	Final CY 2011 Payment Weight	Final CY 2011 Payment
0016T	Thermotx choroid vasc lesion	N	CH	D5		
0017T	Photocoagulat macular drusen	N	CH	D5		

(continued)

TABLE 7-3 *(continued)*

HCPCS Code	Short Descriptor	Subject To Multiple Procedure Discounting	Final CY 2011 Comment Indicator	Final CY 2011 Payment Indicator	Final CY 2011 Payment Weight	Final CY 2011 Payment
0099T*	Implant corneal ring	Y		R2	16.538	$693.59
0100T	Prosth retina receive&gen	Y		G2	37.8357	$1,586.79
0101T	Extracorp shockwv tx hi enrg	Y		G2	29.7869	$1,249.23
0102T	Extracorp shockwv tx anesth	Y		G2	29.7869	$1,249.23
0123T	Scleral fistulization	Y		G2	22.5545	$945.91
0124T*	Conjunctival drug placement	Y		R2	2.3538	$98.72
0176T	Aqu canal dilat w/o retent	N	CH	D5		
0177T	Aqu canal dilat w retent	N	CH	D5		
0186T	Suprachoroidal drug delivery	Y		G2	21.6452	$907.78
0190T	Place intraoc radiation src	Y		G2	21.6452	$907.78

Source: www.cms.gov/center/asc.asp.

TABLE 7-4 *Example of ASC Fee Schedule for Covered Ancillary Services*

HCPCS Code	Short Descriptor	April 2011 Payment Indicator	April 2011 Payment Weight	April 2011 Payment
0042T	Ct perfusion w/contrast cbf	N1		
0073T	Delivery comp imrt	Z2	5.8777	$246.50
0126T	Chd risk imt study	N1		
0159T	Cad breast mri	N1		
0174T	Cad cxr with interp	N1		
0175T	Cad cxr remote	N1		
0182T	Hdr elect brachytherapy	Z2	9.3901	$393.81
0185T	Comptr probability analysis	N1		
70010	Contrast x-ray of brain	N1		
70015	Contrast x-ray of brain	N1		
70030	X-ray eye for foreign body	Z3		$20.05
70100	X-ray exam of jaw	Z3		$23.78
70110	X-ray exam of jaw	Z2	0.6041	$25.34
70120	X-ray exam of mastoids	Z2	0.6041	$25.34
70130	X-ray exam of mastoids	Z2	0.6041	$25.34
70134	X-ray exam of middle ear	Z3		$29.56
70140	X-ray exam of facial bones	Z3		$20.39
70150	X-ray exam of facial bones	Z2	0.6041	$25.34
70160	X-ray exam of nasal bones	Z3		$24.46

(continued)

TABLE 7-4 *(continued)*

HCPCS Code	Short Descriptor	April 2011 Payment Indicator	April 2011 Payment Weight	April 2011 Payment
70170	X-ray exam of tear duct	N1		
70190	X-ray exam of eye sockets	Z3		$25.14
70200	X-ray exam of eye sockets	Z2	0.6041	$25.34
70210	X-ray exam of sinuses	Z3		$22.08
70220	X-ray exam of sinuses	Z2	0.6041	$25.34
70240	X-ray exam pituitary saddle	Z3		$20.05
70250	X-ray exam of skull	Z3		$24.80
70260	X-ray exam of skull	Z3		$30.58
70300	X-ray exam of teeth	Z3		$8.49
70310	X-ray exam of teeth	Z2	0.4089	$17.15
70320	Full mouth x-ray of teeth	Z2	0.4089	$17.15
70328	X-ray exam of jaw joint	Z3		$21.74

Source: www.cms.gov/ASCPayment/.

CMS publishes a listing of covered ASC procedures each year,[2] which includes applicable codes and payment indicator information for each ASC procedure and/or service.

Clinical Laboratory Services

This section will briefly cover clinical laboratory services. Although these services can be performed in a physician's office, freestanding center, hospital, or other facility, outpatient clinical laboratory services are paid based on the clinical lab fee schedule. So, even if performed in a physician's office, the clinical lab fee schedule would be used rather than the physician fee schedule (see Chapter 5). If performed in an outpatient hospital setting, the clinical lab fee schedule would be used instead of the APC (see Chapter 6). Figure 7-2 is a snapshot of the clinical lab fee schedule.

The lesser of the billed amount of the local fee for a geographic area or national limit will be paid. Each year, fees are updated for inflation based on the percent change in the Consumer Price Index. Copayments and deductibles do not apply to services paid under the Medicare clinical laboratory fee schedule; thus the patient cannot be billed for a copayment or a deductible for clinical lab services.

Note

Critical access hospitals (see below) are paid for outpatient laboratory tests on a reasonable cost basis, instead of by the fee schedule.

Critical Access Hospitals (CAHs)

Approximately 20% of the United States' population lives where health care is sparse or absent. Medicare allows a state to establish a rural hospital flexibility program.

A hospital must meet the following criteria to be designated a critical access hospital (CAH):

- Be located in a state that has established a State Flex Program;

FIGURE 7-2 *Snapshot of Clinical Lab Fee Schedule*

					MS	AR	LA	IN
		National	Mid		00512	00520	00528	00630
HCPC	Modifier	Limit	Point	Floor	Loc 00	Loc 00	Loc 00	Loc 00
80047		11.91	16.09	0	$11.91	$11.91	$11.91	$8.99
80047	QW	11.91	16.09	0	$11.91	$11.91	$11.91	$8.99
80048		11.91	16.09	0	$11.91	$11.91	$11.91	$8.99
80048	QW	11.91	16.09	0	$11.91	$11.91	$11.91	$8.99
80051		9.87	13.34	0	$9.87	$9.87	$9.71	$8.99
80051	QW	9.87	13.34	0	$9.87	$9.87	$9.71	$8.99
80053		14.87	20.1	0	$14.87	$14.87	$14.87	$14.65
80053	QW	14.87	20.1	0	$14.87	$14.87	$14.87	$14.65
80061		0	0	0	$18.85	$17.89	$16.82	$18.85
80061	QW	0	0	0	$18.85	$17.89	$16.82	$18.85
80069		12.22	16.51	0	$12.22	$12.22	$12.22	$12.22
80069	QW	12.22	16.51	0	$12.22	$12.22	$12.22	$12.22
80074		0	0	0	$57.92	$67.01	$67.01	$61.51
80076		11.49	15.53	0	$11.49	$11.49	$11.49	$8.99
80100		20.47	27.66	0	$20.47	$20.47	$20.47	$20.47
80102		18.64	25.19	0	$18.64	$18.64	$17.46	$18.64

Source: www.cms.gov/ClinicalLabFeeSched/01_overview.asp.

- Be located in a rural area or be treated as rural (there are some provisions allowing qualified hospitals in urban areas to be treated as rural);
- Have 24-hour emergency care services;
- Have 25 or fewer inpatient beds that can be used for either inpatient or swing bed services. Note that CAHs may also operate a distinct rehabilitation or psychiatric unit, each with up to 10 beds;
- Have an average annual length of stay of 96 hours or less; and
- Be located either more than 35 miles from the nearest hospital or CAH or more than 15 miles in areas with mountainous terrain or only secondary roads.

Medicare pays CAHs for most inpatient and outpatient services primarily on the basis of reasonable cost. CAHs are not subject to the Inpatient Prospective Payment System (IPPS) or to the OPPS nor are they subject to the three-day window for bundling outpatient care into inpatient payment. However, the same deductible and coinsurance rules that are applicable to hospital services also apply to CAHs.

Again, inpatient CAH services are paid on the basis of reasonable cost. There are two methods of outpatient CAH payment under Medicare: (1) Method I: standard or default payment in which professional fees are paid under Part B Medicare professional services benefits; and (2) Method II: elective payment in which a hospital is paid for the facility and the professional fee services (through an agreement with the physicians and/or nonphysician providers not to bill separately). Table 7-5 illustrates the differences between these two methods.

TABLE 7-5 *CAH Payment Methods I and II*

Method I—Standard	Method II—Elective
Facility Payment: 80% of 101% of the outpatient reasonable costs or 101% of the outpatient reasonable costs less the deductible and coinsurance	Facility Payment: 80% of 101% of the outpatient reasonable costs or 101% of the outpatient reasonable costs less the deductible and coinsurance
Professional Services Payment: billed separately and paid under Part B benefits based on the Medicare Physician Fee Schedule	Professional Services Payment: billed by the hospital and paid based on 115% of the Medicare Physician Fee Schedule

Durable Medical Equipment and/or Prosthetic and Orthotic Suppliers

Durable medical equipment (DME) is covered under Part B and is equipment that:

- can withstand repeated use;
- is primarily and customarily used for a medical purpose;
- generally is not useful in the absence of an illness or injury; and
- is appropriate for use in the home.

A durable medical equipment and/or prosthetic and orthotic supplies (DMEPOS) supplier must meet certain requirements and enroll as a supplier of DMEPOS in order to bill Medicare. Separate payment is restricted to items not included in a prospective payment system (PPS) rate. For example, Medicare payments for DME, prosthetic and/or orthotic devices and/or supplies (POS) and oxygen used during a Part A covered inpatient stay in a hospital or skilled nursing facility (SNF) are all included in the Inpatient Prospective Payment System (IPPS) and are not separately billable. Claims for implanted DME, implanted prosthetic devices, replacement parts, accessories, and supplies for the implanted DME must be billed to the local MACs and not the DME MAC.

DMEPOS items use the HCPCS codes to describe these services. See Chapter 9 on HCPCS coding.

Parenteral and enteral nutrition, and related accessories and supplies, are covered under the Medicare program as a prosthetic device. All parenteral and enteral nutrition (PEN) services furnished under Part B are billed to the DME MAC. If a provider provides PEN items under Part B, the provider must qualify for and receive a supplier number and bill as a supplier.

Prosthetic devices (other than dental) are covered under Part B and defined as devices that replace all or part of an internal body organ or replace all or part of the function of a permanently inoperative or malfunctioning internal body organ.

Payment

Medicare Part B pays for DME and for prosthetic and orthotic devices using a fee schedule. Payment is limited to whichever is lower: the actual charge for the equipment or the fee schedule amount for the supply. See Figure 7-3 for an excerpt from the DMEPOS fee schedule.

Note that on the fee schedule, the payment is based on the HCPCS codes used, which is why accuracy in coding is very important.

Table 7-6 lists all the DMEPOS payment classes and their definitions.

FIGURE 7-3 *DMEPOS Fee Schedule Excerpt*

Durable Medical Equipment,										
Prosthetics, Orthotics, and Supplies										
(DMEPOS)										
2011 Fee Schedule										
HCPCS	**Mod**	**Mod2**	**JURIS**	**CATG**	**Ceiling**	**Floor**	**AL**	**AR**	**AZ**	**CA**
A4216			D	OS	$0.47	$0.40	$0.45	$0.47	$0.46	$0.47
A4217			D	SU	$3.29	$2.80	$2.80	$3.29	$3.29	$2.80
A4217	AU		D	OS	$3.29	$2.80	$2.80	$3.29	$3.29	$2.80
A1221			D	SU	$23.75	$20.19	$23.75	$23.75	$23.35	$23.35
A2222			D	SU	$49.02	$41.67	$49.02	$49.02	$46.33	$46.33
A4233	NU		D	IN	$0.84	$0.71	$0.84	$0.84	$0.84	$0.84
A4233	NU	KL	D	IN	$0.72	$0.61	$0.72	$0.72	$0.72	$0.72
A4234	NU		D	IN	$3.81	$3.24	$3.81	$3.81	$3.81	$3.81
A4234	NU	KL	D	IN	$3.29	$2.80	$3.29	$3.29	$3.29	$3.29
A4235	NU		D	IN	$2.46	$2.09	$2.46	$2.46	$2.46	$2.46
A4235	NU	KL	D	IN	$2.12	$1.80	$2.12	$2.12	$2.12	$2.12
A4236	NU		D	IN	$1.76	$1.50	$1.76	$1.76	$1.76	$1.76
A4236	NU	KL	D	IN	$1.52	$1.29	$1.52	$1.52	$1.52	$1.52
A4253	NU		D	IN	$0.00	$0.00	$38.75	$38.75	$37.94	$38.75
A4253	NU	KL	D	IN	$0.00	$0.00	$33.40	$33.40	$32.70	$33.40
A4255			D	SU	$4.32	$3.67	$4.32	$4.32	$4.32	$4.32
A4256			D	SU	$12.00	$10.20	$12.00	$10.20	$10.20	$10.20
A4256	KL		D	SU	$10.34	$8.79	$10.34	$8.79	$8.79	$8.79
A4257			D	SU	$13.38	$11.37	$13.38	$13.38	$13.38	$13.38

Source: www.cms.gov/DMEPOSFeeSched/01_overview.asp.

TABLE 7-6 *DMEPOS Payment Classes*

Payment Class	Definition
IN	DME: Inexpensive/routinely purchased Payment is made for rentals or lump-sum purchases; however the total payment cannot exceed the actual charge or the fee schedule amount for purchase (with the exception of TENS).
FS	DME: Frequency Service Payment is made on rental basis until based on the fee schedule until medical necessity ends.
CR	DME: Capped Rental Payment is made a monthly rental basis not to exceed a period of continuous use of 15 months with an option to purchase in month ten.
OX	OXY: Oxygen and Oxygen Equipment Payment is made on a monthly fee schedule amount per patient.
OS	P/O: Ostomy, Tracheostomy and Urologicals Payment is made on the fee schedule amounts for prosthetic and orthotic devices on a lump-sum purchase basis.
S/D	S/D: Surgical Dressings Payment is made by fee schedule except: • Those applied incident to a physician's professional services; • Those furnished by an HHA; and

(continued)

TABLE 7-6 *(continued)*

Payment Class	Definition
	• Those applied while a patient is being treated in an outpatient hospital department.
P/O	P/O: Prosthetics and Orthotics Payment is made on the fee schedule amounts for prosthetic and orthotic devices on a lump-sum purchase basis.
SU	DME: Supplies
TE	DME: TENS

Source: www.cms.gov/.

Certain Customized Items

Items that require custom fabrication are unsuitable for grouping together for profiling purposes, and therefore, there are no fee schedules established. Contractors usually make lump-sum payments based on individual consideration.

Payment for Parenteral and Enteral Nutrition

Payment for parenteral and enteral nutrition (PEN) is made in a lump-sum for nutrients/supplies purchased and on a monthly basis for equipment that is rented.

Federally Qualified Health Centers and Rural Health Clinics

Rural health clinics (RHCs) are clinics that are located in areas that are designated both by the Bureau of the Census as rural and by the Secretary of Department of Health and Human Services (DHHS) as medically underserved. Federally Qualified Health Center (FQHC) services are services similar to those provided in rural health clinics (RHCs) but include preventive primary services.

Medicare Payments

Payment to independent RHCs and FQHCs for covered services is made by means of an all-inclusive rate for each visit. This rate includes covered services provided by an RHC/FQHC physician, physician assistant, nurse practitioner, clinical nurse midwife, clinical psychologist, clinical social worker, or visiting nurse and related services and supplies. This "visit rate" is calculated from data submitted by the RHC/FQHC. RHCs and FQHCs must submit (via the cost report) statistical visit data and other information necessary to enable Medicare to calculate a cost per visit and apply productivity standards. Providers must identify all incurred costs of furnishing covered services. These costs and the submitted budget will be used to estimate allowable costs to be incurred by the RHC/FQHC during the period as well as the number of visits expected during the reporting period. Then Medicare establishes an interim payment rate calculated by dividing the total allowable costs by the number of total visits for RHC/FQHC services. The rate is paid, subject to the Medicare deductible and coinsurance requirements, for each covered visit with a Medicare beneficiary. No deductible applies to FQHCs.

At the end of the reporting period, RHCs/FQHCs submit a report of actual allowable costs and actual visits for RHC/FQHC services for the reporting period. After reviewing the report, the fiscal intermediary (FI) divides actual allowable costs by the number of actual visits to determine a final rate for the period. At the end of the reporting period, the FI determines the total payment due and the amount necessary to reconcile payments made during the period with the total payment due.

The RHCs and FQHCs bill on the UB-04/CMS 1450 form, using type of bill (TOB) 71x for RHCs and 73x/77x for FQHCs.

What's Next?

Medicare is planning on implementing an FQHC prospective payment system (PPS) in 2014. Beginning with dates of service on or after January 1, 2011, services billed on a 77x type of bill should be listed with the appropriate revenue code and HCPCS code for each line.

Home Health Agencies

Medicare pays home health agencies (HHAs) with a prospective payment system (HH-PPS) based on a predetermined base payment. The payment is adjusted for the health condition and care needs of the patient as well as geographic differences in wages for HHAs across the country.

> **Note**
>
> The adjustment for the health condition, or clinical characteristics, and service needs of the patient is referred to as the case-mix adjustment.

HH-PPS pays for each 60-day episode of care per patient. If a patient is still eligible for care after the end of the first episode, a second episode can begin, and there are no limits to the number of episodes unless a patient becomes ineligible for home health benefits.

While payment for each episode is adjusted to reflect the patient's health needs, there is also a special outlier provision to provide additional payment for patients with expensive care requirements.

HH-PPS Payment

Payment per 60-day episode. The HHA receives half of the estimated base payment for the full 60 days as soon as Medicare receives the initial claim, which is adjusted based on the case-mix. Case-mix is defined as specific sets of patient characteristics during the specific service timeframe. The HHA receives the second half of the payment at the end of the 60-day episode unless an adjustment is applicable.

Case-mix adjustment. A physician prescribes a home health plan, and then, at the beginning of the episode of care, the HHA assesses the patient's condition and needs relative to skilled nursing care, therapy, medical social services, and home health aide services. Each subsequent episode of care also requires an assessment. A nurse or therapist from the HHA uses the Outcome and Assessment Information Set (OASIS) instrument to assess the patient's condition. OASIS items describing the patient's condition and expected therapy needs are used to determine the case-mix adjustment to the standard payment rate.

The HHA must bill for all home health services, including:

- nursing and therapy services;
- routine and nonroutine medical supplies; and
- home health aide and medical social services.

Home Health Care Coding

Health Insurance Prospective Payment System (HIPPS) codes are used in billing home health care using UB-04 forms (see Chapter 3), instead of HCPCS coding. HIPPS codes are not covered in detail in this book, but the following provides fundamental information such as a defintion of and basic insight into these codes.

For HH-PPS, a five-digit HIPPS code is billed. HIPPS is defined as rate codes that "represent specific sets of patient characteristics (or case-mix groups) on which payment determinations are made under several prospective payment systems. Case-mix groups are developed based on research into utilization patterns among various provider types. For the payment systems that use HIPPS codes, clinical assessment data is the basic input used to determine which case-mix group applies to a particular patient. A standard patient assessment instrument is interpreted by case-mix grouping software algorithms, which assign the case mix group. For payment purposes, at least one HIPPS code is defined to represent each case-mix group. These HIPPS codes are reported on claims to insurers. Institutional providers use HIPPS codes on claims in association with special revenue codes. One revenue code is defined for each prospective payment system that requires HIPPS codes. HIPPS codes are placed in data element SV202 on the electronic 837 institutional claims transaction or in Form Locator (FL) 44 ('HCPCS/rate') on a paper UB-04 claims form. The associated revenue code is placed in data element SV201 or in FL 42. In certain circumstances, multiple HIPPS codes may appear on separate lines of a single claim."[3]

Table 7-7 demonstrates what various HIPPS codes represent for HH-PPS.

TABLE 7-7 *Examples of HIPPS Coding for HH-PPS*

HIPPS Code	Code Effective From Date	Code Effective Through Date	Payment System Indicator	Description
1AFKS	1/1/2008		HHA	Early Episode, 0-13 therapies, Clinical Severity Level 1, Functional Severity Level 1, Service Severity Level 1, Supply Severity Level 1, supplies provided
1AFKT	1/1/2008		HHA	Early Episode, 0-13 therapies, Clinical Severity Level 1, Functional Severity Level 1, Service Severity Level 1, Supply Severity Level 2, supplies provided
1AFKU	1/1/2008		HHA	Early Episode, 0-13 therapies, Clinical Severity Level 1, Functional Severity Level 1, Service Severity Level 1, Supply Severity Level 3, supplies provided
1AFKV	1/1/2008		HHA	Early Episode, 0-13 therapies, Clinical Severity Level 1, Functional Severity Level 1, Service Severity Level 1, Supply Severity Level 4, supplies provided
1AFKW	1/1/2008		HHA	Early Episode, 0-13 therapies, Clinical Severity Level 1, Functional Severity Level 1, Service Severity Level 1, Supply Severity Level 5, supplies provided
1AFKX	1/1/2008		HHA	Early Episode, 0-13 therapies, Clinical Severity Level 1, Functional Severity Level 1, Service Severity Level 1, Supply Severity Level 6, supplies provided
1AFK1	1/1/2008		HHA	Early Episode, 0-13 therapies, Clinical Severity Level 1, Functional Severity Level 1, Service Severity Level 1, Supply Severity Level 1, supplies not provided
1AFK2	1/1/2008		HHA	Early Episode, 0-13 therapies, Clinical Severity Level 1, Functional Severity Level 1, Service Severity Level 1, Supply Severity Level 2, supplies not provided

(continued)

TABLE 7-7 *(continued)*

HIPPS Code	Code Effective From Date	Code Effective Through Date	Payment System Indicator	Description
1AFK3	1/1/2008		HHA	Early Episode, 0-13 therapies, Clinical Severity Level 1, Functional Severity Level 1, Service Severity Level 1, Supply Severity Level 3, supplies not provided
1AFK4	1/1/2008		HHA	Early Episode, 0-13 therapies, Clinical Severity Level 1, Functional Severity Level 1, Service Severity Level 1, Supply Severity Level 4, supplies not provided
1AFK5	1/1/2008		HHA	Early Episode, 0-13 therapies, Clinical Severity Level 1, Functional Severity Level 1, Service Severity Level 1, Supply Severity Level 5, supplies not provided
1AFK6	1/1/2008		HHA	Early Episode, 0-13 therapies, Clinical Severity Level 1, Functional Severity Level 1, Service Severity Level 1, Supply Severity Level 6, supplies not provided
1AFLS	1/1/2008		HHA	Early Episode, 0-13 therapies, Clinical Severity Level 1, Functional Severity Level 1, Service Severity Level 2, Supply Severity Level 1, supplies provided
1AFLT	1/1/2008		HHA	Early Episode, 0-13 therapies, Clinical Severity Level 1, Functional Severity Level 1, Service Severity Level 2, Supply Severity Level 2, supplies provided
1AFLU	1/1/2008		HHA	Early Episode, 0-13 therapies, Clinical Severity Level 1, Functional Severity Level 1, Service Severity Level 2, Supply Severity Level 3, supplies provided
1AFLV	1/1/2008		HHA	Early Episode, 0-13 therapies, Clinical Severity Level 1, Functional Severity Level 1, Service Severity Level 2, Supply Severity Level 4, supplies provided
1AFLW	1/1/2008		HHA	Early Episode, 0-13 therapies, Clinical Severity Level 1, Functional Severity Level 1, Service Severity Level 2, Supply Severity Level 5, supplies provided

Source: www.cms.gov/ProspMedicareFeeSvcPmtGen/02_HIPPSCodes.asp.

An example of a HIPPS code is 1AFK1. This code represents the first episode, 0-13 therapy visits, with the lowest scores in the clinical, functional, and service domains (AFK), and the lowest supply severity level, and it indicates that nonroutine supplies were not provided.

As indicated by the example, HIPPS codes are alphanumeric codes of five digits. Certain characters of the code indicate the case-mix group, while other characters provide additional information. The additional information varies among HIPPS codes and pertains to different payment systems, but it

TABLE 7-8 *HIPPS Fifth Character Supplies Options*

Severity Level	Supplies Provided	Supplies Not Provided
Severity Level 1	S	1
Severity Level 2	T	2
Severity Level 3	U	3
Severity Level 4	V	4
Severity Level 5	W	5
Severity Level 6	X	6

often provides information about the clinical assessment, which is used for the code selection. Which characters of the code carry the information of the case-mix group may also vary by payment systems.[3] To simplify, the following reflects what each character of the HIPPS code illustrates:

- The first character in the HIPPS code is a numeric value that represents the grouping step (which episode and how many visits).
- The second, third, and fourth characters of the code remain a one-to-one crosswalk to the three domains of the Home Health Resource Groups (HHRGs), which is captured from the OASIS assessment and projected therapy. HHRG and OASIS guidelines are available from the CMS Web site.[4]
- The fifth character indicates a severity group for nonroutine supplies. There are six available options. Table 7-8 shows the code options for supplies.

Hospice

Hospice care is a Part A elected benefit for patients who meet all of the following requirements:

- Eligible for Part A;
- Certified as having a terminal illness with a prognosis of six months or less;
- Receive care from a Medicare-approved hospice program; and
- Sign a statement indicating that the patient elects the hospice benefit and waives all other rights to Medicare payments for services for the terminal illness and related conditions.*

Hospice includes medical services and items that are provided to a terminally ill individual. In order to be paid by Medicare, there must be a certification of the terminal illness by the medical director of the hospice no later than two calendar days after hospice care begins. Written certification must include:

- A statement certifying the patient as terminally ill with a prognosis of six months or fewer;
- The specific clinical findings/documentation supporting the short life expectancy;
- A brief narrative by the physician explaining the clinical findings; and
- Dated signature of the physician.

Hospice Coverage

Covered hospice services include:

- Nursing care provided by or supervised by a registered nurse;
- Physical, occupational, or speech-language pathology therapy;
- Medical social services under a physician's direction (ie, home health aide services and homemaker services);

* Services for care unrelated to hospice may be paid additionally.

TABLE 7-9 *Example of Hospice Payment*

Revenue Code	Description	Rate	Wage-Adjusted Component	Nonweighted Amount
651	Routine Home Care	$146.63	$100.75	$45.88
652	Continuous Home Care Full Rate = 24 Hours of Care $35.66 = Hourly Rate	$855.84	$588.01	$267.78
655	Inpatient Respite Care	$151.67	$82.10	$69.57
656	General Inpatient Care	$652.27	$417.52	$234.75

- Medical supplies, drugs and biologicals, and use of medical appliances;
- Physicians' services;
- Short-term inpatient care;
- Grief and loss counseling;
- Spiritual counseling;
- Dietary counseling; and
- Other items/services specified in the plan and for which payment may be made.

Hospice care is covered for two periods of 90 days and an unlimited number of subsequent 60-day periods; however, the hospice physician or nonphysician must have a face-to-face encounter with patients who reach the end of the second 90-day recertification (a total of 180 days), and at each recertification thereafter, to determine continued eligibility for the hospice benefit.

Hospice Payments

Medicare pays hospice agencies a daily rate for each day of approved hospice. The daily payments are regardless of the services furnished on any one day as they are intended to cover costs that the hospice incurs in furnishing services in the plan of care. Payments are made based on the level of care required to meet beneficiary and family needs (eg, routine home care, continuous home care, inpatient respite care, and general inpatient care).

The daily hospice payment rates are adjusted to account for differences in wage rates among markets. Hospice services are billed using the UB-04 form (see Chapter 3), and payment is determined by the revenue code and for some services HCPCS coding.

Table 7-9 shows an example of the hospice payment rates.

Inpatient Psychiatric Facility

Inpatient psychiatric hospital services are paid using a prospective payment system (IPF-PPS). The following are requirements that must be met for payment:

- There must be active psychiatric treatment rendered to the patient that is reasonably expected to improve the patient's health;
- A physician must certify at admission (or soon after) that the patient requires daily, active inpatient treatment; and
- A physician must recertify that as of the 12th day of hospitalization and in subsequent recertifications.

Patients treated for psychiatric conditions in specialty facilities are covered for 90 days of care per illness (60-day lifetime reserve) and for 190 days in freestanding psychiatric hospitals.

Payments

Under the IPF-PPS, per diem rates are determined by:

- geographic factors (hospital wage indices);
- patient characteristics (MS-DRG classification, age, comorbidities, and length of stay); and
- facility characteristics (rural facilities, teaching hospitals).

Additional payments may be provided for special circumstances such as:

- facilities that have a qualifying emergency department;
- number of electroconvulsive therapy (ECT) treatments furnished; and
- outlier payments for cases that have extraordinarily high costs.

Partial Hospitalization

Partial hospitalization is an intensive outpatient program of psychiatric services provided to patients as an alternative to inpatient psychiatric care for beneficiaries who have an acute mental illness. Under OPPS, a partial hospitalization program (PHP) may be provided by a hospital to its outpatients or by a Medicare-certified community mental health center. Because a day of care is the unit that defines the structure and scheduling of partial hospitalization services, CMS established a per-diem payment method for the PHP APC. Exclusions from OPPS are different from and more limited than exclusions from the inpatient PPS. Thus, hospitals or distinct parts of hospitals (such as a psychiatric hospital) that are excluded from the inpatient PPS are included in the OPPS, to the extent that the hospital or distinct part of the hospital (eg, psychiatric hospital) furnishes outpatient services.

Inpatient Rehabilitation Facility

Inpatient rehabilitation facility (IRF) services are paid based on a per-discharge PPS. The IRF-PPS payment is based on the IRF Patient Assessment Instrument (PAI) (see Figure 7-4), which contains clinical and demographic information that classifies patients into distinct groups based on clinical characteristics and expected resource needs.

Separate payments are calculated for each group, including the application of case and facility level adjustments. The IRF-PPS includes the following elements:

Per diem rates

- Patient case-mix (resource intensity associated with the patient's clinical condition) as defined through the following:
  - Cases are grouped on the primary condition (ICD-9-CM code) for which the patient was admitted to the IRF;
  - Cases are further grouped into case-mix groups (CMGs), which include patients who are similar in their functional motor and cognitive scores and age; and
  - Cases are grouped into one of four tiers within each CMG, according to patients' comorbidities (ICD-9-CM codes that are secondary to the principal diagnosis).
- Additional adjustments are made for interrupted stays, short stays, transfers, and high-cost outlier cases.

Provider characteristics also impact the rates through geographic wage indices, teaching status, etc.

The following list includes the medical conditions that are approved for IRF:

- Stroke;
- Spinal cord injury;
- Congenital deformity;
- Amputation;
- Major multiple trauma;
- Fracture of femur (hip fracture);

FIGURE 7-4 *CMS Patient Assessment Instrument (PAI)*

DEPARTMENT OF HEALTH AND HUMAN SERVICES
CENTERS FOR MEDICARE & MEDICAID SERVICES

Form Approved
OMB No. 0938-0842

INPATIENT REHABILITATION FACILITY – PATIENT ASSESSMENT INSTRUMENT

Identification Information*

1. Facility Information
   A. Facility Name ________
   B. Facility Medicare Provider Number ________
2. Patient Medicare Number ________
3. Patient Medicaid Number ________
4. Patient First Name ________

5A. Patient Last Name ________

5B. Patient Identification Number ________

6. Birth Date ___/___/___ MM / DD / YYYY
7. Social Security Number ________
8. Gender (*1 - Male; 2 - Female*) ________
9. Race/Ethnicity (*Check all that apply*)
   American Indian or Alaska Native A. ________
   Asian B. ________
   Black or African American C. ________
   Hispanic or Latino D. ________
   Native Hawaiian or Other Pacific Islander E. ________
   White F. ________
10. Marital Status ________
    (*1 - Never Married; 2 - Married; 3 - Widowed; 4 - Separated; 5 - Divorced*)
11. Zip Code of Patient's Pre-Hospital Residence ________

Admission Information*

12. Admission Date ___/___/___ MM / DD / YYYY
13. Assessment Reference Date ___/___/___ MM / DD / YYYY
14. Admission Class ________
    (*1 - Initial Rehab; 2 - Evaluation; 3 - Readmission; 4 - Unplanned Discharge; 5 - Continuing Rehabilitation*)
15. Admit From ________
    (*01 - Home; 02 - Board & Care; 03 - Transitional Living; 04 - Intermediate Care; 05 - Skilled Nursing Facility; 06 - Acute Unit of Own Facility; 07 - Acute Unit of Another Facility; 08 - Chronic Hospital; 09 - Rehabilitation Facility; 10 - Other; 12 - Alternate Level of Care Unit; 13 – Subacute Setting; 14 - Assisted Living Residence*)
16. Pre-Hospital Living Setting ________
    (*Use codes from item 15 above*)
17. Pre-Hospital Living With ________
    (*Code only if item 16 is 01 - Home; Code using 1 - Alone; 2 - Family/Relatives; 3 - Friends; 4 - Attendant; 5 - Other*)
18. Pre-Hospital Vocational Category ________
    (*1 - Employed; 2 - Sheltered; 3 - Student; 4 - Homemaker; 5 - Not Working; 6 - Retired for Age; 7 - Retired for Disability*)
19. Pre-Hospital Vocational Effort ________
    (*Code only if item 18 is coded 1 - 4; Code using 1 - Full-time; 2 - Part-time; 3 - Adjusted Workload*)

Payer Information*

20. Payment Source
    A. Primary Source ________
    B. Secondary Source ________
    (*01 - Blue Cross; 02 - Medicare non-MCO; 03 - Medicaid non-MCO; 04 - Commercial Insurance; 05 - MCO HMO; 06 - Workers' Compensation; 07 - Crippled Children's Services; 08 – Developmental Disabilities Services; 09 - State Vocational Rehabilitation; 10 - Private Pay; 11 - Employee Courtesy; 12 - Unreimbursed; 13 - CHAMPUS; 14 - Other; 15 - None; 16 – No-Fault Auto Insurance; 51 – Medicare MCO; 52 - Medicaid MCO*)

Medical Information*

21. Impairment Group ________ Admission ________ Discharge
    Condition requiring admission to rehabilitation; code according to Appendix A, attached.
22. Etiologic Diagnosis ________
    (*Use an ICD-9-CM code to indicate the etiologic problem that led to the condition for which the patient is receiving rehabilitation*)
23. Date of Onset of Impairment ___/___/___ MM / DD / YYYY
24. Comorbid Conditions; Use ICD-9-CM codes to enter up to ten medical conditions
    A. ________ B. ________
    C. ________ D. ________
    E. ________ F. ________
    G. ________ H. ________
    I. ________ J. ________

Medical Needs

25. Is patient comatose at admission? ________ 0 - No, 1 - Yes
26. Is patient delirious at admission? ________ 0 - No, 1 - Yes
27. Swallowing Status ________ Admission ________ Discharge
    3 - Regular Food: solids and liquids swallowed safely without supervision or modified food consistency
    2 - Modified Food Consistency/ Supervision: subject requires modified food consistency and/or needs supervision for safety
    1 - Tube /Parenteral Feeding: tube / parenteral feeding used wholly or partially as a means of sustenance
28. Clinical signs of dehydration ________ Admission ________ Discharge
    (Code 0 – No; 1 – Yes) e.g., *evidence of oliguria, dry skin, orthostatic hypotension, somnolence, agitation*

(continued)

FIGURE 7-4 *(continued)*

DEPARTMENT OF HEALTH AND HUMAN SERVICES
CENTERS FOR MEDICARE & MEDICAID SERVICES

INPATIENT REHABILITATION FACILITY – PATIENT ASSESSMENT INSTRUMENT

Function Modifiers*

Complete the following specific functional items prior to scoring the FIM™ Instrument:

	ADMISSION	DISCHARGE
29. Bladder Level of Assistance (Score using FIM Levels 1 - 7)	☐	☐
30. Bladder Frequency of Accidents (Score as below)	☐	☐

7 - No accidents
6 - No accidents; uses device such as a catheter
5 - One accident in the past 7 days
4 - Two accidents in the past 7 days
3 - Three accidents in the past 7 days
2 - Four accidents in the past 7 days
1 - Five or more accidents in the past 7 days

Enter in Item 39G (Bladder) the lower (more dependent) score from Items 29 and 30 above.

	ADMISSION	DISCHARGE
31. Bowel Level of Assistance (Score using FIM Levels 1 - 7)	☐	☐
32. Bowel Frequency of Accidents (Score as below)	☐	☐

7 - No accidents
6 - No accidents; uses device such as an ostomy
5 - One accident in the past 7 days
4 - Two accidents in the past 7 days
3 - Three accidents in the past 7 days
2 - Four accidents in the past 7 days
1 - Five or more accidents in the past 7 days

Enter in Item 39H (Bowel) the lower (more dependent) score of Items 31 and 32 above.

	ADMISSION	DISCHARGE
33. Tub Transfer	☐	☐
34. Shower Transfer	☐	☐

(Score Items 33 and 34 using FIM Levels 1 - 7; use 0 if activity does not occur) *See training manual for scoring of Item 39K (Tub/Shower Transfer)*

	ADMISSION	DISCHARGE
35. Distance Walked	☐	☐
36. Distance Traveled in Wheelchair	☐	☐

(Code items 35 and 36 using: 3 - 150 feet; 2 - 50 to 149 feet; 1 - Less than 50 feet; 0 – activity does not occur)

	ADMISSION	DISCHARGE
37. Walk	☐	☐
38. Wheelchair	☐	☐

(Score Items 37 and 38 using FIM Levels 1 - 7; 0 if activity does not occur) See training manual for scoring of Item 39L (Walk/Wheelchair)

*The FIM data set, measurement scale and impairment codes incorporated or referenced herein are the property of U B Foundation Activities, Inc. ©1993, 2001 U B Foundation Activities, Inc. The FIM mark is owned by UBFA, Inc.

39. FIM™ Instrument*

	ADMISSION	DISCHARGE	GOAL
SELF-CARE			
A. Eating	☐	☐	☐
B. Grooming	☐	☐	☐
C. Bathing	☐	☐	☐
D. Dressing - Upper	☐	☐	☐
E. Dressing - Lower	☐	☐	☐
F. Toileting	☐	☐	☐
SPHINCTER CONTROL			
G. Bladder	☐	☐	☐
H. Bowel	☐	☐	☐
TRANSFERS			
I. Bed, Chair, Whlchair	☐	☐	☐
J. Toilet	☐	☐	☐
K. Tub, Shower	☐	☐	☐
LOCOMOTION (W - Walk; C - wheelChair; B - Both)			
L. Walk/Wheelchair	☐ ☐	☐ ☐	☐
M. Stairs	☐	☐	☐
COMMUNICATION (A - Auditory; V - Visual; B - Both)			
N. Comprehension	☐ ☐	☐ ☐	☐
O. Expression (V - Vocal; N - Nonvocal; B - Both)	☐ ☐	☐ ☐	☐
SOCIAL COGNITION			
P. Social Interaction	☐	☐	☐
Q. Problem Solving	☐	☐	☐
R. Memory	☐	☐	☐

FIM LEVELS

No Helper
7 Complete Independence (Timely, Safely)
6 Modified Independence (Device)

Helper - Modified Dependence
5 Supervision (Subject = 100%)
4 Minimal Assistance (Subject = 75% or more)
3 Moderate Assistance (Subject = 50% or more)

Helper - Complete Dependence
2 Maximal Assistance (Subject = 25% or more)
1 Total Assistance (Subject less than 25%)

0 Activity does not occur; Use this code only at admission

(continued)

FIGURE 7-4 *(continued)*

DEPARTMENT OF HEALTH AND HUMAN SERVICES
CENTERS FOR MEDICARE & MEDICAID SERVICES

INPATIENT REHABILITATION FACILITY – PATIENT ASSESSMENT INSTRUMENT

Discharge Information*

40. Discharge Date ______/______/______ MM / DD / YYYY

41. Patient discharged against medical advice? ______ *(0 - No, 1 -Yes)*

42. Program Interruption(s) ______ *(0 - No; 1 - Yes)*

43. Program Interruption Dates *(Code only if Item 42 is 1 - Yes)*

A. 1st Interruption Date [ ] MM / DD / YYYY — B. 1st Return Date [ ] MM / DD / YYYY

C. 2nd Interruption Date [ ] MM / DD / YYYY — D. 2nd Return Date [ ] MM / DD / YYYY

E. 3rd Interruption Date [ ] MM / DD / YYYY — F. 3rd Return Date [ ] MM / DD / YYYY

44A. Discharge to Living Setting ______
(01 - Home; 02 - Board and Care; 03 - Transitional Living; 04 - Intermediate Care; 05 - Skilled Nursing Facility; 06 - Acute Unit of Own Facility; 07 - Acute Unit of Another Facility; 08 - Chronic Hospital; 09 - Rehabilitation Facility; 10 - Other; 11 - Died; 12 - Alternate Level of Care Unit; 13 - Subacute Setting; 14 - Assisted Living Residence)

44B. Was patient discharged with Home Health Services? ______ *(0 - No; 1 - Yes)*
(Code only if Item 44A is 01 - Home, 02 - Board and Care, 03 - Transitional Living, or 14 - Assisted Living Residence)

45. Discharge to Living With ______
(Code only if Item 44A is 01 - Home; Code using 1 - Alone; 2 - Family / Relatives; 3 - Friends; 4 - Attendant; 5 - Other

46. Diagnosis for Interruption or Death ______
(Code using ICD-9-CM code)

47. Complications during rehabilitation stay
(Use ICD-9-CM codes to specify up to six conditions that began with this rehabilitation stay)

A. ______ B. ______
C. ______ D. ______
E. ______ F. ______

Quality Indicators

RESPIRATORY STATUS
(Score items 48 to 50 as 0 - No; 1 - Yes)

	Admission	Discharge
48. Shortness of breath with exertion	______	______
49. Shortness of breath at rest	______	______
50. Weak cough and difficulty clearing airway secretions	______	______

* The FIM data set, measurement scale and impairment codes incorporated or referenced herein are the property of U B Foundation Activities, Inc. ©1993, 2001 U B Foundation Activities, Inc. The FIM mark is owned bv UBFA, Inc.

Quality Indicators

PAIN

51. Rate the highest level of pain reported by the patient within the assessment period:
Admission: ______ Discharge: ______

(Score using the scale below; report whole numbers only)

0 1 2 3 4 5 6 7 8 9 10

No Pain (0) — *Moderate Pain* (5) — *Worst Possible Pain* (10)

Pressure Ulcers

52A. Highest current pressure ulcer stage
Admission ______ Discharge ______

(0 - No pressure ulcer; 1 - Any area of persistent skin redness (Stage 1); 2 - Partial loss of skin layers (Stage 2); 3 - Deep craters in the skin (Stage 3); 4 - Breaks in skin exposing muscle or bone (Stage 4); 5 - Not stageable (necrotic eschar predominant; no prior staging available)

52B. Number of current pressure ulcers
Admission ______ Discharge ______

PUSH Tool v. 3.0 ©

SELECT THE CURRENT LARGEST PRESSURE ULCER TO CODE THE FOLLOWING. Calculate three components (C through E) and code total score in F.

52C. Length multiplied by width (open wound surface area)
Admission ______ Discharge ______

(Score as 0 - 0 cm^2; 1 - < 0.3 cm^2; 2 - 0.3 to 0.6 cm^2; 3 - 0.7 to 1.0 cm^2; 4 - 1.1 to 2.0 cm^2; 5 - 2.1 to 3.0 cm^2; 6 - 3.1 to 4.0 cm^2; 7 - 4.1 to 8.0 cm^2; 8 - 8.1 to 12.0 cm^2; 9 - 12.1 to 24.0 cm^2; 10 - > 24 cm^2)

52D. Exudate amount
Admission ______ Discharge ______
0 - None; 1 - Light; 2 - Moderate; 3 - Heavy

52E. Tissue type
Admission ______ Discharge ______
0 - Closed/resurfaced: The wound is completely covered with epithelium (new skin); 1 - Epithelial tissue: For superficial ulcers, new pink or shiny tissue (skin) that grows in from the edges or as islands on the ulcer surface. 2 - Granulation tissue: Pink or beefy red tissue with a shiny, moist, granular appearance. 3- Slough: Yellow or white tissue that adheres to the ulcer bed in strings or thick clumps or is mucinous. 4 - Necrotic tissue (eschar): Black, brown, or tan tissue that adheres firmly to the wound bed or ulcer edges.

52F. TOTAL PUSH SCORE (Sum of above three items -- C, D and E)
Admission ______ Discharge ______

SAFETY

	Admission	Discharge
53. Balance problem *(0 - No; 1 - Yes) e.g., dizziness, vertigo, or light-headedness*	______	______
54. Total number of falls during the rehabilitation stay		______

Source: www.cms.gov/InpatientRehabFacPPS/04_IRFPAI.asp.

- Brain injury;
- Neurological disorders, including multiple sclerosis, motor neuron diseases, polyneuropathy, muscular dystrophy, and Parkinson's disease;
- Burns;
- Active, polyarticular rheumatoid arthritis, psoriatic arthritis, and seronegative arthropathies resulting in significant functional impairment of ambulation and other activities of daily living that have not improved after an aggressive and sustained course of outpatient therapy services;
- Systemic vasculidities with joint inflammation, resulting in significant functional impairment of ambulation and other activities of daily living that have not improved after an aggressive and sustained course of outpatient therapy services;
- Severe or advanced osteoarthritis involving two or more major weight-bearing joints with joint deformity and substantial loss of range of motion, atrophy of muscles surrounding the joint, and significant functional impairment of ambulation and other activities of daily living that have not improved after an aggressive and sustained course of outpatient therapy services; and
- Knee or hip joint replacement (specific requirements must be met).

Long-Term Care Hospital

Long-term care hospitals (LTCHs) treat patients with multiple comorbidities that require long-stay hospital-level care. For a hospital to be designated as a LTCH, Medicare requires that the hospital typically demonstrate that it has an average length of stay (ALOS) greater than 25 days for its Medicare patients. The LTCH-PPS uses Medicare severity long-term care diagnosis related groups (MS-LTC-DRGs) as a patient classification system. Each patient-stay is grouped into a single MS-LTC-DRG, which is based on the diagnoses (including secondary diagnoses), procedures performed, age, gender, and discharge status.

The facility receives payment based on the MS-LTC-DRG to which each patient's stay is grouped. Each MS-LTC-DRG has a relative weight that is multiplied by a payment rate (national rate adjusted for geographic wage variations) for the final payment.

Each bill from a LTCH must contain the complete diagnosis and procedure coding for each patient's complete stay (from admittance through discharge). Final PPS payment is based on the discharge bill.

Skilled Nursing Facility

Medicare Part A skilled nursing facility (SNF) services are paid through case-mix–adjusted per-diem prospective payment rates. The payment rates are payments in full subject to applicable coinsurance for all costs other than costs associated with operating approved educational activities.

SNF-PPS uses a PPS classification system based on resource utilization known as the resource utilization group (RUG) version. SNFs utilize information from the Minimum Data Set (MDS) and Resident Assessment Instrument (RAI) to classify residents into the RUG groups. The MDS is an assessment tool that contains a core set of screening, clinical, and functional status elements used in the assessment of residents. This process provides a comprehensive assessment of each resident's functional capabilities and helps nursing home staff identify health problems. The MDS includes evaluating the patient's cognitive status, communication/hearing patterns, physical functioning, structural problems, and disease diagnosis.

The RAI helps staff gather information on a resident's strengths and needs to be addressed in an individualized care plan. It also assists in evaluating goal achievement in order to revise care plans.

The RUG classification system utilizes patient characteristics and health status information (eg, diagnosis, ability to perform Activities of Daily Living [ADLs], and treatment received) to place the resident into a resource utilization group for payment purposes.

For Medicare billing purposes, there is a payment code associated with each RUG group. There are eight major classification groups:

- Rehabilitation Plus Extensive Services
- Rehabilitation
- Extensive Services
- Special Care
- Clinically Complex
- Impaired Cognition
- Behavior Only
- Physical Function Reduced

These groups are subdivided by the intensity of the resident's ADL needs and by the presence of depression.

SNF Payment: HIPPS Codes

A HIPPS code for SNF payment consists of a two-digit assessment indicator and a RUG code, which is outlined and explained below. SNF claims include:

- **Principal diagnosis code.** SNFs enter the ICD-9-CM code for the principal diagnosis in the appropriate item on a UB-04 claims form.
- **Other diagnosis codes required.** The SNF enters the full ICD-9-CM codes for up to eight additional conditions in the appropriate item on a UB-04 claims form. Medicare does not have any additional requirements regarding the reporting or sequence of the codes beyond those contained in the ICD-9-CM guidelines.
- **RUGs.** "Effective October 1, 2010, under the skilled nursing facility prospective payment system (SNF PPS), a case-mix adjusted payment for varying numbers of days of SNF care is made using one of 66 Resource Utilization Groups, Version IV (RUG-IV)."[3] (See Table 7-11.) On claims to Medicare and other payers, these RUG-IVs are represented as the first three characters of HIPPS codes. Valid values for these characters are as follows:
  - **Rehabilitation Plus Extensive Services:** RUX, RUL, RVX, RVL, RHX, RHL, RMX, RML, RLX
  - **Rehabilitation:** RUC, RUB, RUA, RVC, RVB, RVA, RHC, RHB, RHA, RMC, RMB, RMA, RLB, RLA
  - **Extensive Services:** SE3, SE2, SE1
  - **Special Care:** SSC, SSB, SSA
  - **Clinically Complex:** CC2, CC1, CB2, CB1, CA2, CA1
  - **Impaired Cognition:** IB2, IB1, IA2, IA1
  - **Behavior Problems:** BB2, BB1, BA2, BA1
  - **Reduced Physical Function:** PE2, PE1, PD2, PD1, PC2, PC1, PB2, PB1, PA2, PA1
  - **Default:** AAA
- **Assessment indicator.** "The fourth and fifth positions of the [HIPPS] code represent an assessment indicator [see Table 7-10], identifying the reason and timeframe for the completion of the MDS. These positions may be numeric or alphabetical."[3]

SNF Payments Under Part B

SNFs must include on the Part A bill all Medicare-covered services furnished to a resident during the course of a covered stay. There is a list of "excluded" services that can be billed separately under Part B. Services that may be billed outside the Part A SNF bill are:

- Physician and nonphysician provider services (eg, physician assistants, psychologists, nurse practitioners), including the professional component of diagnostic tests;
- Home dialysis supplies and equipment, self-care home dialysis support services, and institutional dialysis services and supplies;

(continued on page 118)

TABLE 7-10 *Assessment Indicators and Definitions*

Assessment Indicator	Definition
00	No assessment completed/default code
11	Medicare 5 day assessment (comprehensive) AND initial admission assessment
01	Medicare 5 day assessment (Full)
07	Medicare 14 day assessment (Full or comprehensive)
02	Medicare 30 day assessment (Full)
03	Medicare 60 day assessment (Full)
04	Medicare 90 day assessment (Full)
54	Quarterly review assessment-Medicare 90 day assessment (Full)
38	[7/98 def.] Significant Change in Status Assessment (SCSA), [10/98 def.] OMRA replacing 60-day Medicare required assessment
08	Other Medicare Required Assessment (OMRA)
41	Significant Correction of Prior Full Assessment/Medicare 5 Day Assessment
47	Significant Correction of Prior Full Assessment/Medicare 14 Day Assessment
42	Significant Correction of Prior Full Assessment/Medicare 30 Day Assessment
43	Significant Correction of Prior Full Assessment/Medicare 60 Day Assessment
44	Significant Correction of Prior Full Assessment/Medicare 90 Day Assessment
31	[7/98 def.] SCSA or OMRA/ Medicare 5 Day Assessment (Replacement), [10/00 def.] Significant change assessment REPLACES 5-day Medicare required assessment
37	[7/98 def.] SCSA or OMRA/ Medicare 4 Day Assessment (Replacement), [10/00 def.] Significant change assessment REPLACES 14-day Medicare required assessment
32	[7/98 def.] SCSA or OMRA/ Medicare 30 Day Assessment (Replacement), [10/00 def.] Significant change assessment REPLACES 30-day Medicare required assessment
33	[7/98 def.] SCSA or OMRA/ Medicare 60 Day Assessment (Replacement), [10/00 def.] Significant change assessment REPLACES 60-day Medicare required assessment
34	[7/98 def.] SCSA or OMRA/ Medicare 90 Day Assessment (Replacement), [10/00 def.] Significant change assessment REPLACES 90-day Medicare required assessment
05	Readmission/Return Medicare assessment
17	14-day Medicare assessment AND initial admission assessment
18	OMRA replacing 5-day Medicare assessment
28	OMRA replacing 30-day Medicare assessment
30	Off-cycle significant change assessment (outside assessment window)
35	Significant change assessment REPLACES a readmission/return Medicare-required assessment
40	Off-cycle significant change correction assessment of a prior assessment (outside assessment window)
45	Significant correction of a prior assessment REPLACES a readmission/return assessment

(continued)

TABLE 7-10 *(continued)*

Assessment Indicator	Definition
48	OMRA replacing 90-day Medicare-required assessment
78	OMRA replacing 14-day Medicare-required assessment
19	Special payment situation 5-day assessment
29	Special payment situation 30-day assessment
39	Special payment situation 60-day assessment
49	Special payment situation 90-day assessment
79	Special payment situation 14-day assessment
8A	TRICARE 120-day assessment
8B	TRICARE 150-day assessment
8C	TRICARE 180-day assessment
8D	TRICARE 210-day assessment
8E	TRICARE 240-day assessment
8F	TRICARE 270-day assessment
8G	TRICARE 300-day assessment
8H	TRICARE 330-day assessment
8I	TRICARE 360-day assessment
8X	TRICARE Post 360-day assessments with 30-day interval

Source: www.cms.gov/transmittals/downloads/A01124.pdf; www.cms.gov/SNFPPS/Downloads/sbmanual112005-RUG53.pdf.

TABLE 7-11 *Examples of RUG Rates*

RUG-IV Category	Nursing Index	Therapy Index	Nursing Component	Therapy Component	Non-Case Mix Therapy Comp.	Non-Case Mix Component	Total Rate
RUX	3.55	1.87	551.07	218.66		79.22	848.95
RUL	3.41	1.87	529.33	218.66		79.22	827.21
RVX	3.48	1.28	540.20	149.67		79.22	769.09
RVL	2.92	1.28	453.27	149.67		79.22	682.16
RHX	3.40	0.85	527.78	99.39		79.22	706.39
RHL	2.86	0.85	443.96	99.39		79.22	622.57
RMX	3.28	0.55	509.15	64.31		79.22	652.68
RML	2.92	0.55	453.27	64.31		79.22	596.80
RLX	3.01	0.28	467.24	32.74		79.22	579.20
RUC	2.08	1.87	322.88	218.66		79.22	620.76
RUB	2.08	1.87	322.88	218.66		79.22	620.76

Source: www.cms.gov/SNFPPS/02_Spotlight.asp.

(continued from page 115)

- Epoetin Alfa (EPO) and Darbepoetin Alfa;
- Rural Health Clinic or Federally Qualified Health Center services;
- Hospice care related to a resident's terminal condition;
- Ambulance services transporting the patient initially to the SNF for the initial admission or from the SNF following a final discharge (or transport to/from an excluded service's site);
- Cardiac catheterization;
- Computerized axial tomography scans;
- Magnetic resonance imaging services;
- Ambulatory surgery requiring an operating room or comparable setting;
- Emergency services;
- Radiation therapy;
- Angiography;
- Certain lymphatic and venous procedures;
- Chemotherapy;
- Radioisotope services;
- Customized prosthetic devices; and
- Zevalin and Bexxar.

Definitions and Acronyms

ASC. Ambulatory Surgery Center.

CAHs. Critical Access Hospitals.

DMEPOS. Durable Medical Equipment/ Prosthetic and Orthotic Supplies.

FQHC. Federally Qualified Health Center.

HIPPS. Health Insurance Prospective Payment System (HIPPS) codes represent specific sets of patient characteristics on which payment determinations are made under several prospective payment systems.

HH-PPS. Home Health Prospective Payment System.

HHRG. Home Health Resource Group.

LTCH. Long-Term Care Hospital.

OASIS. Outcome and Assessment Information Set.

RHC. Rural Health Clinic.

SNF-PPS. Skilled Nursing Facility Prospective Payment System.

REFERENCES

1. Electronic Code of Federal Regulations. Ambulatory Surgery Centers. 416.65b. Available at: http://ecfr.gpoaccess.gov/cgi/t/text/text-idx?c=ecfr&rgn=div5&view=text&node=42:3.0.1.1.3&idno=42#42:3.0.1.1.3.4.1.3. Accessed February 28, 2011.
2. Centers for Medicare and Medicaid Services. Ambulatory Surgery Center. Available at: www.cms.gov/ASCPayment/11_Addenda_Updates.asp. Accessed January 12, 2011.
3. Centers for Medicare and Medicaid Services. Available at: www.cms.gov/ProspMedicareFeeSvcPmtGen/02_HIPPSCodes.asp. Accessed January 13, 2011.
4. Centers for Medicare and Medicaid Services. Home Health Agency Center. Available at: www.cms.gov/HomeHealthPPS/. Accessed January 13, 2011.

Chapter 8

Medical Record Documentation

Documentation Overview

Documentation is what every coder and insurer desires, but it seems to be ever elusive. The patient is the soul of health care, but documentation is the skin and bones, ie, what can be seen, or the projection of the patient's health care. Without intelligible, strong, accurate, and comprehensive documentation within every patient's chart, there is a breakdown in health care. From a quality of care perspective to payment and compliance, documentation is a vital part of the process.

Documentation affects every element of patient care during every part of life from birth to death. Medical record documentation should be honored, respected, and given the effort it deserves.

Health Insurance Portability and Accountability Act (HIPAA)

Medical records and information must be protected from public access, and any information released must comply with HIPAA guidelines. Every health care provider, regardless of size, who electronically transmits health information in connection with certain transactions, is a covered entity under HIPAA. These transactions include claims, benefit eligibility inquiries, referral authorization requests, and other transactions for which the Department of Health and Human Services (HHS) has established standards under HIPAA. The HIPAA Privacy Rule covers a health care provider whether it electronically transmits these transactions directly or uses a billing service or other third party to do so on its behalf. This is to keep personal health and billing information for individuals that is considered protected health information (PHI) private. Health care providers include all providers of medical or health services as defined by Medicare and any other person or organization that furnishes, bills, or is paid for health care. PHI is individually identifiable health information, including demographic data that relates to:

- The individual's past, present, or future physical or mental health or condition;
- The provision of health care to the individual; or
- The past, present, or future payment for the provision of health care to the individual.

Key Uses for Medical Record Documentation

Medical records chronologically document the care of patients and are an important element contributing to high quality care and accurate payment. Some of the purposes of medical records are listed below and summarized in Figure 8-1. Many aspects of medical record documentation could be added to the given list, but these are the most prevalent.

Ongoing patient care. Medical records help prompt a provider's memory about the provider's history with the patient from one encounter to the next (whether in the office or within a facility). Often providers see so many patients a day, sometimes for very similar conditions, that the nuances of an individual patient's condition and history are important reminders.

Communications between providers. Documentation helps promote continuity of care if well recorded. One provider can review another's documentation to get a great view of what the patient's immediate or long-term medical history includes. Patients cannot always remember the drug one provider gave them or the precise procedure performed, so the medical record becomes their spokesperson, so to speak.

Provides data for research/education. Decisions are better made with accurate data to support them. Medical documentation is used to make future decisions regarding insurance coverage, research and development of new pharmaceuticals or procedures, and where federal monies will be spent in health care.

Claims payment. Although documentation is not usually submitted with a claim for payment, payers reserve the right to request and review the supporting documentation for claims submissions. Medical records are the source of information for the patient's condition being treated as well as the services provided. If the condition or service is not well supported in the documentation, the payment level can be altered or, worse yet, a penalty for noncompliance could be levied against the billing provider.

Medical malpractice litigation. The record is a legal document and can be used for or against a provider in litigation of any kind, malpractice or otherwise. Many malpractice insurance carriers will have documentation requirements that policyholders must abide by in order to have coverage.

Malpractice Insurance Note

Providers should review their policies to determine if the malpractice insurance carrier has documentation requirements. If those requirements are not met and the unfortunate circumstance of a litigation case being filed occurs, the malpractice insurance may not provide any legal or financial assistance.

FIGURE 8-1 *Key Uses for Medical Documentation*

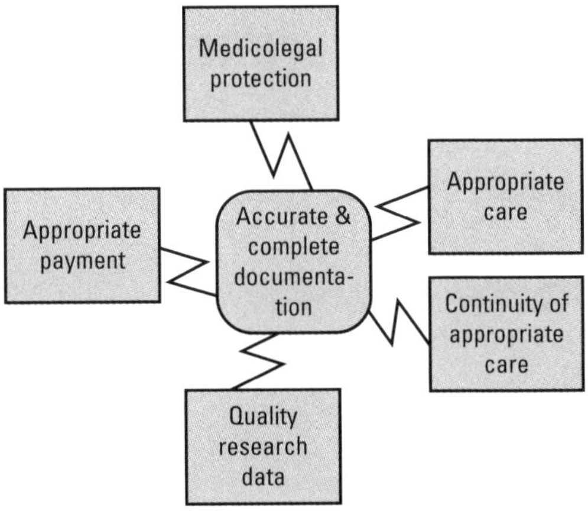

General Principles to Document Clinical Services

This section addresses general guidelines regarding the documentation of clinical services. There may be licensure, scope of practice, supervision, malpractice liability, and other requirements that are more or less stringent than what is presented here, and those must be considered in addition to these general guidelines.

Conditions of Participation (CoPs) are rules governing the eligibility of someone or an entity to be involved in a particular activity or organization. For participation in Medicare and/or Medicaid programs, CoPs have very specific guidelines on documentation. The guidelines vary a bit between providers, but there are some common principles that should be followed. CoPs may be accessed through the Code of Federal Regulations.[1] In addition, many payers have specific instructions on documentation requirements. The following are general principles taken from the CoPs, CMS manuals, the National Committee for Quality Assurance (NCQA),[2] and personal experience.

Overall Organization

Medical records should be organized in a consistent manner to make certain:

- The record is clearly organized;
- The records are organized in chronological order; and
- The medical record does not contain information for other patients (exception: family members in one record must be clearly separated).

Confidentiality and Security

The following guidelines should be followed to ensure confidentiality and security of medical records:

- All medical records must be stored out of reach and view of unauthorized persons.
- Staff must receive periodic training in patient information and confidentiality.
- All providers with electronic health records (EHRs) must have access to compatible electronic hardware and software to enable the generation of a legible copy of the record.
- All providers with EHRs must prepare and maintain a current backup copy of the electronic medical record.
- After having met the minimum mandated record retention periods, records should be discarded as follows:
  - For paper records, by incineration, shredding, pulping, or other comparable process that renders the records permanently unreadable;
  - For electronic or magnetic media, by completely sanitizing the media and not just by deletion (ie, all data should be totally destroyed from the source such as by demagnetizing an old hard drive); and
  - For other media, such as film, photos, or compact disks (CDs), by destroying the media with no possibility of recovery, such as by shredding CDs and photos.

Clinical Content

In order to improve quality of care and documentation efficiency while maximizing the accuracy of billing, it is important to observe some fundamental rules and/or guidelines for the content of medical records:

- The record must be legible to someone other than the writer.
- All entries in the medical record must be authenticated. Note that authentication requires an actual signature or a password-protected electronic signature and the provider's credentials. Many insurers (eg, Medicare) have policies against rubber-stamped signatures since the stamps are not always secured to one individual, ie, a staff member could pick up a stamp and use it.

Entries should include a complete date (month, day, and year) and time. The person responsible for providing or evaluating the service is responsible for the authentication. If there are multiple clinicians who are documenting within a patient's record, there must be a way to clearly establish the author of each entry. For example, all physicians and nonphysician providers documenting in medical records should be required to provide a sample of their signature on a blank piece of paper to the compliance officer. Initials are not acceptable as signatures without further documentation (attestation, signature log, typed or printed name next to the initials, and so forth).

- The medical record should be accurate, consistent, and complete. Services rendered should be documented during or as soon as practicable after they are provided in order to maintain an accurate medical record.[2] Documentation should be made as close to the time of the actual event as possible; therefore, timeliness is a crucial component of accuracy. When documenting services, always keep in mind that ***medical necessity*** of a service is the overarching criterion for payment in addition to the individual requirements of the reported CPT code.[3] Payers hold providers responsible for providing and supporting the medical necessity of the services for which they are billing. Audits have shown that medical necessity is a theme of the weakness in most documentation. Although clinicians can differ in terms of how they treat conditions, the necessity of the treatment (diagnostic or therapeutic) must be well documented.
- The date of each entry (orders, reports, notes, etc) must be accurately documented. Also, in a hospital setting, entries should be timed. Timing establishes when an order was given, when an activity happened, or when an activity is to take place.

Note

Some services are coded with HCPCS based on time (eg, critical care, psychotherapy). For those services, the time involved in the care should be clearly documented regardless of site of service.

- The patient should be identified on all pages within the record. Each page in the record must contain the patient's name or ID number.
- The overall patient record should also contain:
  - Patient name, date of birth, and medical record number;
  - Personal biographical data including the patient's address, employer, home and work telephone numbers, and marital status;
  - Notation of any agent to which the patient has a history of reacting unfavorably (eg, allergies and adverse reactions). Allergies and adverse reactions should be prominently noted in the record. If the patient has no known allergies or history of adverse reactions, this should be noted;
  - Significant illnesses and medical conditions;
  - Past medical history (if known), including serious accidents, operations, and illnesses. For children, history relating to prenatal care, birth, operations, and childhood illnesses should be included;
  - Medications;
  - Up-to-date immunization records;
  - Calls between the clinician and the patient (clinicians could include nonphysician providers);
  - Correspondence between clinicians and between clinicians and patients;
  - Advance directives, if available;
  - A summary or copy of other providers' records that are relevant to the condition for which the patient is being treated; and
  - Patient demographics.

- The documentation of each patient encounter should include:
  - Reason for the encounter and relevant subjective history (eg, appropriate health risk factors), objective physical examination findings, and prior diagnostic test results;
  - Working diagnoses consistent with findings;
  - Treatment plans consistent with diagnoses;
  - Notations regarding follow-up care when indicated with the specific time of return noted;
  - Notes indicating that unresolved problems from previous office visits are addressed in subsequent visits;
  - Assessment, clinical impression, or diagnosis;
  - Plan for care; and
  - The patient's progress, response to and changes in treatment, and revision of diagnosis.
- For all services (medical, surgical, testing, injections, etc) provided or ordered:
  - The medical necessity and appropriateness of the service must be documented;
  - Abnormal findings should have explicit notations in the record for follow-up plans; and
  - The CPT and ICD-9-CM codes reported on the claim form should be supported by the documentation in the medical record, and the site of service should be clearly documented (office, ASC, hospital).

The following are some basic things that should **not** be documented in medical records:

- Assignment of blame to other caregivers or clinicians;
- Self-serving remarks;
- Critical remarks about a patient's personality or appearance that have no clinical relevance;
- Use of excuses, rationalizations, or denials of wrongdoing;
- Bills and/or correspondence about billing; and
- Alterations, unless they are made through the approved amendment policies discussed below.

Corrections to Medical Records

By law, record falsification and/or tampering is viewed as an illegal activity and potentially as a false claim. Record tampering undermines a clinician's credibility in the event of litigation. Do not make the integrity of a patient's medical record vulnerable by using a poor correction method.

The following guidelines outline how to make appropriate medical record corrections and/or amendments (see Figure 8-2):

- Do not add to an entry after you have received a subpoena for records.
- Never make entries in pencil or erasable ink.
- Never attempt a correction by erasing, obliterating, or using correction fluid.
- When a correction or amendment becomes necessary, merely draw a single line through the entry so that the original entry is still legible. Make a notation explaining the correction and/or where the appropriate addendum can be found (see below for amendments).
- Date and sign the correction.
- When making amendments:
  - Do not annotate in the margins to add information. Instead, create a new entry for the additional information;
  - Keep all entries in chronological order;
  - Add the title "Addendum";
  - Use the actual date of the addendum;
  - Reference the original entry by indicating the date of the service; and
  - Always sign the additional entry or document.

Improvement Opportunities

Often physicians do not record everything they do or observe during a patient encounter. They probably are not even cognizant of everything they do to arrive at an assessment and treatment plan. It is not a

FIGURE 8-2 *Example of Appropriate Amendment of a Medical Record*

Original Record

Progress Notes	
11/6/xx 4:38 am	GS awake and following commands except will not move lt arm. VS: temp 101.5 bp 125/52 Lungs clear Abd obese, soft, BSO Ext no edema Neuro much more awak A/P s/p MVA Resp failure – he looks ready to initiate INV Closed head injury – mental status much better Nutrition Infection – fever down on ABX Anemia, blood loss, may need transfusion again C6,7 facet fx and bilateral rib fracture Looks better Val, PA-C Smith, MD

Amended Record

Progress Notes	
11/6/xx 4:38 am ↑ *Amended 11/9/xx – see 11/9/xx documentation . . . Val, PA-C*	GS awake and following commands except will not move lt arm. VS: temp 101.5 bp 125/52 Lungs clear Abd obese, soft, BSO Ext no edema Neuro much more awak A/P s/p MVA Resp failure – he looks ready to initiate INV Closed head injury – mental status much better Nutrition Infection – fever down on ABX Anemia, blood loss, may need transfusion again C6,7 facet fx and bilateral rib fracture Looks better *Correction - MD did not provide any face to face. Smith* Val, PA-C Smith, MD
11/9/xx 6:05 am	amended note for service 11/8/xx On 11/8/xx, patient's family also shared that patient was recently diagnosed with a stroke, not known previously. Neurology is being consulted. Val, PA-C

deliberate misstep on their part; it's easy to forget to write things down when they are often seeing one patient right after the next (whether in their office or a facility). That, unfortunately, does not dismiss the need for good documentation, nor does it excuse poor documentation.

Consultants, experienced office staff, and other clinicians can help physicians who may be missing vital documentation needs.

Templates

Developing encounter templates that prompt a physician to record information might be helpful. Filling out a form with spaces can spur a physician to record information obtained that might otherwise be lost from the documentation. The form can (and should) have a lot of free space for writing with simple labels, such as for the history of the present illness or the organ systems for a physical exam. Another option would be for the form to have checklists for the physician to indicate findings (normal or abnormal). One important aspect of checklists is that the physician must further explain any abnormalities documented; a check box is not sufficient. Figure 8-3 is an example of a template with a combination of free spaces and checklists for a medical visit.

Templates will vary from practice to practice and from office to hospital or other facility. All forms should be reviewed on an annual basis to ensure they reflect current documentation requirements as well as the current practice needs of the facility. For more information and additional resources about developing templates see AMA's *Practical EHR*[4] and *Practical E/M*.[5]

Shadowing

By shadowing a physician, an objective observer can identify some areas where improvement can be made. Shadowing simply means following the physician during the patient encounter and offering suggestions on how documentation can be improved.

The different steps of shadowing are as follows:

1. Begin at the initial clinical interaction with the patient during that encounter. If this is in the office, begin when the patient is brought back for triage (vitals, etc).
2. Observe the physician's interaction with the patient and write down notes on everything the physician asks, examines, orders, or discusses with the patient.
3. Immediately after the patient encounter, review the physician's documentation and compare it to the notes you made. Note any omissions or disconnects.
4. Discuss your findings immediately with the physician and offer suggestions for improvement.

Scribes

Scribes can help a physician by taking over the written part of the documentation. They are essentially dynamic human Dictaphones. It is important to note that the scribe's only purpose is to write down what the physician dictates—nothing more, nothing less. The physician is providing the care; the scribe has no personal input into the documentation.

Just about anyone can act as a scribe; however, at times it is difficult to justify using a midlevel provider or resident as a scribe. Their cost and the value of their time may make it counterintuitive to use them as scribes.

Another potential problem with using a clinician as a scribe is that no personal opinion or information from the scribe should enter the record. If the scribe is also a physician, it may be difficult to limit documentation to what transpires in the encounter. This requirement is sometimes difficult to defend if a nurse practitioner is used as a scribe.

If a scribe is used to record the provider's information, this should be noted within the documentation. An example of the attestation that could be used by the scribe would be "In the presence of (Enter Provider's Name) I am taking down these notes verbatim.

(*continued on page 131*)

FIGURE 8-3 *Example of Documentation Template*

Patient Name:______________________ Account No.______________ DOB:___/___/___

Initial Visit Form (p. 1): Please provide the following medical information to the best of your ability:

Date:	Age:	List any ALLERGIES TO MEDICATIONS:
What problems are you here for today?		

Past Medical History:

1) Please check the "Yes" or "No" box to indicate if you have any of the following illnesses; for "Yes" answers, please explain.

	Yes	No			Yes	No	
Diabetes (Circle: type I/type II)	☐	☐	______	Stomach or Intestinal problems	☐	☐	______
Hypertension (high blood press)	☐	☐	______	Allergy problems/therapy	☐	☐	______
Thyroid problems	☐	☐	______	Kidney problems	☐	☐	______
Heart Disease/cholesterol probs	☐	☐	______	Neurological problems	☐	☐	______
Respiratory problems	☐	☐	______	Cancer	☐	☐	______
Bleeding disorder	☐	☐	______	Other Medical Diagnosis	☐	☐	______

2) Please list any operations (and dates) you have ever had *(including tonsils & adenoids)*:

3) Please list any current medications (and amounts, times per day):
(include aspirin, antacids, vitamins, hormone replacement, birth control, herbal supplements, OTC meds including sinus/allergy/weight loss meds):

Social History:	Yes	No		Please list details below:
Do you use tobacco?	☐	☐	List type and how much:	
If no, did you use it previously?	☐	☐	List type and how much:	When did you quit?
Do you drink alcohol?	☐	☐	List type and how much:	
Do you use recreational drugs?	☐	☐	List type and how much:	

What is your occupation?______________________

Family History:

Please check the "Yes" or "No" box to indicate whether any relatives have any of the following illnesses:
If yes, please indicate which relative(s) have the problem.

	Yes	No	
Heart problems/murmurs	☐	☐	______
Allergy	☐	☐	______
Diabetes	☐	☐	______
Cancer	☐	☐	______
Bleeding disorder	☐	☐	______
Anesthesia problems	☐	☐	______

☐ See attached dictation | Reviewed by:

FIGURE 8-3 *(continued)*

Date____/____/____

Patient Name:________________________________ **Account No.**________________ **DOB:**____/____/____

Outpatient Initial Visit Form (p. 2): Please provide the following medical information to the best of your ability:

Review of Systems:

1) Please check the "Yes" or "No" box to indicate whether you presently have any of the following symptoms:

2) For any "yes" responses, please check the "Current" box if this symptom relates to the reason for your visit today.

		Yes	No	Current		Yes	No	Current
GENERAL	chills	☐	☐	☐	weight loss or gain	☐	☐	☐
	fatigue	☐	☐	☐	daytime sleepiness	☐	☐	☐
ALLERGY	environmental allergy	☐	☐	☐	sneezing fits	☐	☐	☐
NEURO	headache	☐	☐	☐	weakness	☐	☐	☐
	passing out	☐	☐	☐	numbness, tingling	☐	☐	☐
EYES	eye pain/pressure	☐	☐	☐	vision changes	☐	☐	☐
	watery or itchy eyes	☐	☐	☐				
ENT	hearing loss	☐	☐	☐	ear noises	☐	☐	☐
	dizziness	☐	☐	☐	lightheadedness	☐	☐	☐
	nasal congestion	☐	☐	☐	sinus pressure or pain	☐	☐	☐
	hoarseness	☐	☐	☐	problem snoring, apnea	☐	☐	☐
	throat clearing	☐	☐	☐	throat pain	☐	☐	☐
RESPIR	cough	☐	☐	☐	coughing blood	☐	☐	☐
	wheezing	☐	☐	☐	shortness of breath	☐	☐	☐
CARDIAC	chest pain	☐	☐	☐	palpitations	☐	☐	☐
	wake short of breath	☐	☐	☐	ankle swelling	☐	☐	☐
GI	difficulty swallowing	☐	☐	☐	heartburn	☐	☐	☐
	abdominal pain	☐	☐	☐	nausea/vomiting	☐	☐	☐
	bowel irregularity	☐	☐	☐	rectal bleeding	☐	☐	☐
GU	frequent urination	☐	☐	☐	painful urination	☐	☐	☐
	blood in urine	☐	☐	☐	prostate problems	☐	☐	☐
HEME/LYM	swollen glands	☐	☐	☐	sweating at night	☐	☐	☐
	bleeding problems	☐	☐	☐	easy bruising	☐	☐	☐
ENDO	feel warmer than others	☐	☐	☐	feel cooler than others	☐	☐	☐
MSK	joint aches	☐	☐	☐	muscle aches	☐	☐	☐
SKIN	rash	☐	☐	☐	hives	☐	☐	☐
	itching	☐	☐	☐	skin or hair changes	☐	☐	☐
PSYCH	depression	☐	☐	☐	anxiety or panic	☐	☐	☐

PLEASE STOP HERE ☐ See attached dictation

Reviewed by:

(continued)

FIGURE 8-3 *(continued)*

Date ___/___/___ Patient States Consultation Requested By______________________

Patient Name:______________________ Account No.______________ DOB:___/___/___

Outpatient Initial Visit Form (p. 3):

PRESENT ILLNESS — Chronology with: 1. one to three elements (level 2) 2. four to eight elements; OR status of 3 chronic or inactive conditions (level 3, 4 or 5)
(1) duration (2) timing (3) severity; (4) location (5) quality (6) context (7) modifying factors (8) assoc. signs & symptoms

☐ See attached dictation

PHYSICAL EXAMINATION: **General Multisystem Exam**

GENERAL (at least 3 measurements of vital signs) HT___ft___in WT______lbs

BP sitting-standing ___/___mm Hg BP supine___/___mm Hg

PULSE _____/min regular - irregular RESP _____/min TEMP _____° (F-C)

System	Element	Description	Normal	AB
	GENERAL APPEARANCE	Stature, nutrition	☐	☐
EYES	CONJUNCTIVAE & LIDS	Appearance, color	☐	☐
	PUPILS & IRISES	Size, reactivity	☐	☐
	OPTIC DISCS	Fundi, vessels	☐	☐
ENT	EARS & NOSE, EXTERNAL	Appearance	☐	☐
	OTOSCOPY	Canals, tymp membranes	☐	☐
	HEARING	Response to sound	☐	☐
	INTERNAL NOSE	Septum, mucosa, turbs	☐	☐
	LIPS,TEETH, & GUMS	Mucosa, dentition	☐	☐
	OROPHARYNX	Mucosa, tonsils, palate	☐	☐
NECK	MASSES & TRACHEA	Symmetry, masses	☐	☐
	THYROID	Size, nodules	☐	☐
RESP	RESPIRATORY EFFORT	Inspiratory-expiratory	☐	☐
	CHEST PALPATION	Movement	☐	☐
	CHEST PERCUSSION	Sound	☐	☐
	AUSCULTATION	Lung sounds	☐	☐
CVS	HEART PALPATION	Rhythm	☐	☐
	HEART AUSCULTATION	Sounds	☐	☐
	CAROTID ARTIERIES	Pulsation	☐	☐
	ABDOMINAL AORTA	Pulsation	☐	☐
	FEMORAL ARTERIES	Pulsation	☐	☐
	PEDAL PULSES	Pulsation	☐	☐
	EDEMA,VARICES, LE	Appearance	☐	☐

System	Element	Description	Normal	AB
CHEST/	BREAST INSPECTION	Symmetry, color	☐	☐
BREASTS	BREAST/AXILLAE PALP	Nodules, masses	☐	☐
GI/ABD	MASSES/TENDERNESS	Palpation	☐	☐
	LIVER/SPLEEN	Size, tenderness	☐	☐
	HERNIA EVAL	Inspection, palpation	☐	☐
	ANUS/RECTUM/PERIN	Appearance, palpation	☐	☐
	STOOL, HEMACULT	Eval for blood	☐	☐
LYMPH	NECK/AXILLAE/GROIN/OTHER	Adenopathy	☐	☐
	(circle areas examined; requires exam in 2 or more regions)			
MSKEL	GAIT & STATION	Stability & smoothness	☐	☐
(partial)	DIGITS & NAILS	Color & appearance	☐	☐
SKIN/	INSPECTION	Head, trunk, RUE	☐	☐
SUBCU		LUE, RLE, LLE	☐	☐
	PALPATION	Head, trunk, RUE	☐	☐
		LUE, RLE, LLE	☐	☐
NEURO	CRANIAL NERVES	II - XII	☐	☐
	DEEP TENDON REFLEXES	Knee, ankle, Babinski	☐	☐
	SENSATION	Light touch	☐	☐
PSYCH	JUDGEMENT & INSIGHT	Subjectively	☐	☐
	ORIENTATION	Person, place, time	☐	☐
	MEMORY	Recent & remote	☐	☐
	MOOD & AFFECT	Comments	☐	☐

☐ Continued on supplemental page ☐ See attached dictation

1. Problem focused = 1-5 elements (level 1) 2. Expanded = 6-11 elements (level 2) 3. Detailed = 12 or more elements [in 2 or more systems] (level 3)
4. Comprehensive = document two (or more) elements in each of nine (or more) systems (level 4 or 5) *Optional

FIGURE 8-3 *(continued)*

Date____/____/____

Patient Name:________________________________ **Account No.**__________________ **DOB:**____/____/____

Outpatient Initial Visit Form (p. 4):

MEDICAL DECISION MAKING — 2 of the 3 sections (a vs a', b vs b' vs b", c vs c' vs c") must meet or exceed indicated level of care

DATA REVIEWED (c): 1. Minimal (level 2) 2. Limited (level 3) 3. Moderate (level 4) 4. Extensive (level 5)

☐ X-ray/CT scan ☐ See attached dictation

☐ MRI

☐ Lab/blood work

IMPRESSIONS/DIFFERENTIAL DIAGNOSES (a): PLANS/MANAGEMENT OPTIONS (a')

1. Minimal (level 2) 2. Limited (level 3) 3. Multiple (level 4) 4. Extensive (level 5)

☐ See attached dictation

IMPRESSIONS/DIFFERENTIAL DIAGNOSES (a)	PLANS/MANAGEMENT OPTIONS (a')
1)	1)
2)	2)
3)	3)
4)	4)
5)	5)

DATA ORDERED (c'): 1. Minimal or none (level 2) 2. Limited (level 3) 3. Moderate (level 4) 4. Extensive (level 5)

☐ ☐ ☐ ☐ ☐

☐ See attached dictation

Information Sheets Given:

COMPLEXITY OF DATA REVIEWED OR ORDERED (c")

1. Minimal (level 2)	2. Limited (level 3)	3. Moderate (level 4)	4. Extensive (level 5)
1. min	2. limited	3. mod	4. extensive

RISK OF COMPLICATIONS &/OR MORBIDITY OR MORTALITY (see examples in Table of Risk)

	1. Minimal (level 2)	2. Low (level 3)	3. Moderate (level 4)	4. High (level 5)
risk of presenting problem(s) (b):	1. min	2. low	3. mod	4. high
risk of diagnostic procedure(s) ordered (b'):	1. min	2. low	3. mod	4. high
risk of management option(s) selected (b"):	1. min	2. low	3. mod	4. high

NATURE OF PRESENTING PROBLEM(S)

1. minor	(level 1)	Problem runs definite and prescribed course, is transient in nature, and is not likely to permanently alter health status; OR, has a good prognosis with management and compliance.
2. low	(level 1)++	Problem in which the risk of morbidity without treatment is low; there is little to no risk of mortality without treatment; full recovery without functional impairment is expected.
3. low - mod	(level 2)	Problem in which the risk of morbidity without treatment is low to moderate; there is low to moderate risk of mortality without treatment; full recovery without functional impairment is expected in most cases, with low probability of prolonged functional impairment
4. moderate	(level 3)	Problem in which the risk of morbidity without treatment is moderate; there is moderate risk of mortality without treatment; prognosis is uncertain, or there is an increased probability of prolonged functional impairment.
5. mod - high	(levels 4, 5)	Problem in which the risk of morbidity without treatment is moderate to high; there is moderate risk of mortality without treatment; uncertain prognosis or increased probability of prolonged functional impairment
6. high	(level 5)	Problem in which the risk of morbidity without treatment is high to extreme; there is moderate to high risk of mortality without treatment, or high probability of severe prolonged functional impairment.

++ For Consultation, a low NPP is equal to a level 2

Complete this section only if documented below > 50% of visit time involved counseling and/or coordinating care.

TIME: ____________ minutes ☐ > 50% of visit time involved counseling and/or coordination of care

Clinician's signature:

(continued)

FIGURE 8-3 *(continued)*

Date: ____/____/______

Patient Name:______________________________ Account No.________________ DOB:____/____/____

Outpatient Initial Visit Form (Supplement):

PHYSICAL EXAMINATION: **General Multisystem Exam (continued)**

			Normal	AB				Normal	AB
GU MALE	SCROTAL CONTENTS	Appearance, palpation	☐	☐	MSKEL	RT UPPER EXTREMITY	Inspec., palp., percussion	☐	☐
	PENIS	Appearance, palpation	☐	☐			Range of motion	☐	☐
	PROSTATE	Palpation	☐	☐			Stability or laxity	☐	☐
GU FEMALE (PELVIC)	EXT GENITALIA	Appearance, palpation	☐	☐			Muscle strength & tone	☐	☐
	URETHRA	Inspection	☐	☐		LT UPPER EXTREMITY	Inspec., palp., percussion	☐	☐
	BLADDER	Palpation	☐	☐			Range of motion	☐	☐
	CERVIS	Palpation	☐	☐			Stability or laxity	☐	☐
	UTERUS	Palpation	☐	☐			Muscle strength & tone	☐	☐
	ADNEXA/PARAMET	Palpation	☐	☐		RT LOWER EXTREMITY	Inspec., palp., percussion	☐	☐
MSKEL	HEAD & NECK	Inspec., palp., percussion	☐	☐			Range of motion	☐	☐
		Range of motion	☐	☐			Stability or laxity	☐	☐
		Stability or laxity	☐	☐			Muscle strength & tone	☐	☐
		Muscle strength & tone	☐	☐		LT LOWER EXTREMITY	Inspec., palp., percussion	☐	☐
	SPINE, RIBS, PELVIS	Inspec., palp., percussion	☐	☐			Range of motion	☐	☐
		Range of motion	☐	☐			Stability or laxity	☐	☐
		Stability or laxity	☐	☐			Muscle strength & tone	☐	☐
		Muscle strength & tone	☐	☐			☐ See attached dictation		

1. Problem focused = 1-5 elements (level 1) 2. Expanded = 6-11 elements (level 2) 3. Detailed = 12 or more elements [in 2 or more systems] (level 3)
4. Comprehensive = document two (or more) elements in each of nine (or more) systems (level 4 or 5) *Optional

Source: Levinson, SR. Practical *E/M: Documentation and Coding Solutions for Quality Patient Care.* Second Edition. Chicago, IL: American Medical Association; 2008.

(*continued from page 125*)

(Signed by the scribe)." Any variation of this could be used by the scribe; however, it must be clear that the provider is performing the service and the scribe is simply and only recording the information. The provider must authenticate the documentation with a signature.

National Committee for Quality Assurance (NCQA). An organization that develops quality standards and performance measures for health care entities.

Protected health information (PHI). Individual-specific information protected under HIPAA.

Bottom Line

Documentation is the story of the patient's health care experience and must be precise and complete. When billing for services, the documentation must support each diagnosis assigned as well as the service provided. Each claim submitted and every service/supply on the claim must stand alone and be supported by documentation clearly showing the intent of the clinician and the reasons for performing or ordering the service.

Definitions and Acronyms

Health Insurance Portability and Accountability Act (HIPAA). Act that serves to protect the privacy of individually identifiable health information.

REFERENCES

1. Code of Federal Regulations. Conditions of Participation. Available at: www.gpoaccess.gov/cfr/. Accessed January 14, 2011.
2. National Committee for Quality Assurance. About NCQA. Available at: http://ncqa.org/tabid/675/Default.aspx. Accessed January 15, 2011.
3. Centers for Medicare and Medicaid Services. Medicare Claims Processing Manual, Chapter 12: Physicians/Nonphysician Practitioners. Available at: www.cms.gov/Manuals/IOM/itemdetail.asp?itemID=CMS018912. Accessed January 15, 2011.
4. Levinson, SR. Practical *EHR: Electronic Record Solutions for Compliance and Quality Care*. Chicago, IL: American Medical Association; 2008.
5. Levinson, SR. Practical *E/M: Documentation and Coding Solutions for Quality Patient Care*. Second Edition. Chicago, IL: American Medical Association; 2008.

Chapter 9

Healthcare Common Procedure Coding System (HCPCS)

Background of HCPCS

HIPAA (see Chapter 8), in addition to mandating privacy requirements, also demands that standard coding classifications be used when submitting or processing health care claims (see Chapter 1). HCPCS coding is divided into two categories or subsystems, which are referred to as Level I and Level II HCPCS (see Figure 9-1).

Level I HCPCS consists of the CPT codes. These codes are maintained by the AMA. CPT codes are used to identify medical services and procedures as well as for performance measurements.

Level II HCPCS is composed of alphanumeric codes representing supplies, pharmaceuticals, special services (eg, ambulance, chiropractor, dental), and many other items.

Note

Prior to HIPAA, HCPCS also had a Level III subsystem that was maintained at a local level. It was discarded since all code sets must now be nationally recognized.

Level II HCPCS codes are maintained by the CMS.

HCPCS is the approved coding classification for billing outpatient facility and professional fee services that include but are not limited to:

- Physician and nonphysician provider services;
- Radiological procedures;
- Clinical laboratory tests;

FIGURE 9-1 *HCPCS Levels*

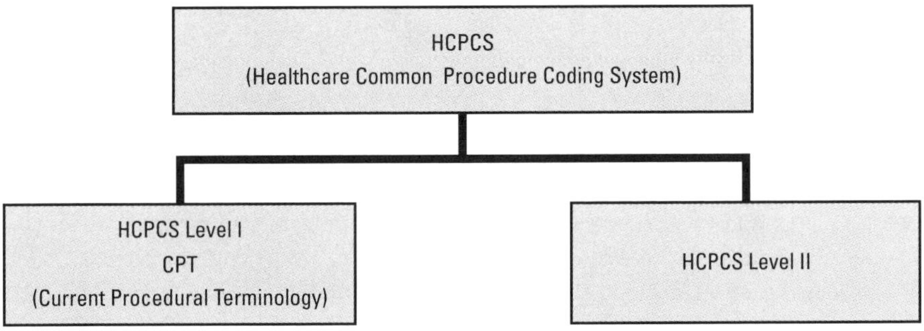

- Other medical diagnostic procedures;
- Hearing and vision services;
- Transportation services including ambulance;
- Supplies, durable medical equipment, and other devices; and
- Pharmaceuticals.

HCPCS is a uniform coding classification consisting of descriptions paired with codes that are used to identify medical services, supplies, and procedures furnished by physicians and other health care professionals.

As illustrated in this example, HCPCS codes, at only five characters long, provide an enormous amount of information:

99213 **Office or other outpatient visit** for the evaluation and management of an established patient, which requires at least two of these three key components:

- **An expanded problem focused history;**
- **An expanded problem focused examination; and**
- **Medical decision making of low complexity.**

Counseling and/or coordination of care with other providers or agencies are provided consistent with the nature of the problem(s) and the patient's and/or family's needs.

Usually, the presenting problem(s) are of low to moderate severity. Physicians typically spend 15 minutes face-to-face with the patient and/or family.

CPT Category I, CPT Category II, and HCPCS Level II codes are updated at least annually for implementation in January of each year. There can be more frequent updates; therefore, both the CMS and AMA Web sites should be referenced often to determine any mid-year updates. For example, twice a year, the AMA issues Category III CPT codes, which the AMA defines as temporary codes for emerging technology, services, and procedures. In addition, AMA issues midyear Category I CPT codes for vaccines for which FDA approval is imminent, to ensure timely availability of a code. CMS modified its process for implementing the Category III codes that the AMA releases each January for implementation in July to ensure timely collection of data pertinent to services described by the codes; to ensure patient access to the services the codes describe; and to eliminate potential redundancy between Category III CPT codes.

HCPCS Level I (CPT) Codes

As noted previously, Level I of the HCPCS is composed of CPT codes, which are maintained by the AMA. CPT codes are used to identify medical services and procedures furnished by physicians and other health care professionals. CPT codes do not include codes needed to separately report medical items or services that are regularly billed by suppliers other than physicians and nonphysician providers. Level II HCPCS serves that role.

The CPT coding system includes more than just codes. It also provides cross-reference instructions (see examples of CPT Category I codes below) and guidelines that may be used to ensure proper use of CPT codes. It is imperative that providers as well as payers review all instructional guidance found in the CPT codebook when coding or deciphering codes. Failure to observe these guidelines can result in erroneous coding of services and a misrepresentation of the patient encounter.

For example, CPT coding instructions under lesion excisions read:

> Excision is defined as full-thickness (through the dermis) removal of a lesion, including margins, and includes simple (non-layered) closure when performed.

If a lesion was excised and the simple repair of the site where the lesion was removed was coded separately, that would violate CPT guidelines and be incorrect.

The CPT codebook lists specific procedures represented by assigned code numbers following an introduction or guidelines. The three categories of CPT codes are described below.

Category I Codes

Category I codes are five-digit numeric codes that are found within the main body of the CPT codebook. These codes represent procedures and services that have met certain criteria:

- They must be approved by the Food and Drug Administration (FDA);
- They must be commonly performed by health care professionals nationwide; and
- They must have proven and documented clinical efficacy.

Category I codes are then further separated into six sections, which are:

1. Evaluation and Management
2. Anesthesiology
3. Surgery
4. Radiology
5. Pathology and Laboratory
6. Medicine

Some examples of the CPT Category I codes are as follows (note the parent and child codes [these are further indented, eg, 81007]), and the cross-reference instructions (under 81005):

99238 Hospital discharge day management; 30 minutes or less

00100 Anesthesia for procedures on salivary glands, including biopsy

66984 Extracapsular cataract removal with insertion of intraocular lens prosthesis (1 stage procedure), manual or mechanical technique (eg, irrigation and aspiration or phacoemulsification)

78491 Myocardial imaging, positron emission tomography (PET), perfusion; single study at rest or stress

81005 Urinalysis; qualitative or semiquantitative, except immunoassays

(For nonimmunoassay reagent strip urinalysis, see 81000, 81002)

(For immunoassay, qualitative or semiqualitative, use 83518)

(For microalbumin, see 820343, 82044)

81007 bacterium screen, except by culture or dipstick

90804 Individual psychotherapy, insight oriented, behavior modifying and/or supportive, in an office or outpatient facility, approximately 20 to 30 minutes face-to-face with the patient

Within each section of the CPT codebook, many services, procedures, and tests are included. However, there are occasional circumstances in which no code exists to exactly match the service provided. In these cases, the CPT codebook provides unlisted service or procedure codes in the specific section guidelines that precede each section. Within the guidelines of each section, information is provided for the use of the unlisted codes. Unlisted codes provide the means of reporting and tracking services and procedures until a more specific code is established in the CPT coding system to describe the procedure in question.

Unlisted codes do not describe a specific procedure or service, so when using these codes, it is necessary to submit supporting documentation (eg, an operative report, office notes) when filing the claim, unless instructed differently by a payer. Such documentation or operative report serves to identify the specific information regarding the procedure(s) identified by the unlisted code. Relevant information should include an adequate definition or description of the nature, extent, and need for the procedure or service, as well as the time, effort, and equipment necessary to provide the service. The information may also include:

1. The specific service performed (including any assistance necessary to carry out the service);
2. Whether the procedure was performed independent of other services provided, or if it was performed at the same surgical site or through the same surgical opening;

3. The number of times the service was provided; and
4. Any extenuating circumstances that may have complicated the service(s) or procedure.

Because unlisted codes do not include descriptor language that specifies the components of a particular service, these codes are reported without modifiers. Modifiers are used to indicate that a service or procedure performed was altered by some specific circumstance but not changed in its definition or code. When using unlisted codes, there is no need to "alter" the meaning of the code.

It is very important that the reported CPT code accurately describe the service that was performed. For that reason, it is equally important that a code that is "close" to the procedure performed **not** be selected in lieu of an unlisted code. Note that there are some coders who maintain that they are not allowed to use unlisted codes or that the use of the unlisted codes is undesirable. While the use of an unlisted procedure code **will** require a special report or documentation to describe the service, correct coding demands that you use a code that is appropriate for the service being provided (ie, a code that most accurately represents the service provided), and not a code that is similar but actually represents another service.

Some examples of unlisted service or procedure CPT codes are as follows:

15999 Unlisted procedure, excision pressure ulcer

17999 Unlisted procedure, skin, mucous membrane and subcutaneous tissue

19499 Unlisted procedure, breast

Category II Codes

Category II codes are tracking codes to be used for performance measurement, specifically in Medicare's Physician Quality Reporting System (PQRS).[1] PQRS is an incentive program where Medicare offers additional payment for providers who report data on quality measures for Medicare patients. Category II codes facilitate collection of information concerning the quality of care. The codes reflect services or test results regarding performance measures that have been determined to contribute to good care. The use of these codes is optional, but the incentive payment is only applicable to providers who choose to use these codes on their Medicare claims.

Category II codes are alphanumeric and consist of four digits followed by the letter "F."

CPT Category II codes are arranged according to the following categories:

1. Composite codes
2. Patient management
3. Patient history
4. Physical examination
5. Diagnostic/screening processes or results
6. Therapeutic, preventive, or other interventions
7. Follow-up or other outcomes
8. Patient safety
9. Structural measures

These codes are used to report performance measures and are not in and of themselves services. Category I and Category III codes as well as HCPCS Level II codes are used to bill for services. Therefore, Category II codes will not have relative value units (RVUs). (See Chapter 5 on physician payment.) Category II codes are not recognized for hospital facility billing and should not be billed on the UB-04 (see Chapter 3 on claim forms).

The Category II codes are released annually as part of the general CPT code set and are published twice a year, on January 1 and July 1, on the AMA Web site.[2]

Some examples of Category II codes are as follows:

0500F Initial prenatal care visit (report at first prenatal encounter with health care professional providing obstetrical care). Report also date of visit and, in a separate field, the date of the last menstrual period [LMP] (Prenatal)

2001F Weight recorded (CHF, PAG)

3008F Body Mass Index (BMI), documented (PV)

Category III Codes

Category III codes are developed to represent new and emerging technologies that have yet to demonstrate they deserve a Category I status (eg, they may not have been approved by the FDA or may not have proven clinical efficacy). Category III codes are used for data collection (how often they are used and who uses them). These codes have five characters, ie, four numbers followed by the letter "T" in the last field (eg, 0002T). The intention of these codes is that they are to be temporary codes and will be retired if the service is not converted to a Category I code.

Note

Category III codes must be used over unlisted Category I codes.

Note

If there is a HCPCS Level II code, it should be used instead of a CPT code for Medicare billing.

Some examples of Category III codes as as follows:

0199T Physiologic recording of tremor using accelerometer(s) and/or gyroscope(s) (including frequency and amplitude), including interpretation and report

0200T Percutaneous sacral augmentation (sacroplasty), unilateral injection(s), including the use of a balloon or mechanical device, when used, 1 or more needles

Figure 9-2 illustrates CPT code categories.

FIGURE 9-2 *CPT Code Categories*

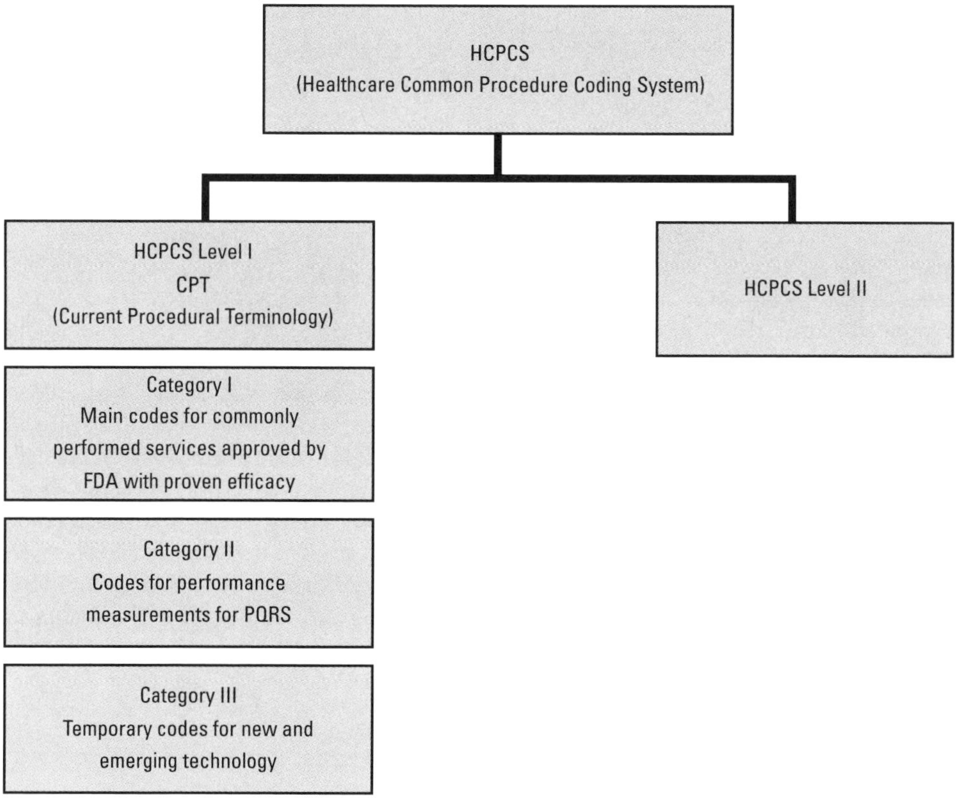

HCPCS Level II Codes

Level II of the HCPCS is a standardized coding system used to identify products, supplies, and services not included in the CPT codes (Level I HCPCS). Such services include ambulance transportation and care; durable medical equipment, prosthetics, orthotics, and supplies (DMEPOS); and pharmaceuticals used in chemotherapy. Unlike CPT codes, HCPCS Level II codes are alphanumeric with a leading alpha character (all codes consist of a letter followed by four numbers).

Some examples of HCPCS Level II codes are as follows:

A0080 Non-emergency transportation, per mile; vehicle provided by volunteer (individual or organization), with no vested interest

J0120 Injection, tetracycline, up to 250 mg

Q0083 Chemotherapy administration by other than infusion technique only (eg, subcutaneous, intramuscular, push), per visit

There are four types of HCPCS Level II codes:

- Permanent National Codes: codes used for all health insurers, whether public or private. These codes are maintained by the CMS HCPCS Workgroup;
- Dental Codes: codes maintained by the American Dental Association (ADA) similar to the way Level I HCPCS codes are maintained by the AMA. Also known as CDT codes;
- Miscellaneous Codes: codes similar to CPT unlisted codes. These are considered miscellaneous or not otherwise classified codes; and
- Temporary National Codes: codes to meet immediate operational needs of an insurer for a short period of time. These codes may or may not be replaced with permanent codes. There is no expiration timeline for temporary codes.

HCPCS Level II codes are arranged in alphanumeric code order as follows:

A Codes: Transportation services including ambulance, medical and surgical supplies, helmets, administrative, miscellaneous and investigational

B Codes: Enteral and parenteral therapy

C Codes: Temporary codes for use with OPPS

D Codes: Dental procedures

E Codes: Durable medical equipment

G Codes: Temporary procedures/professional services

H Codes: Alcohol and drug abuse treatment services

J Codes: Drugs administered other than by oral method

K Codes: Durable medical equipment, prosthetics, orthotics, supplies and dressings

L Codes: Orthotic procedures

M Codes: Medical services

P Codes: Pathology and laboratory services

Q Codes: Temporary codes

R Codes: Diagnostic radiology services

S Codes: Temporary national codes (non-Medicare)

T Codes: Codes established for the state Medicaid agencies

V Codes: Vision services, hearing services

Unlike the CPT coding system, there are limited guidelines within the HCPCS Level II code system. Individual payers (eg, Medicare, BlueCross BlueShield) will usually provide instructions through transmittals, memoranda, and manuals. Therefore, knowing the payer and the payer's guidelines is important. Most payers will notify providers of updated instructions via e-mails, which should be screened to determine what changes need to be made from a coding, documentation, or billing perspective.

Code Modifiers

For both levels of HCPCS, there some situations that require an additional code appended to the HCPCS code. These are called modifiers. HCPCS modifiers help to further describe a HCPCS code without changing the base definition of the code. They provide further information on the code and the patient encounter. There are many HCPCS modifiers within CPT and HCPCS Level II.

For example, modifiers can be used to identify when a procedure has increased work involved than what is usual for the particular code (see modifier 22), if an assistant surgeon is billing for his or her work (see modifiers 80, 81, 82, and AS), or if a service should not be bundled with another because the circumstances of the encounter warrant both (see modifier 59).

Modifiers can be used for information only or can impact payment, so the use of these appended codes is critical for compliance and revenue. The documentation within the patient's medical record should support the modifier just as the documentation should support the HCPCS or ICD-9-CM codes billed.

Table 9-1 shows some of the available HCPCS modifiers. Instructions on using the modifiers are available within the CPT codebook, payer memoranda and/or manuals, and the *CPT Assistant*[3] monthly newsletters. Using modifiers appropriately is vital to being compliant in billing.

TABLE 9-1 *Modifier Examples*

Modifier	Description
22	Increased Procedural Services
23	Unusual Anesthesia
24	Unrelated E/M by Same Physician within Postoperative Period
25	Significant, Separately Identifiable E/M by Same Physician on the Same Day of the Procedure or Other Service
26	Professional Component
27	Multiple Outpatient Hospital E/M Encounters on the Same Date
32	Mandated Services
47	Anesthesia by Surgeon
50	Bilateral Procedure
51	Multiple Procedures
52	Reduced Services
53	Discontinued Procedure
54	Surgical Care Only
55	Postoperative Management Only
56	Preoperative Management Only
57	Decision for Surgery
58	Staged or Related Procedure/Service by Same Physician During Postoperative period
59	Distinct Procedural Service

(continued)

TABLE 9-1 *(continued)*

Modifier	Description
62	Two Surgeons
63	Procedure Performed on Infants less than 4 kg
66	Surgical Team
73	Discontinued OutPatient Hospital/Ambulatory Surgery Center (ASC) Procedure Prior to the Administration of Anesthesia
74	Discontinued OutPatient Hospital/Ambulatory Surgery Center (ASC) Procedure After Administration of Anesthesia
76	Repeat Procedure/Service by Same Physician
77	Repeat Procedure/Service by Another Physician
78	Unplanned Return to the Operating/Procedure Room by the Same Physician Following Initial Procedure for a Related Procedure During the Postoperative Period
79	Unrelated Procedure or Service by the Same Physician During the Postoperative Period
80	Assistant Surgeon
81	Minimum Assistant Surgeon
82	Assistant Surgeon (when qualified resident surgeon not available)
90	Reference (Outside) Laboratory
91	Repeat Clinical Diagnostic Laboratory Test
92	Alternative Laboratory Platform Testing
99	Multiple Modifiers
Physical Status Modifier P1	A normal healthy patient
Physical Status Modifier P2	A patient with mild systemic disease
Physical Status Modifier P3	A patient with severe systemic disease
Physical Status Modifier P4	A patient with severe systemic disease that is a constant threat to life
Physical Status Modifier P5	A moribund patient who is not expected to survive without the operation
Physical Status Modifier P6	A declared brain-dead patient whose organs are being removed for donor purposes
E1	Upper left, eyelid
E2	Lower left, eyelid
E3	Upper right, eyelid
E4	Lower right, eyelid
F1	Left hand, second digit
F2	Left hand, third digit
F3	Left hand, fourth digit

(continued)

TABLE 9-1 *(continued)*

Modifier	Description
F4	Left hand, fifth digit
F5	Right hand, thumb
F6	Right hand, second digit
F7	Right hand, third digit
F8	Right hand, fourth digit
F9	Right hand, fifth digit
FA	Left hand, thumb
GG	Performance and payment of a screening mammogram and diagnostic mammogram on the same patient, same day
GH	Diagnostic mammogram converted from screening mammogram on same day
LC	Left circumflex coronary artery
LD	Left anterior descending coronary artery
LT	Left side
QM	Ambulance service provided under arrangement by a provider of services
QN	Ambulance service furnished directly by a provider of services
RC	Right coronary artery
RT	Right side
T1	Left foot, second digit
T2	Left foot, third digit
T3	Left foot, fourth digit
T4	Left foot, fifth digit
T5	Right foot, great toe
T6	Right foot, second digit
T7	Right foot, third digit
T8	Right foot, fourth digit
T9	Right foot, fifth digit
TA	Left foot, great toe

Definitions and Acronyms

American Medical Association (AMA). This is an association whose mission is to promote the art and science of medicine and the betterment of public health. It is also responsible for maintaining the Level I HCPCS (CPT) code set.

CPT. Current Procedural Terminology.

HCPCS. Healthcare Common Procedure Coding System.

Health Insurance Portability and Accountability Act (HIPAA). Act that serves to protect the privacy of individually identifiable health information.

REFERENCES

1. Centers for Medicare and Medicaid Services. Physician Quality Reporting Initiative (PQRI). www.cms.gov/pqri/. Accessed January 24, 2011.
2. American Medical Association. Category II Codes. www.ama-assn.org/ama/pub/physician-resources/solutions-managing-your-practice/coding-billing-insurance/cpt/about-cpt/category-ii-codes.shtml. Accessed January 24, 2011.
3. American Medical Association. *CPT Assistant 1990–2009*. Chicago, IL: American Medical Association; 2010.

Chapter 10

International Classification of Diseases

"The International Classification of Diseases (ICD) is the international standard for diagnostic classification for all general epidemiological [purposes], many health management purposes and clinical use. These include the analysis of the general health situation of population groups and monitoring of the incidence and prevalence of diseases and other health problems in relation to other variables such as the characteristics and circumstances of the individuals affected, payment, resource allocation, quality and guidelines. It is used to classify diseases and other health problems recorded on many types of health and vital records including death certificates and health records. In addition to enabling the storage and retrieval of diagnostic information for clinical, epidemiological and quality purposes, these records also provide the basis for the compilation of national mortality and morbidity statistics by WHO Member States."[1]

This chapter focuses on both ICD-9-CM and ICD-10-CM/PCS. ICD-9-CM is used to represent the diagnoses, signs, symptoms, and conditions responsible for or that impact patient care. Physicians, hospitals, ambulatory surgery centers, and all other providers use ICD-9-CM on their insurance claim forms. These codes represent "why" care was given, rather than "what" service was provided. From a medical necessity level, ICD-9-CM also helps support the type and level of care provided. As mentioned in Chapter 6, ICD-9-CM is also a key driver of the level of payment received. "ICD-10 was endorsed by the Forty-third World Health Assembly in May 1990 and came into use in WHO Member States [in] 1994. The classification is the latest in a series which has its origins in the 1850s. The first edition, known as the International List of Causes of Death, was adopted by the International Statistical Institute in 1893. WHO took over the responsibility for the ICD at its creation in 1948 when the Sixth Revision, which included causes of morbidity for the first time, was published. The World Health Assembly adopted in 1967 the WHO Nomenclature Regulations that stipulate use of ICD in its most current revision for mortality and morbidity statistics by all Member States."[1] In the United States, ICD-10 codes will soon be replacing the ICD-9-CM codes for all claims with dates of service or for inpatient claims with dates of discharge on and after October 1, 2013.

International Classification of Diseases, Ninth Revision, Clinical Modification (ICD-9-CM)

As discussed in Chapter 1, ICD-9-CM is one of the principal coding sets for health care in the United States. ICD-9-CM is the United States' version of ICD-9, which was maintained by the World Health Organization (WHO). WHO no longer maintains ICD-9 since the international conversion to ICD-10. Although many countries are using a derivative of ICD-10, the United States, until October 1, 2013, is still using ICD-9-CM for claims submission.[2]

The CM suffix represents the Clinical Modifications made by the United States from the ICD-9. ICD-9 is international, ICD-9-CM is the United States' version, ICD-9-AM represents the Australian version, etc.

ICD-9-CM Documentation

In order to use ICD-9-CM codes correctly, the documentation must:

- Be specific in describing the patient's condition, disease, illness, or injury;
- Distinguish between a chronic versus an acute condition; and
- Identify, when possible or applicable, the reason for the condition and/or an occurring manifestation of the condition.

The more specific and complete the documentation, the better it is for code assignment. However, conditions noted within an encounter's record that do not directly impact the care for that encounter should not be coded.

For example, if a physician is seeing a patient for a spider bite and the physician also indicates that the patient is allergic to spiders, that bite plus the allergy would be important to code. If the physician also noted that the patient suffered but has recovered from a fracture two years ago, that would not be important to the current encounter and should not be coded.

ICD-9-CM Manual

There are three volumes in ICD-9-CM as illustrated in Figure 10-1.

Although the index is called Volume II of ICD-9-CM, it appears first in the ICD-9-CM manual. The volume contains an alphabetic index of diseases and injuries, a table of drugs and chemicals, and an index of external causes.

Note

As with any index, its purpose is to point the user in the right direction, but one should never code from the index. The tabular description and instructions must be referred to prior to assigning a code.

Volume I, which is the tabular listing, is subdivided into:

- 19 chapters, consisting of 17 chapters for diseases and injuries plus two special chapters:
  - The 17 chapters for diseases and injuries are in numeric order:
    1. Infectious and Parasitic Diseases
    2. Neoplasms
    3. Endocrine, Nutritional, and Metabolic Diseases and Immunity Disorders
    4. Diseases of the Blood and Blood-Forming Organs
    5. Mental Disorders
    6. Diseases of the Nervous System and Sense Organs
    7. Diseases of the Circulatory System
    8. Diseases of the Respiratory System
    9. Diseases of the Digestive System

FIGURE 10-1 *Structure of ICD-9-CM Manual*

Volume I	Volume II	Volume III
Tabular List of Diseases	Alphabetic Index to Diseases	Tabular List and Alphabetic Index for Procedures
Used in billing for most providers (physicians, hospitals, etc)		Used in billing for inpatient hospital facility services; not used in physicians' offices
Contain codes for diagnoses and symptoms, factors influencing health		Contains codes for surgical and nonsurgical procedures

10. Diseases of the Genitourinary System
11. Complications of Pregnancy, Childbirth, and the Puerperium
12. Diseases of the Skin and Subcutaneous Tissue
13. Diseases of the Musculoskeletal System and Connective Tissue
14. Congenital Anomalies
15. Certain Conditions Originating in the Perinatal Period
16. Symptoms, Signs, and Ill-Defined Conditions
17. Injury and Poisoning

- A special chapter of V codes (codes beginning with the letter V) for factors influencing health status and contact with health services. V codes are used when an encounter falls into a category other than a disease or injury, which would be coded from the main section of ICD-9-CM (chapters 1 through 17). There are three ways this can occur:
  1. When a person who is not currently sick has a health service for a specific purpose (eg, to receive prophylactic service);
  2. When a person who has a disease or injury has a health service for a specific treatment (eg, dialysis for renal disease); and
  3. When there exists a circumstance that influences the person's health status but is not a current illness or injury (eg, personal history of colon cancer).
- A special chapter of E codes (codes beginning with the letter E) for supplemental classification of external causes of injury and poisoning. This section allows the coding of environmental events, circumstances, and conditions as the cause of injury, poisoning, and other adverse effects (eg, automobile accident, skiing accident).

• Appendices include:
  - Appendix A: Morphology of Neoplasms
  - Appendix B: Glossary of Mental Disorders (deleted as of October 1, 2004)
  - Appendix C: Classification of Drugs
  - Appendix D: Classification of Industrial Accidents
  - Appendix E: List of Three-Digit Categories

The manual is set up by chapter as shown above and, within the chapters, by section. For example, Chapter 7, "Diseases of the Circulatory System," has sections for acute rheumatic fever, chronic rheumatic heart disease, hypertensive disease, etc.

Within each section, the diagnoses are divided into three-digit categories, also called rubrics.

Note

Rubric represents a three-digit category of ICD-9-CM (Volume I) coding that provides an overall category of diagnosis.

The following is an example of a category code:

Hypertensive Disease (401-405.99)

401 Essential hypertension

Most of the category codes have a subcategory (fourth digit) and often a subclassification (fifth digit) further specifying the diagnosis. The subcategory is indicated by the addition of a decimal point and a fourth digit after the category code.

The following is an example of the fourth-digit subcategory level of specificity:

Hypertensive Disease (401-405.99)

401 Essential hypertension

401.0 Malignant

401.1 Benign

401.9 Unspecified

If there is not a subclassification (fifth digit) option, then the four-digit code most appropriately reflecting the documentation would be used. However, if there is a subclassification available, it must be used.

The following is an example of the fifth-digit subclassification level of specificity:

Hypertensive Disease (401-405.99)

402 Hypertensive heart disease

402.0 Malignant

402.00 Without heart failure

402.01 With heart failure

In the examples above, essential hypertension only has options for four-digit subcategory specificity, but malignant hypertensive heart disease has options for fifth-digit specificity. Therefore, for malignant hypertensive heart disease a fifth digit is required. Remember, ICD-9-CM codes can be three, four, or five characters long. If a fifth digit is available, it must be used. You cannot use a three-digit code if a fourth or fifth digit is available.

Volume III includes a tabular listing and index of surgical and nonsurgical procedures. This volume is used for inpatient facility coding and should not be used on outpatient hospital or physician bills. Its chapters are:

0. Procedures and interventions, not elsewhere classified
1. Operations on the Nervous System
2. Operations on the Endocrine System
3. Operations on the Eye
4. Operations on the Ear
5. Operations on the Nose, Mouth, and Pharynx
6. Operations on the Respiratory System
7. Operations on the Cardiovascular System
8. Operations on the Hemic and Lymphatic System
9. Operations on the Digestive System
10. Operations on the Urinary System
11. Operations on the Male Genital Organs
12. Operations on the Female Genital Organs
13. Obstetrical Procedures
14. Operations on the Musculoskeletal System
15. Operations on the Integumentary System
16. Miscellaneous Diagnostic and Therapeutic Procedures

ICD-9-CM, Volume III procedure codes consist of three or four digits, and the decimal falls after the second digit. Since most of this volume is divided by body system, the first two digits of the code represent the

FIGURE 10-2 *ICD-9-CM Code Structure*

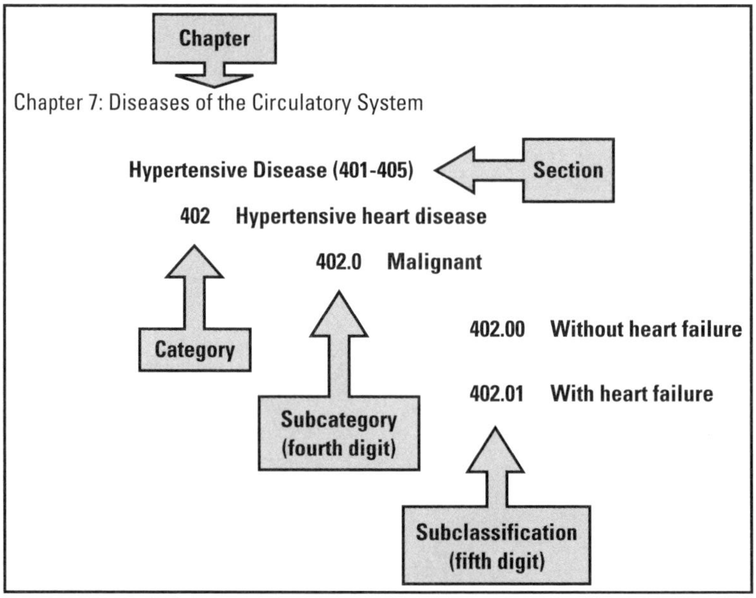

body system or anatomic site (except for chapters 0, 13, and 16). The third and, when applicable, fourth digits represent the type of procedure, the technique used, or a more specific site. Figure 10-3 shows an example of an ICD-9-CM procedure code.

ICD-9-CM Code Guidelines

Accurate ICD-9-CM coding depends on understanding the meaning of coding conventions, terms, notes, guidelines, and abbreviations. Conventions are the general rules for using ICD-9-CM codes. These conventions are not the same as the guidelines; rather they are basic constructs of how ICD-9-CM is to be used and referenced along with definitions of instructions found within the manual. The conventions give definitions for key terms and symbols used within ICD-9-CM. Figure 10-4 shows a few of the conventions within ICD-9-CM (not an all-inclusive list).

FIGURE 10-3 *ICD-9-CM Procedure Code Structure*

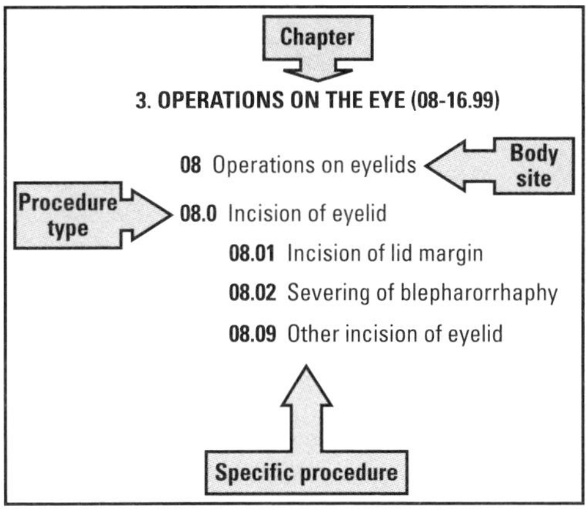

In addition, each year the National Center for Health Statistics (NCHS) produces updated guidelines[3] for coding within ICD-9-CM. These are released for October implementation (to coincide with the code updates). These guidelines must be reviewed each year and compared to the prior year's guidelines for changes. Accuracy depends on coders' staying current with the rules and regulations of coding. Figure 10-5 is a snapshot of the first page of one year's guidelines.

Lastly, the American Hospital Association (AHA) also publishes *Coding Clinic*.[4] *Coding Clinic* is a quarterly publication that provides the official ICD-9-CM coding guidelines developed by the AHA, the American Health Information Management Association (AHIMA), the Centers for Medicare and Medicaid Services (CMS), and NCHS.

FIGURE 10-4 *Example of ICD-9-CM Conventions*

Abbreviations

a. Index Abbreviations

NEC "Not elsewhere classifiable"

This abbreviation in the index represents "other specified." When a specific code is not available for a condition the index directs the coder to the "other specified" code in the tabular.

b. Tabular Abbreviations

NEC "Not elsewhere classifiable"

This abbreviation in the tabular represents "other specified." When a specific code is not available for a condition the tabular includes an NEC entry under a code to identify the code as the "other specified" code.

Punctuation

[ ] Brackets are used in the tabular list to enclose synonyms, alternative wording or explanatory phrases. Brackets are used in the index to identify manifestation codes.

( ) Parentheses are used in both the index and tabular to enclose supplementary words which may be present or absent in the statement of a disease or procedure without affecting the code number to which it is assigned. The terms within the parentheses are referred to as nonessential modifiers.

FIGURE 10-5 *Snapshot of NCHS ICD-9-CM Guidelines*

> **ICD-9-CM Official Guidelines for Coding and Reporting**
> **Effective October 1, 2010**
> **Narrative changes appear in bold text**
> **Items underlined have been moved within the guidelines since October 1, 2009**
>
> The Centers for Medicare and Medicaid Services (CMS) and the National Center for Health Statistics (NCHS), two departments within the U.S. Federal Government's Department of Health and Human Services (DHHS) provide the following guidelines for coding and reporting using the International Classification of Diseases, 9th Revision, Clinical Modification (ICD-9-CM). These guidelines should be used as a companion document to the official version of the ICD-9-CM as published on CD-ROM by the U.S. Government Printing Office (GPO).
>
> These guidelines have been approved by the four organizations that make up the Cooperating Parties for the ICD-9-CM: the American Hospital Association (AHA), the American Health Information Management Association (AHIMA), CMS, and NCHS. These guidelines are included on the official government version of the ICD-9-CM, and also appear in "*Coding Clinic for ICD-9-CM*" published by the AHA.

Bottom Line

ICD-9-CM coding is vitally important in coding and payment. It helps support the medical necessity of care provided. Coverage is dependent upon diagnosis coding. For inpatient hospital facility payment, it drives the MS-DRG classification. Most importantly, when an ICD-9-CM code is assigned, the patient is labeled with that diagnosis. Care here is critical.

International Classification of Diseases, Tenth Revision (ICD-10)

As mentioned at the beginning of this chapter, ICD-10-CM/PCS codes will replace ICD-9-CM codes for all claims with dates of service or for inpatient claims with dates of discharge on and after October 1, 2013. Claims that do not use ICD-10-CM/PCS codes on October 1, 2013 will be rejected. In order to transition to ICD-10-CM/PCS, both health care providers and payers need to begin preparing as soon as possible. This can include updates to software, clinical, coding, billing, and adjudication. ICD-10-CM/PCS is much more granular, with specific details of diagnoses and conditions, which requires more available codes. ICD-10-CM provides approximately five times as many codes as ICD-9-CM. This classification coding system will easily be able to expand when new conditions are discovered or when new procedures are introduced. ICD-9-CM has very limited expansion capabilities.

There are two parts to ICD-10-CM/PCS:

ICD-10-CM. The clinical modification (CM) to the international ICD-10 includes diagnosis codes similar to Volumes I and II of ICD-9-CM.

ICD-10-PCS. PCS is the procedure coding system portion of ICD-10. This replaces Volume III of ICD-9-CM. This will be used for inpatient hospital coding only.

Figure 10-6 shows that ICD-10-CM will be maintained by the NCHS and ICD-10-PCS will be the responsibility of CMS.

FIGURE 10-6 *Entities Responsible for Maintenance ICD-10-CM/PCS*

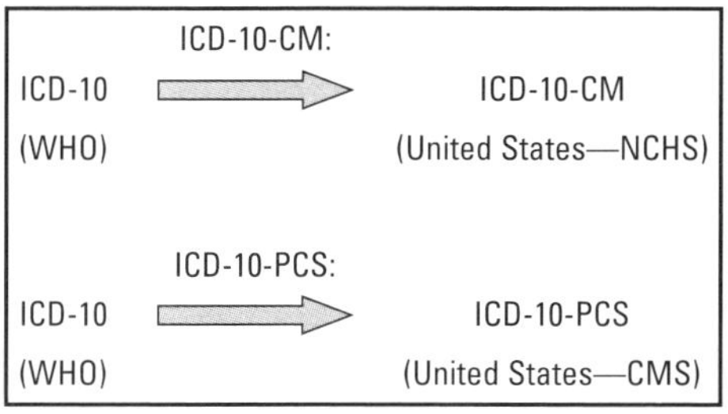

Structural Differences Between ICD-9-CM and ICD-10-CM/PCS

Figure 10-7 highlights the differences between ICD-9-CM Volumes I and II and ICD-10-CM.

Figure 10-8 highlights the differences between ICD-9-CM (Volume III) and ICD-10-PCS.

The ICD-10-CM manual has an index and a tabular listing. There are 21 chapters, and the current manual may be downloaded electronically by visiting the NCHS ICD-10-CM Web site.[5]

Note

Do not print the files as they can be quite large. Save the files to your computer or purchase them from one of the many vendors offering hardcopy manuals.

Figure 10-9 provides a snapshot of the index, tabular, chapter heading, and code detail of ICD-10-CM manual.

ICD-10-CM coding is very different from ICD-9-CM coding. For example, ICD-10-CM code M22.8x1 represents a diagnosis of other disorders of the left patella as represented in Figure 10-10. Notice the lowercase *x* in this code; this is the placeholder, which means that there was no applicable fifth character, but a sixth character was needed to specify the laterality of this code.

FIGURE 10-7 *Differences Between ICD-9-CM (Volumes I and II) and ICD-10-CM*

ICD-9-CM (Volumes I and II)	ICD-10-CM
≈14,500 total codes	≈ 69,000 codes
3 to 5 characters per code – maximum 5 characters	3 to 7 characters per code – maximum 7 characters
Numeric except for supplementary codes (V and E)	All codes are alphanumeric (1st character will always be a letter)
17 chapters with two supplementary chapters – total 19 chapters	21 chapters – no supplementary chapters
No laterality within code nomenclature	Laterality is codeable
Trimesters for pregnancy are not addressed	Trimesters for pregnancy are included
Example: 250.00 - Diabetes mellitus without mention of complication, type II or unspecified type, not stated as uncontrolled	Example: E11.9 - Type 2 diabetes mellitus without complications
Example: V23.49 - Pregnancy with other poor obstetric history	Example: O09.10 - Supervision of pregnancy with history of ectopic or molar pregnancy, unspecified trimester

FIGURE 10-8 *Differences Between ICD-9-CM (Volume III) and ICD-10-PCS*

ICD-9-CM (Volume III)	ICD-10-PCS
≈3,000 codes available	≈87,000 codes available
3-4 characters per code with a decimal after the 2nd character	Always 7 characters per code – no decimal
All numeric	All alphanumeric
Example: 36.14 - (Aorto)coronary bypass of four or more coronary arteries	Examples: 02130AF – bypass coronary artery, four or more sites to abdominal artery with autologous arterial tissue, open approach OR 02130AW – bypass coronary artery, four or more sites to aorta with Autologous arterial tissue, open approach OR Many other options

FIGURE 10-9 *Snapshot of ICD-10-CM Manual*

ICD-10-CM INDEX TO DISEASES and INJURIES

A | B | C | D | E | F | G | H | I | J | K | L | M | N | O | P | Q | R | S | T | U | V | W | X | Y | Z

A

Aarskog's syndrome Q87.1
Abandonment —*see* Maltreatment, abandonment
Abasia (-astasia) (hysterical) F44.4
Abderhalden-Kaufmann-Lignac syndrome (cystinosis) E72.04
Abdomen, abdominal —*see also* condition
- acute R10.0
- angina K55.1
- muscle deficiency syndrome Q79.4
Abdominalgia —*see* Pain, abdominal
Abduction contracture, hip or other joint —*see* Contraction, joint
Aberrant (congenital) —*see also* Malposition, congenital
- adrenal gland Q89.1
- artery (peripheral) Q27.8
- - basilar NEC Q28.1
- - cerebral Q28.3
- - coronary Q24.5
- - digestive system Q27.8
- - eye Q15.8
- - lower limb Q27.8

ICD-10-CM TABULAR LIST of DISEASES and INJURIES

Table of Contents

1 Certain infectious and parasitic diseases (A00-B99)
2 Neoplasms (C00-D49)
3 Diseases of the blood and blood-forming organs and certain disorders involving the immune mechanism (D50-D89)
4 Endocrine, nutritional and metabolic diseases (E00-E89)
5 Mental and behavioral disorders (F01-F99)
6 Diseases of the nervous system (G00-G99)
7 Diseases of the eye and adnexa (H00-H59)
8 Diseases of the ear and mastoid process (H60-H95)
9 Diseases of the circulatory system (I00-I99)
10 Diseases of the respiratory system (J00-J99)
11 Diseases of the digestive system (K00-K94)
12 Diseases of the skin and subcutaneous tissue (L00-L99)
13 Diseases of the musculoskeletal system and connective tissue (M00-M99)
14 Diseases of the genitourinary system (N00-N99)
15 Pregnancy, childbirth and the puerperium (O00-O99)
16 Certain conditions originating in the perinatal period (P00-P96)
17 Congenital malformations, deformations and chromosomal abnormalities (Q00-Q99)
18 Symptoms, signs and abnormal clinical and laboratory findings, not elsewhere classified (R00-R99)
19 Injury, poisoning and certain other consequences of external causes (S00-T88)
20 External causes of morbidity (V00-Y99)
21 Factors influencing health status and contact with health services (Z00-Z99)

FIGURE 10-9 *(continued)*

Chapter 1

Certain infectious and parasitic diseases (A00-B99)

Includes: diseases generally recognized as communicable or transmissible

Use additional code for any associated drug resistance (Z16)

Excludes1: carrier or suspected carrier of infectious disease (Z22.-)
certain localized infections - see body system-related chapters
infectious and parasitic diseases complicating pregnancy, childbirth and the puerperium (O98.-)
influenza and other acute respiratory infections (J00-J22)

Excludes2: infectious and parasitic diseases specific to the perinatal period (P35-P39)

This chapter contains the following blocks:

A00-A09	Intestinal infectious diseases
A15-A19	Tuberculosis
A20-A28	Certain zoonotic bacterial diseases
A30-A49	Other bacterial diseases
A50-A64	Infections with a predominantly sexual mode of transmission
A65-A69	Other spirochetal diseases
A70-A74	Other diseases caused by chlamydiae
A75-A79	Rickettsioses
A80-A89	Viral and prion infections of the central nervous system
A90-A99	Arthropod-borne viral fevers and viral hemorrhagic fevers
B00-B09	Viral infections characterized by skin and mucous membrane lesions
B10	Other human herpesviruses
B15-B19	Viral hepatitis
B20	Human immunodeficiency virus [HIV] disease
B25-B34	Other viral diseases
B35-B49	Mycoses

Intestinal infectious diseases (A00-A09)

A00 Cholera

A00.0 Cholera due to Vibrio cholerae 01, biovar cholerae
Classical cholera

A00.1 Cholera due to Vibrio cholerae 01, biovar eltor
Cholera eltor

A00.9 Cholera, unspecified

A01 Typhoid and paratyphoid fevers

A01.0 Typhoid fever
Infection due to Salmonella typhi

A01.00 Typhoid fever, unspecified

A01.01 Typhoid meningitis

A01.02 Typhoid fever with heart involvement
Typhoid endocarditis
Typhoid myocarditis

A01.03 Typhoid pneumonia

A01.04 Typhoid arthritis

As an example of ICD-10-PCS coding, code 072KX0Z represents a medical/surgical procedure performed (first character 0) on the lymphatic and hemic systems (second character 7) specifically the thoracic duct (fourth character K) to change a device (third character 2) using an external approach (fifth character X) to reach the site, and the type of device changed was a drainage device (sixth character 0). There was no qualifier applicable (seventh character Z), as illustrated by the ICD-10-PCS table in Figure 10-11.

FIGURE 10-10 *Example of ICD-10-CM Code*

M22.4 Chondromalacia patellae
- **M22.40 Chondromalacia patellae, unspecified knee**
- **M22.41 Chondromalacia patellae, right knee**
- **M22.42 Chondromalacia patellae, left knee**

M22.8 Other disorders of patella
- **M22.8x Other disorders of patella**
  - **M22.8x1 Other disorders of patella, right knee**
  - **M22.8x2 Other disorders of patella, left knee**
  - **M22.8x9 Other disorders of patella, unspecified knee**

M22.9 Unspecified disorder of patella
- **M22.90 Unspecified disorder of patella, unspecified knee**
- **M22.91 Unspecified disorder of patella, right knee**
- **M22.92 Unspecified disorder of patella, left knee**

ICD-10-CM/PCS Guidelines

There is a wealth of information, including guidelines on ICD-10-CM/PCS, on the CMS Web site.[6] As providers move toward the adoption of ICD-10-CM/PCS, a current understanding of the guidelines is incredibly important.

Definitions and Acronyms

AHA *Coding Clinic*.[4] Quarterly publication of the joint efforts of the American Hospital Association (AHA), the American Health Information Management Association (AHIMA), the Centers for Medicare and Medicaid Services (CMS), and NCHS.

Centers for Medicare & Medicaid Services (CMS). This is an agency within the Department of Health and Human Services (HHS) in charge of managing the Medicare and Medicaid federal health care programs. Responsible for overseeing the United States' ICD-10-PCS coding system.

ICD-10-CM. Diagnosis coding system to replace Volumes I and II of ICD-9-CM in the United States on October 1, 2013.

ICD-10-PCS. Hospital inpatient procedure coding system to replace Volume III of ICD-9-CM in the United States on October 1, 2013.

National Center for Health Statistics (NCHS). An agency primarily responsible for the nation's health statistics. Responsible for coordinating the United States' ICD-10-CM coding guidelines.

World Health Organization (WHO). Organization responsible for maintaining the International Classification of Diseases (ICD).

FIGURE 10-11 *Example of ICD-10-PCS Table*

Section **0** Medical and Surgical *Body System* **7** Lymphatic and Hemic Systems *Operation* **2** Change: Taking out or off a device from a body part and putting back an identical or similar device in or on the same body part without cutting or puncturing the skin or a mucous membrane			
Body Part	*Approach*	*Device*	*Qualifier*
K Thoracic Duct **L** Cisterna Chyli **M** Thymus **N** Lymphatic **P** Spleen **T** Bone Marrow	**X** External	**0** Drainage Device **Y** Other Device	**Z** No Qualifier

REFERENCES

1. World Health Organization (WHO). International Classification of Diseases (ICD). Available at: www.who.int/classifications/icd/en/. Accessed January 13, 2011.
2. National Center for Health Statistics (NCHS). International Classification of Diseases, 9th Revision, Clinical Modification (ICD-9-CM). Available at: www.cdc.gov/nchs/icd/icd9cm.htm. Accessed January 18, 2011.
3. National Center for Health Statistics (NCHS). International Classification of Diseases, 9th Revision, Clinical Modification (ICD-9-CM). ICD-9-CM Guidelines. Available at: www.cdc.gov/nchs/data/icd9/icdguide10.pdf. Accessed January 3, 2011.
4. American Hospital Association (AHA). *Coding Clinic* Products. Available at: www.ahacentraloffice.org/ahacentraloffice/shtml/Products.shtml. Accessed January 18, 2011.
5. National Center for Health Statistics (NCHS). International Classification of Diseases, 10th Revision, Clinical Modification (ICD-10-CM). Available at: www.cdc.gov/nchs/icd/icd10cm.htm. Accessed January 18, 2011.
6. Centers for Medicare and Medicaid Services (CMS). ICD-10 Web site. Available at: www.cms.gov/ICD10/. Accessed January 19, 2011.

Chapter 11

Electronic Health Records

Overview of Electronic Health Records

An electronic health record (EHR), also known as an electronic medical record (EMR), is a patient's medical record in electronic format. The EHR helps make the clinician's workflow more efficient, makes retrieval of data easier, and facilitates the sharing of information with other caregivers, as well as insurance companies. At the same time, storing medical records electronically has some definite advantages and disadvantages.

As shown in Table 11-1, there are quite a few advantages and some significant disadvantages. One advantage is that by having medical records stored electronically, there is a reduced need for the physical space required for hardcopy records. Paper records require significant amounts of space for storage, especially considering how long patient records must be saved. Electronic records make it much easier to share information with other caregivers. Distributing paper records usually requires photocopying, faxing, and other manual steps, which consume considerable resources and heighten the concern over patient confidentiality.

Finally, this book would be remiss if it did not point out a significant positive aspect of electronic records. They are almost always legible, while handwritten documentation might prove difficult to read depending on the author's handwriting.

Among the disadvantages is the charge of transferring paper records to an EHR to effectively incorporate older paper records into the new electronic record. One common option providers are using to incorporate paper records into the EHR is by scanning the documents and retaining them as images. This saves the time needed to convert them to an electronic format, but of course, the records are not fully integrated using this method.

Another potential disadvantage or challenge of EHRs is when a patient has care provided at different facilities. Updating records at both will need to be coordinated.

A different challenge is a financial one. There are initial and ongoing expenditures necessary to convert to and maintain an EHR system. Computers, storage, software, training, and security are just a few.

Perhaps the biggest concern is maintaining the patient's privacy in EHRs. Everyone has heard the horror stories of electronic banking systems, credit cards, and other computerized information being accessed by nefarious entities. This is a potential with any data stored electronically.

Another consideration when using EHRs is ensuring the integrity of the documentation. There must be adequate policies in place to help ensure key documentation principles are met (see Chapter 8 on documentation). A few of the documentation integrity points to watch out for include:

- ***Authentication.*** There can be no room for someone other than the authenticating author to add to the record. Most medical records will have multiple entries by multiple providers; however, there must be a way to unmistakably establish the author of each entry.

TABLE 11-1 *Advantages and Disadvantages of Electronic Health Records*

Advantages of EHRs	Disadvantages of EHRs
EHRs reduce the physical space required for storing records.	Incorporating old paper records into the EHR can prove challenging.
Records can be easily shared with other providers to coordinate care (paper records require photocopying, faxing, etc).	The ability to share records for coordinating care creates an additional concern of patient confidentiality.
Documenting within the electronic record is often easier than documenting on paper.	Ease of documenting sometimes makes the integrity of the documentation questionable (too easy to overdocument).
Legibility is sometimes an issue with handwritten notes—not the case with EHRs.	The potential for errors (typo or error in documenting) still exists.
Sorting and searching is much easier in electronic format (paper is stored in one place, hopefully with cross-references).	Costs are higher.
	The learning curve is higher as compared to paper record documenting.

- ***Current documentation.*** The documentation of each patient encounter should be dynamically created and not simply pulled forward from another visit.

There should be policies and procedures in place to ensure compliance with proper documentation requirements in the EHR including:

- What medical information can be copied from within a patient's record from one encounter to the next;
- How corrections, amendments, and other changes can be made; and
- How to ensure confidentiality is maintained.

There are many policies that should be carefully implemented to make certain documentation purity is protected.

EHR Adoption Incentives

CMS is offering incentives for providers to convert to EHRs as long as specific requirements are met.[1] These requirements primarily are focused on ensuring the incentives induce the appropriate implementation of an EHR. The requirements are divided by provider type and are outlined in Table 11-2.

Meaningful Use

There are three elements of meaningful use[2]:

1. The EHR must be used in a meaningful manner (eg, e-prescribing);
2. The EHR must be used to electronically exchange health information to improve quality of care; and
3. The EHR must be used to submit clinical quality and other measures, such as in the Physician Quality Reporting Initiative (PQRI).

Certified EHR

In order to qualify for the incentives, the EHR must be certified.[3] This is to help assure providers and CMS that the EHR is capable, functional, and secure.

TABLE 11-2 *CMS Incentive Requirements for EHR Conversion*

Provider Type	Requirements
Professional Services	Licensure of MD, DO, DC, DPM, NP, PA, CNM, Optometrist. Meet a specified percentage of Medicare/Medicaid patient volume. Must demonstrate meaningful use of the EHR. Must adopt a certified EHR.
Hospital Services	Hospitals that are reimbursed under Inpatient Prospective Payment Systems (IPPS) or Critical Access Hospitals (CAH). Have a certain percentage of Medicare or Medicaid patient volume. Must demonstrate meaningful use of the EHR. Must adopt a certified EHR.

> The way Medicare looks at an EMR, nothing has changed in its rules from using paper. Instead of pencil and paper, it's pixels and bytes.[4]

Definitions and Acronyms

Centers for Medicare and Medicaid Services (CMS). This is an agency of the Department of Health and Human Services (HHS) responsible for overseeing the Medicare and Medicaid federal health care programs.

Electronic health record (EHR). Medical record stored in an electronic format.

Eligible Providers (EPs). Doctors that CMS deems eligible for incentive payments to transition to EHRs.

Eligible Hospitals (EHs). Hospitals that CMS deems eligible for incentive payments to transition to EHRs.

meaningful use. Using, through certified technology, an EHR in a meaningful manner and with submission of clinical quality measures.

REFERENCES

1. Centers for Medicare and Medicaid Services. Meaningful Use. Available at: www.cms.gov/EHRIncentivePrograms/30_Meaningful_Use.asp. Accessed January 20, 2011.
2. Centers for Medicare and Medicaid Services. EHR Incentive Programs. Available at: www.cms.gov/EHRIncentivePrograms/01_Overview.asp#TopOfPage. Accessed January 20, 2011.
3. The Office of the National Coordinator for Health Information Technology. Standards and Certification for Electronic Health Records. Available at: http://healthit.hhs.gov/portal/server.pt?open=512&objID=2884&parentname=CommunityPage&parentid=357&mode=2&in_hi_userid=12059&cached=true. Accessed January 20, 2011.
4. Dr. Debra Patterson, Medicare Medical Director. TrailBlazer Health Enterprises' Medicare Compliance Alert. June 2, 2008.

Chapter 12

Fraud and Abuse Issues in Health Care Coding, Payment, and Documentation

Fraud and Abuse Overview

Most providers deliver great patient care and conduct business (eg, billing insurance, coding services and diagnoses) in a highly ethical manner. However, there have been cases of unscrupulous billing. Through audits by the government and private insurers, unfortunate situations of misrepresenting services have been discovered. Although there are relatively few occurrences, this does taint the entire process of billing for payment and being paid. Medicare and Medicaid, as well as private payers, have a responsibility to ensure monies spent on paying claims are appropriate. It is important to remember that tax dollars are used to pay Medicare and Medicaid claims.

Insurers have undertaken measures to discover deceptions in billing. Most insurance companies have departments devoted to "program integrity" or "fraud and abuse" to audit providers for compliance with coding and billing guidelines. Billions of dollars over the past decade have been recovered just by the federal government in cases of billing errors.

Fraud and abuse in health care has serious consequences if providers are found to be guilty. According to the Health Care Fraud and Abuse Control Program (HCFAC) report of fiscal year 2009,[1,2] the federal government successfully obtained over $1.6 billion in judgments and settlements in health care fraud cases. Also, for 2009, there were over 1,000 new fraud investigations opened with another 1,621 pending. These are big numbers, and health care fraud earns a lot of attention.

Fraud is defined as a deliberate falsification that causes another person to suffer damages (usually monetary losses). Fraud means the misrepresentation was intentional.

Abuse means the falsification was an innocent mistake, but nonetheless misrepresentative.

An example of fraud in health care billing might be when a provider bills for services that were not provided or charges for patient visits that never occurred. An example of abuse could be when the provider coded for a more complex service than was performed due to a misunderstanding of the coding system.

Regardless of whether the error is considered fraudulent or abusive, monies received would need to be returned, and potential fines and a prospect of jail time could result, depending on the extent of the misrepresentation. Overall, errors are best to be avoided.

Office of Inspector General (OIG)

The Office of Inspector General (OIG) was established in the U.S. Department of Health and Human Services (HHS). One of the OIG's primary purposes is to identify and eliminate fraud, waste, and abuse in the department's programs. To accomplish this, the OIG performs or oversees audits, inspections, and other investigations. In addition, the OIG has the authority to exclude providers from participation in federal health care programs. The OIG can also impose civil monetary penalties (CMPs).

Medicare Claims Review Programs

Centers for Medicare & Medicaid Services (CMS) has been on the forefront of combating deceptive practices within health care billing, and several initiatives are ongoing to prevent improper payments. Medicare efforts are divided into two primary categories: prepayment and postpayment reviews.[3] Prepayment reviews are performed before the claim is processed for payment. If there are discoveries of potential problems, the claim is corrected and paid appropriately or rejected and returned to the provider for correction. Postpayment reviews are performed after a claim has been paid and if there are problems with the payments, recoveries of overpayments, or additional payments, or if a claim was underpaid.

The entities that are responsible for reviewing inappropriate payments are shown in Table 12-1 and Table 12-2.

TABLE 12-1 *Medicare Prepayment Reviewers*

Prepayment Reviews	Responsible Party
National Correct Coding Initiative (NCCI) Edits	Medicare Administrative Contractors (MACs)
Medically Unlikely Edits (MUEs)	MACs
Medical Review	MACs

TABLE 12-2 *Medicare Postpayment Reviewers*

Postpayment Reviews	Responsible Party
Recovery Audit Contractor (RAC) Audits	Recovery Audit Contractors (RACs)
Comprehensive Error Rate Testing (CERT) program	Comprehensive Error Rate Testing Review and Documentation Contractors
Medical Review	Medicare Administrative Contractors (MACs)

National Correct Coding Initiative Edits

The National Correct Coding Initiative (NCCI) was developed by CMS to help ensure correct coding methodologies were followed to avoid inappropriate payments for Medicare Part B claims (eg, physician and outpatient hospital services). These edits are automated prepayment edits that are reached by analyzing every pair of codes billed for the same patient on the same service date by the same provider to see if an edit exists in the NCCI. If there is an NCCI edit, one of the codes is denied unless the edit is bypassed with an NCCI modifier (see Chapter 9 on HCPCS coding).

An example of an NCCI edit would be if a provider billed for a lesion excision and skin repair on the same patient on a single service date. In CPT coding guidelines, simple repairs are included in the excision codes; therefore, separately coding the repair would be incorrect and would generate an NCCI edit. However, if the repair was performed on a different site from where the lesion was removed, both may be billed and a modifier appended to the repair to alert the payer that procedure was indeed separate from the excision.

Another example would be if a provider billed for a diagnostic colonoscopy and a screening colonoscopy on a single patient on a single date of service. It would be highly unlikely for two colonoscopies to be performed on a single date, and therefore, that billing would generate an NCCI edit resulting in denial of payment for one of the colonoscopies. In this example, the billing was incorrect, and the payment was appropriately denied.

Medically Unlikely Edits

Medically Unlikely Edits (MUEs) are edits that limit the number of services (also known as units of service) allowed for a single patient on a single date of service. The MUE basically represents the allowed maximum number of services reported on a single date of service, which is also a prepayment edit that is automatically assessed when a claim is submitted. This edit is driven by HCPCS code, and to expedite the process, rather than look for pairs of codes erroneously billed together, the MUE looks for a single HCPCS code that is erroneously billed in multiple units.

Similar to the NCCI edits, if a diagnostic colonoscopy was performed and billed with two units of service for the same patient on a single date of service, the MUE would be triggered. Again, the trigger is the oddity of having two colonoscopies performed on a single date. It is important to note and distinguish the difference from the preceding example. Here, it was not two different colonoscopies (ie, screening and diagnostic) that was billed; instead, it was a single colonoscopy billed as two units.

As with NCCI edits, there are modifiers that may be used, **when appropriate**, to bypass these edits as long as the services are billed as separate line items.

Comprehensive Error Rate Testing Program

Comprehensive Error Rate Testing (CERT) is a postpayment random audit only performed on fee-for-service (FFS) claims to develop an error rate and to help make education, policy, and review decisions going forward.

Recovery Audit Contractor (RAC) Program

A Medicare Recovery Audit Contractor (RAC) detects and corrects improper payments on Medicare FFS claims. Each RAC uses its own proprietary software to identify claims in which there is a likelihood of inappropriate payment. RACs are tasked with discovering both underpayments and overpayments and are currently paid based on a percentage of what is identified as either overpayments or underpayments.

Medicare Administrative Contractor (MAC) Medical Review Program

Medicare uses information gleaned from findings within other programs (CERT, RAC), patient complaints, etc, to target areas for manual review. If a MAC performs a medical review and finds discrepancies, the MAC can provide feedback and training to the provider to avert future problems. In these cases, the providers are often placed on a systematic prepayment review of their claims until the problems are found to be resolved.

Fraud and Abuse Laws

"The five most important Federal fraud and abuse laws that apply to physicians are the False Claims Act (FCA), the Anti-Kickback Statute (AKS), the Physician Self-Referral Law (Stark law), the Exclusion Authorities, and the Civil Monetary Penalties Law (CMPL). Government agencies, including the Department of Justice, the Department of Health & Human Services Office of Inspector General (OIG), and the Centers for Medicare & Medicaid Services (CMS), are charged with enforcing these laws. As you begin your career, it is crucial to understand these laws not only because following them is the right thing to do, but also because violating them could result in criminal penalties, civil fines, exclusion from the Federal health care programs, or loss of your medical license from your State medical board."[4]

For more information on federal fraud and abuse laws, go to www.ama-assn.org/ama/pub/physician-resources/legal-topics/regulatory-compliance-topics/health-care-fraud-abuse/federal-fraud-enforcement-physician-compliance/federal-fraud-abuse-laws.page.

The Federal Civil Monetary Penalties Statute (Section 1128A of the Social Security Act/42 USC 1320a-7aa)

"Health care professionals and entities are prohibited from presenting or causing to be presented claims for services that the individual or entity 'knows or should know' were not provided as claimed. This provision applies to persons or entities that know or should know that the claims are false or fraudulent, and it prohibits anyone from providing false or misleading information on coverage that could reasonably be expected to influence a decision regarding when to discharge a person from inpatient hospital services. Civil monetary penalties (CMPs) may be applied in situations where the service was not provided as claimed or where the service was provided during a period in which the professional or entity was excluded from the program. Violation may result [in] CMPs of up to $10,000 per claim, or $15,000 for each individual with respect to whom false or misleading information was given, and assessment payments (with part going for restitution) of up to three times the amount claimed. Physicians who certify the need for home health services and who know that all of the requirements for this care are not met, are subject to CMPs of not more than the greater of $5,000 or three times the amount of payments for services that are made pursuant to the certification. The Health Insurance Portability and Accountability Act of 1996, Public Law 104–191 (HIPAA), clarified that the term 'should know' includes, with respect to information set out in a claim, 'acts in deliberate ignorance' or in 'reckless disregard of the truth or falsity' and 'no proof of specific intent to defraud is required.'"[5]

Federal Civil False Claims Act (31 USC 3829–3733)

"The Act imposes liability upon anyone who knowingly makes, uses, or causes to be made or used, a false record or statement to get a false or fraudulent claim paid or approved by the Government. Depending on the applicable part of the statute, a false statement may or may not be necessary on the claim submitted to the Government for payment for liability."[5]

Essentially, the False Claims Act (FCA) protects the government from being overcharged or billed for poor services. If a billing entity knows the claim being submitted for payment is fraudulent, that is illegal activity.

The fines may result in three times the overpaid amount plus $11,000 per claim. Because of the potential fines, and repayment plus likely legal fees, filing false claims certainly does not pay.

Note

The FCA defines "knowingly" to include reckless disregard of the truth. If you are expected to have known better, that is good enough.

There is also a Qui Tam provision in the FCA. This allows for a private citizen to file a suit in the name of the United States government charging fraud against someone receiving government funds, for example, a hospital billing Medicare. Qui Tam allows the private citizen to receive recompense via a percentage of the government's recoupment.

Qui Tam is *Latin for He who sues on behalf of the king as well as for himself.*

"Anti-Kickback" Law/Criminal Penalties for Acts Involving Federal Health Care Programs (Section 1128B of the Social Security Act/42 USC 1320a-7b)

"Individuals and entities are prohibited from 'knowingly and willfully' making false statements or representations in applying for benefits or payments under all federal and state health care programs. Individuals also are prohibited from fraudulently concealing or failing to disclose knowledge of an event relating to an initial or continued right to benefits or payments. There is also a prohibition against knowingly and willfully soliciting or receiving any remuneration (including any kickbacks, bribe or rebate) directly or indirectly, in cash or in kind in exchange for referrals; or in return for purchasing, leasing, ordering, or arranging for or recommending purchasing, leasing, or ordering any good, facility, service, or item for which payment may be made in whole or in part under a federal health care program. Violations may result in a felony conviction, with penalties including imprisonment for up to five years and a fine of up to $25,000. (Related safe harbor regulations define payment practices that are not within the meaning of prohibited 'remuneration.' The regulations provide immunity from criminal prosecution and civil exclusion for payment practices that fall within the safe harbor. Failure to fall within a safe harbor, however, does not mean that a payment arrangement necessarily violates the statute. Current safe harbors address: investment interests; space rental; equipment rental; personal services and management contracts; practice sale; referral services; warranties; discounts; employment relationships; waiver of co-insurance and deductible amounts; group purchasing organizations; increased coverage or reduced cost sharing under a risk-basis or prepaid plan; and charge reduction agreements with health plans.)"[5]

"Stark I, II"/Self-Referral Law/Limitations on Certain Physician Referrals (Section 1877 of the Social Security Act/42 USC 1395nn)

"'Stark I' became effective in 1995 and prevents physicians and their immediate family members who have an ownership or compensation relationship with a clinical laboratory services facility from making referrals to it. 'Stark II' is broader, preventing physicians and immediate family members who have an ownership or compensation relationship with an entity providing 'designated health services' from referring patients for these services where payment may be made under Medicare. An entity providing a designated health service is prohibited from billing for the provision of a service based on a prohibited referral. Designated health service includes: clinical laboratory services; physical therapy services; occupational therapy services; radiology services, including magnetic resonance imaging, computerized axial tomography scans, and ultrasound services; radiation therapy services and supplies; durable medical equipment and supplies; parenteral and enteral nutrients, equipment and supplies; prosthetics, orthotics, prosthetic devices and supplies; home health services; outpatient prescription drugs; and inpatient and outpatient hospital services. Penalties for violation of this provision include denial of payment for the designated health services, refund of amounts collected in violation of the provision and CMPs of up to $15,000 for each service. Physicians and entities that enter into an arrangement to circumvent the referral restriction law shall be subject to a CMP of up to $100,000 per occurrence. There are numerous exceptions to this provision, including: personally providing or supervising the provision of the service; in-office ancillary services provided by the physician or another physician or an employee in the same group practice; and referrals through a prepaid health plan."[5]

Exclusion From Federal Health Care Programs (Section 1128(a),(b) and (c) of the Social Security Act/42 USC 1320a-7a)

"Individuals or entities convicted for a program related crime, a criminal offense relating to patient abuse or neglect, a felony offense related to health care fraud, or a felony offense related to controlled substances must be excluded from Medicare and Medicaid for a minimum of 5 years. If there is one prior conviction, the exclusion will be for 10 years, and the exclusion will be permanent where there are two prior convictions. Exclusion will be discretionary only for misdemeanor health care fraud and controlled substance offenses and for criminal offenses related to fraud, theft, embezzlement, breach of fiduciary responsibility, or other financial misconduct in non-health care government programs. Discretionary exclusions also are authorized for: license revocation or suspension; exclusion or suspension from a federal or state health care program; excessive charges or the provision of medically unnecessary services; and failure to provide required information. The minimum period of discretionary exclusion would be three years, unless the Secretary of the federal Department of Health and Human Services (HHS) determines (pursuant to regulations) that a longer or shorter period is appropriate."[5]

Coding and Billing Issues

Fraud and abuse issues cannot be discussed without an emphasis on or at least a conversation about coding and billing issues. Coding drives billing, which determines payment levels, and therefore, if coding and/or billing are erroneous, there is a risk of fraud or abuse.

Coding

Providers' documentation of patient care is the basis for billing claims for payment. This was discussed in Chapter 8 on documentation. When a claim is filed and diagnoses, services, and supplies are coded, the billing entity is certifying that the claim is correct and in compliance with billing requirements. The billing entity is responsible to ensure the claim is truthful and accurate. Coding errors are among the most prevalent findings in reviews.

Claim Assignment

Accepting assignment means the provider accepts the Medicare allowance as the total allowance for a service. Because Medicare pays 80% of the allowed amount, the patient or the secondary insurer is responsible for any required copayment or deductible. The

80-20 (80% by Medicare and 20% by the patient or secondary insurer) ratio is considered as payment in full for the services rendered. Note that the provider may not charge or seek any extra payment (beyond the copayment or deductible) from the patient and doing so is a violation of the assignment agreement, which could lead to penalties.

Physician Relationships with Vendors

Drug companies may give free samples to a provider to offer patients free of charge. This is acceptable as long as the provider does not bill the patient for that which was received for free.

Examples of Fraudulent or Abusive Billing From the OIG[5]

- A psychiatrist was fined $400,000 and permanently excluded from participating in the federal health care programs for misrepresenting that he provided therapy sessions requiring 30 or 60 minutes of face-to-face time with the patient, when he had provided only medication checks for 15 minutes or less. The psychiatrist also misrepresented that he provided therapy sessions when in fact a nonlicensed individual conducted the sessions.[6]
- A cardiologist paid the government $435,000 and entered into a five-year Integrity Agreement with OIG to settle allegations that he knowingly submitted claims for consultation services that were not supported by patient medical records and did not meet the criteria for a consultation. The physician also allegedly knowingly submitted false claims for evaluation and management (E/M) services when he had already received payment for such services in connection with previous claims for nuclear stress testing.[6]

(continued)

(continued)

- A physician paid $107,000 to resolve potential liability for charging patients, including Medicare beneficiaries, an annual fee. In exchange for the fee, the physician offered: (1) an annual physical; (2) same- or next-day appointments; (3) dedicated support personnel; (4) around-the-clock physician availability; (5) prescription facilitation; (6) expedited and coordinated referrals; and (7) other amenities at the physician's discretion. The physician's activities allegedly violated the assignment agreement because some of the services outlined in the annual fee were already covered by Medicare.[6]
- Several urologists pled guilty to charges of conspiracy, paid restitution in the tens of thousands of dollars, and received sanctions against their medical licenses for billing Medicare for injectable prostate cancer drugs they received for free from two pharmaceutical companies. The pharmaceutical companies paid $1.4 billion for their part of the alleged scheme to give urologists free samples and encourage them to bill Medicare at an inflated price. The pharmaceutical companies also provided urologists with additional inducements to use their drugs over the competitor's products, including drug rebates, education grants, volume discounts, free goods, and debt forgiveness.[7]

Compliance Plans

Providers are encouraged to develop and follow a compliance plan to help avoid actions that might be considered questionable. The OIG offers examples of compliance plans for physicians, hospitals, and other provider entities, which are available on the OIG's Web site.[8] Basically, all compliance plans should include, at a minimum:

FIGURE 12-1 *Types of Compliance Policies for Health Care Providers*

Regulatory Compliance Policies

- Policy # xx.xxx Hospital Discharge/Transfer Policy for Medicare Patients
- Policy # xx.xx1 Waivers of Copayments and Deductibles
- Policy # xx.xx2 Chart Completion, Documentation, and Security
- Policy # xx.xx3 Medicare Secondary Payer Provisions
- Policy # xx.xx4 Medicare Bundling Requirements
- Policy # xx.xx5 Electronic Patient Record Policy
- Policy # xx.xx6 Medical Billing Audit

Coding Compliance Policies

- Policy # dd.dd1 Required Tools and Resources for HIM Coding
- Policy # dd.dd2 HIM Coding Continuing Education Requirements
- Policy # dd.dd3 General Coding and Documentation Policies
- Policy # dd.dd4 Physician Queries and Clinical Documentation Improvement

- Internal monitoring and auditing;
- Implementation of compliance standards;
- A designee as a compliance contact;
- Appropriate and consistent education;
- Method of responding appropriately to detected offenses and development of corrective action;
- Open lines of communication with employees; and
- Enforcement of disciplinary standards.

Figure 12-1 shows an example of some compliance policies for a billing provider. Policies will obviously vary by specialty and type of provider (physician, hospital, SNF).

Definitions and Acronyms

abuse. Innocent falsification that causes damages to another.

Civil Monetary Penalty (CMP). "A punitive fine imposed by a civil court on an entity that has profited from illegal or unethical activity."[9]

fraud. Deliberate falsification that causes damages (usually monetary losses) to another.

Office of Inspector General (OIG). Part of the Department of Health and Human Services (HHS) responsible for auditing and investigating federal programs to confirm appropriate spending of tax dollars on those programs.

Qui Tam**.** The ability for an individual to sue another individual or entity on behalf of the government and share in any recovered monies (also known as whistleblower).

REFERENCES

1. The Department of Health and Human Services and the Department of Justice. Health Care Fraud and Abuse Control Program Annual Report for Fiscal Year 2009. Available at: www.justice.gov/dag/pubdoc/hcfacreport2009.pdf. Accessed January 20, 2011.
2. Office of Inspector General. Health Care Fraud and Abuse Control Program Report. Available at: http://oig.hhs.gov/publications/hcfac.asp. Accessed January 23, 2011.
3. Centers for Medicare and Medicaid Services. Medicare Claims Review Program. Available at: www.cms.gov/MLNProducts/downloads/MCRP_Booklet.pdf. Accessed January 23, 2011.
4. The Department of Health and Human Services Office of Inspector General. "A Roadmap for New Physicians Avoiding Medicare and Medicaid Fraud and Abuse: Fraud & Abuse

Laws." Available at: http://oig.hhs.gov/fraud/PhysicianEducation/01laws.asp. Accessed April 11, 2011.

5. American Medical Association. Physician Resources: Federal Fraud Enforcement Physician Compliance. Available at: www.ama-assn.org/ama/pub/physician-resources/legal-topics/regulatory-compliance-topics/health-care-fraud-abuse/federal-fraud-enforcement-physician-compliance/federal-fraud-abuse-laws.page. Accessed April 11, 2011.
6. The Department of Health and Human Services Office of Inspector General. "A Roadmap for New Physicians Avoiding Medicare and Medicaid Fraud and Abuse: I. Physician Relationships With Payers." Available at: http://oig.hhs.gov/fraud/PhysicianEducation/02payers.asp. Accessed May 15, 2011.
7. The Department of Health and Human Services Office of Inspector General. "A Roadmap for New Physicians Avoiding Medicare and Medicaid Fraud and Abuse: III. Physician Relationships With Vendors." Available at: http://oig.hhs.gov/fraud/PhysicianEducation/04vendors.asp. Accessed May 15, 2011.
8. Office of Inspector General (OIG). *Compliance Guidance*. Available at: http://oig.hhs.gov/fraud/complianceguidance.asp. Accessed January 23, 2011.
9. Investopedia Dictionary. Investopedia®. Available at: www.investopedia.com/terms/c/civilmoneypenalty.asp. Accessed January 23, 2011.

Chapter 13

Pulling It All Together: Coding, Payment, and Documentation

Now that you have a good overview of the different concepts such as HIPAA and EHRs, and what is involved in coding, payment, and documentation, it's time to start pulling the pieces together for an accurate reporting process. The following are five fundamental tips to pull it all together to achieve the desired and required process.

As noted in previous chapters, this book is meant to give an introduction and overview of some of the basic fundamentals, which can be used to build a foundation for further information and knowledge. Therefore, this concluding chapter will provide some succint and useful tips to bring together the information outlined herein to enable the progression to the next step.

Five Tips to Success with Coding, Payment, and Documentation

1. Know the Rules
2. Ensure Excellent Accounts Receivable Management
3. Invest in Education
4. Listen to Clinicians
5. Expand Your Perspective

It's perfectly acceptable to not know everything about coding, payment, and documentation—and here's a secret: no single individual knows absolutely everything about this business—so you should not feel pressured or expect to know everything. But if all of this is new to you, recognize that and seek out more knowledge and information.

1. Know the Rules

This book has shared some of the standards expected in health care coding, payment, and documentation. Nevertheless, it is up to every facility and practice to continually update and increase their knowledge base. In the world of health care billing, **ignorance is not bliss**. Not maintaining current knowledge of regulations will cause providers and payers to be stagnant and more than likely to be noncompliant. The risk is great.

Throughout this book, many Web sites and resources have been referenced that provide information about the accepted standards for coding, payment, and documentation. To help visually sum it up, Figure 13-1 identifies the nationally acknowledged and accepted organizations that offer guidance on coding.

FIGURE 13-1 *Guidelines From Recognized Organizations*

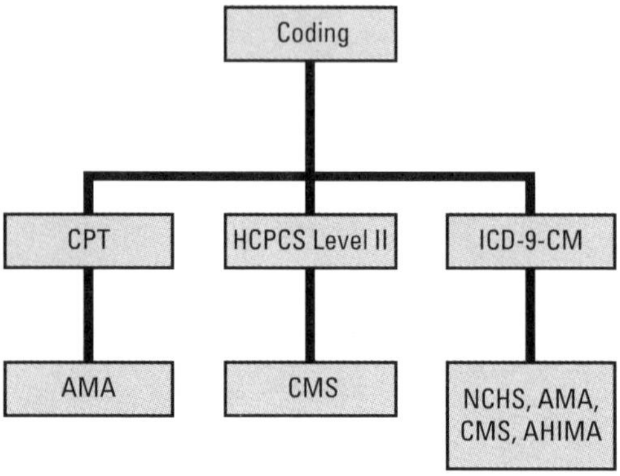

The AMA is responsible for maintaining CPT coding guidelines, and instructions are offered through various products that are available (eg, *CPT Changes: An Insider's View*, *CPT Assistant*, CPT codebook, *Principles of CPT Coding*). CMS is in charge of maintaining the code set for HCPCS Level II coding, and in addition, CMS provides instructions on using this code set through manual instructions, memoranda, transmittals, and webinars. ICD-9-CM coding directives are a joint effort of CMS, AHA, NCHS, and AHIMA. This information is available in the coding guidelines available on the NCHS Web site as well as through the AHA's *Coding Clinic*.

Nonetheless, individual payers can also choose to make adjustments to the guidelines above. As important as official guidelines are to coding and payment, so is awareness of individual payer rules. Obviously, coding is only a piece of the puzzle, and additional information is available from many other sources. Use Table 13-1 as a quick guide and checklist to resources that should be reviewed when billing for services.

Bottom line: it's important to remember that by knowing the rules, you master the conversation of health care billing.

TABLE 13-1 *Quick Resource Guide Checklist*

Resources	Current and Reviewed?
AMA: CPT codebook, *CPT Assistant*, *CPT Changes: An Insider's View*, *Principles of CPT Coding*	
AHA: *Coding Clinic*	
NCHS: Coding guidelines for ICD-9-CM	
CMS: manuals, program transmittals, Web site, memoranda, fee schedules	
CMS MACs: manuals, memoranda, webinars, newsletters	
RACs: Web sites, memoranda	
OIG: Web site, work plans, corporate integrity agreements (CIAs)	
Individual payers: memoranda, contracts, Web sites	
Specialty societies: manuals, newsletters, FAQs	
Trusted vendors	
Medical dictionary	
Anatomy and physiology books	
[Add your own]	

2. Ensure Excellent Accounts Receivable Management

Connecting the different pieces of the puzzle requires a proactive approach. One of the best ways a provider can determine when something is amiss (payment, coding, billing, or documentation) is to take a look at the accounts receivable (A/R) process. A/R is the point in which all payments and denials come in. Implementing good A/R measures gives you a flash of insight into improving at each step of the revenue cycle (see Chapter 1).

You have to identify the problems and trace them to the point of origin (eg, when a patient registration missed important insurance information that caused payment delays, or perhaps a code was incorrectly keyed into the system, which caused an erroneous level of payment) in order to fix the problems.

> Important! Don't just fix a claim; focus on fixing the problem that caused the error or inaccuracy.

The person(s) assigned to the role of A/R should have the tools needed and the skills to determine if the claim was correctly processed by the payer. If there was a problem, consider if it was the way the claim was submitted that caused the problem or whether it was a hitch on the payer's part. Having the necessary A/R tools and skills needed and consciously being aware of such considerations will help mold the provider into a finely tuned billing machine.

3. Invest in Education

This is where both payers and providers cannot afford substandard quality. Staff members responsible for patient care, coding, billing, and A/R need good resources and ongoing education. Changes are constantly made to guidelines, and staying on top of the constant changes is invaluable and of immeasurable importance.

Coders need thorough education not only in coding guidelines but also in anatomy and physiology as well as the disease process. Billers and adjudicators need to be provided with the latest information in claims submission. Each of these individuals and any other individuals who are involved in the revenue cycle need expertise in order to help the provider be compliant, efficient, and effective.

4. Listen to Clinicians

All health care coding, payment, and documentation hinges on the clinician, ie, the individual who is in the room with the patient. When improvement is needed in patient care or documentation, start by listening and not telling. The best way to help clinicians improve is to listen and hear what they have to say. There may be roadblocks to a clinician's success at times, but if you listen, you can uncover those roadblocks and work on removing them.

> **Note**
>
> When there are areas for improvement, eg, in documentation, the best method to teach and reach out to the clinician is to be sure to use real live examples (recent ones) and the official guidelines (pertinent sections). Otherwise, the lesson is just theory and lacks practicality.

Tip: *When highlighting a perceived problem with a clinician's documentation or coding, it is good practice to begin by telling the clinician you must have missed something. Ask for the clinician's help in pointing out what you may have missed. This helps the clinician be less defensive. Also, you may have actually missed something, in which case you are not setting yourself up for failure.*

5. Expand Your Perspective

Perspective is in the eye of the beholder. Thinking through issues in each affected person's mind is important. If you are a payer, how easy will it be for a provider to implement a guideline? If you are a provider, how do you think a payer would view your documentation? Is it sufficient? How do your decisions, whether you are a payer or provider, impact the patient? When preparing information to be conveyed, remember to take a breath and put yourself in the recipient's mindset. Make sure you are clear, concise, and fair.

Individuals often tend to become frustrated at the "other side" of the process without considering the other side's perspective. An individual who is alert to and aware of these different perspectives can be a catalyst for improvement.

Moving From What to How

Ultimately, this book is all about understanding the individual components of and the intertwined relationships between and among coding, payment, and documentation. This chapter is a gathering of essential tips on how to effectively use this book to work better within the health care environment. You have to know the "what" (guidelines, resources, terminology) in order to move to the "how" so that the process can be improved. Without understanding the "what" portion of the equation, moving to the "how" portion is tough.

When reviewing the chapters of this book, think not only about the information presented but about how will it impact the practice, the clinicians, the payment, and the adjudication, and then think through the details of what may need to be changed to effectively incorporate the best practice for that particular piece of information.

Index

A

B

C

D

E

F

G

H

I

J

L

M

N

O

P

Q

R

S

T

U

V

W